# BEAUTY OR STATISTICS

## Practice and Science in Dutch Livestock Breeding, 1900–2000

# Beauty or Statistics

## *Practice and Science in Dutch Livestock Breeding, 1900–2000*

BERT THEUNISSEN

With the collaboration of Steven van der Laan, Jesper Oldenburger, and Liesbeth van der Waaij

UNIVERSITY OF TORONTO PRESS
Toronto Buffalo London

Toronto Buffalo London
utorontopress.com

ISBN 978-1-4875-0700-8 (cloth)
ISBN 978-1-4875-3539-1 (EPUB)
ISBN 978-1-4875-3538-4 (PDF)

**Library and Archives Canada Cataloguing in Publication**

Title: Beauty or statistics : practice and science in Dutch livestock breeding, 1900–2000 / Bert Theunissen ; with the collaboration of Steven van der Laan, Jesper Oldenburger, and Liesbeth van der Waaij.
Names: Theunissen, Bert, 1955– author.
Description: Includes bibliographical references and index.
Identifiers: Canadiana (print) 20190204605 | Canadiana (ebook) 20190204664 | ISBN 9781487507008 (hardcover) | ISBN 9781487535384 (PDF) | ISBN 9781487535391 (EPUB)
Subjects: LCSH: Livestock – Breeding – Netherlands – History – 20th century. | LCSH: Livestock – Netherlands – History – 20th century.
Classification: LCC SF105.25.N4 T44 2019 | DDC 636.08/2 – dc23

University of Toronto Press acknowledges the financial assistance to its publishing program of the Canada Council for the Arts and the Ontario Arts Council, an agency of the Government of Ontario.

Conseil des Arts
du Canada

Funded by the Government of Canada
Financé par le gouvernement du Canada
Canada

# Contents

# Illustrations

# Acknowledgments

This book brings together the results of a project on the history of Dutch livestock breeding supported by a grant from the Netherlands Organisation for Scientific Research NWO (dossier no. 360-69-030). The chapters on pig breeding and sheep breeding synthesize the findings of two PhD theses written by Steven van der Laan and Jesper Oldenburger, respectively, and the chapter on chicken breeding is based on the results of a postdoc project carried out by Liesbeth van der Waaij. I have fond memories of the time we worked together and of our numerous discussions, ranging from the secrets of successful insemination in sows to the rhetoric of agricultural modernization.

Over the years that I worked on this book, I have incurred many debts. I want to thank the farmers, breeders, and animal breeding experts who shared their expertise with us, in particular Gerard Albers, Courtney P. Allen, Ton Bos, Anton Bosgoed, Pim Brascamp, Nico Bons, Wim Dekkers, Bart Ducro, Marleen Felius, Jan Geluk, Frans Kuijpers, Ferry Leenstra, Hans Lenstra, Koos van Middeldorp, Mart Nijssen, Kor Oldenbroek, Theo Peters, the late Rommert Politiek, Frans van Sambeek, Piet Scheer, Henk Slaghuis, Reimer Strikwerda, Hans van Tartwijk, Rienk van der Berg, Addie Vereijken, Jan Vosjan, and Chris Willems.

For their interest in my work, for many stimulating discussions, and for their comments on parts of the manuscript I want to express my warmest thanks to my colleagues at the Descartes Centre for the History and Philosophy of the Sciences and the Humanities at Utrecht University, in particular David Baneke, Floor Haalboom, Hieke Huistra, Noortje Jacobs, Peter Koolmees, Jorieke Savelkouls, and Daan Wegener. I am also grateful to the many colleagues who have commented on my work at conferences and workshops, and during informal conversations. The list is too long to mention them all here, but I want to single out Margaret Derry, whose enthusiasm and suggestions have been a great help.

Thanks, also, to Sara Butler for swiftly and diligently correcting the English text, to Lindsay Norton for advice on technical terms, to Suus van de Kar for checking references and compiling the bibliography, to Gillian Scobie and Barb Porter for their careful copy-editing, and to Pierke Bosschieter for making the index; I greatly enjoyed our collaboration.

Earlier versions of (parts of) chapters 1, 2, and 5 were published in *Agricultural History, Isis, Journal of the History of Biology,* and *Studium.* I thank the publishers for permission to reuse material from these papers in this book.

My deepest gratitude goes to Lian, for being there, and everything else.

# Abbreviations

*AI* Artificial Insemination
*BLUP* Best Linear Unbiased Prediction
*BPH* *Bedrijfspluimveehouder* (chicken husbandry journal)
*B/V* *Boerderij/Varkenshouderij* (pig husbandry journal)
*CBS* Centraal Bureau voor de Schapenfokkerij (umbrella organization of the Dutch sheep breeders' societies)
*CBV* Centraal Bureau voor de Varkenshouderij (umbrella organization of the Dutch pig breeders' societies)
*CPI* Coöperatief Pluimvee Instituut (chicken breeders' cooperative)
*CR Delta* Coöperatieve Rundveeverbetering Delta (cattle breeders' cooperative)
*FRS* Friesch Rundvee Stamboek (Friesian Cattle Herd Book Society)
*FV* *Friese Veefokkerij* (Friesian cattle breeding journal)
*IdS* *In de Strengen* (horse breeding journal of the WPN)
*IVO* Instituut voor Veeteeltkundig Onderzoek (Institute for Animal Sciences)
*KS* *Keurstamboeker* (cattle breeding journal of the NRS)
*MRIJ* Maas-Rijn-IJssel Cattle (Dutch red-and-white dairy cattle)
*MV* *Maandblad voor de Varkensfokkerij* (pig breeding journal of the CBV)
*NRS* Nederlandsch Rundvee Stamboek (Dutch Cattle Herd Book Society)
*NTS* Nederlands Texels Schapenstamboek (Dutch Texel Sheep Flock Book Society)

| | |
|---|---|
| *RRS* | Reciprocal Recurrent Selection |
| *SFA* | Archives of the Swifter Sheep Flock Book Society |
| *V/M* | *Varkenshouderij/Mesterij* (pig husbandry journal) |
| *WPN* | Warmbloed Paardenstamboek Nederland (Dutch Warmblood Stud Book Society) |

# BEAUTY OR STATISTICS

Practice and Science in Dutch Livestock Breeding, 1900–2000

# Introduction

This book was born out of curiosity. As I was rereading the chapter on artificial selection in Charles Darwin's *Origin of Species* for a seminar, it struck me that there was something odd about Darwin's ideas on how breeders create new varieties of domestic species. In his view, there was an analogy between artificial and natural selection: just as breeders used artificial selection to modify the characteristics of domestic breeds, nature used natural selection to change species in the wild. The analogy implied that it takes a long time to develop a new domestic breed: selecting small individual variations, generation after generation, is a very slow process. Indeed, Darwin believed that the most important domestic breeds had a history that spanned centuries, millennia even. I also knew, however, that a dazzling number of new domestic varieties have been introduced since the early nineteenth century, so I wondered how this was possible. Curiously enough, I found that not only historians but also biologists writing about Darwin's analogy seemed to accept it without questioning its accuracy. Popular expositions of evolutionary theory also routinely use the analogy as a didactic tool to explain the principles of variation and selection in nature. For instance, in a BBC documentary about Darwin's work, David Attenborough takes his audience to a dog show and a poultry show to illustrate what can be accomplished by the sustained selection of minute variations.[1]

The opportunity to delve deeper into the matter presented itself when I was studying the work of the Dutch geneticist and livestock breeding expert Arend Hagedoorn (1885–1953), a pupil of Hugo de Vries, one of the "rediscoverers" of Mendelian genetics.[2] Historical literature on livestock breeding proved to be scarce, but once I had discovered the works of, among others, Juliet Clutton-Brock, Robert Trow-Smith, and, more recently, Nicholas Russell, Harriet Ritvo,

Margaret Derry, Roger Wood, and Vítězslav Orel, it soon dawned on me that Darwin had been mistaken.[3]

To be sure, selection is crucial in domestic breeding, but that is not the whole story. Few domestic breeds can convincingly be shown to be any older than 200 years, and a great many of them were created in the twentieth century. So the slow, incremental processes of variation and artificial selection alone cannot account for their origin. Breeders used other methods besides selection to produce new breeds and to improve existing ones, namely inbreeding and crossing, in various forms and combinations, and were thus able to make much faster progress. The creation of a new breed took a number of years, or at most a few decades, depending on its generation interval. So there was indeed something odd about Darwin's analogy. How could the man who fraternized with breeders for so many years have been unaware of how breeding actually works? Returning to his writings, I found that he was not entirely unaware of the breeders' methods, but assumed, incorrectly, that selection was far more important than crossing and inbreeding. Darwin needed the analogy with natural selection, one might say, and this slanted his interpretation of the breeding literature. As a result, he underestimated the role of inbreeding and crossing in domestic breeding.[4]

Having sorted this out, reading about Hagedoorn's lifelong disputes with breeders over the proper ways of improving livestock prompted me to look more closely into the practical side of animal breeding and the interactions between commercial breeders and scientists. The twentieth-century world of breeders that Hagedoorn confronted proved to be perfectly suited for my investigation. The Netherlands is a leading agricultural country and, after the United States, the world's largest agricultural exporting economy. In the twentieth century, it was among the world's foremost livestock breeding countries. At various times, breeds such as Friesian dairy cattle (the foundation stock of American Holsteins), Texel sheep, and Dutch Warmblood horses, were touted as the best in the world. In the second half of the century, farm animal breeding became a global enterprise, yet among the select few multinational corporations that dominate cattle, pig, and chicken breeding today some are still companies based in the Netherlands, while Texel sheep and the Dutch sport horse are among the world's premier breeds in their sectors.

This long and rich tradition of stockbreeding has generated ample archival and published sources for historical study that have remained virtually untapped until now. Among these, the journals and magazines issued by the major livestock breeders' societies and professional organizations are of particular importance. They were published biweekly or monthly and reported on the practical, technical, scientific, and economic aspects of livestock breeding. They also included reports on shows and meetings, as well as sections in which society board members, studbook inspectors, scientific breeding experts, government officials, and the breeders themselves voiced their opinion on current issues and affairs. Thus the journals may rightly be called the "arena" where the "social worlds" of breeders, scientists, and policymakers encountered each other.[5] For any study of what happened at the crossroads between science and practice, breeding journals thus provide a rich starting point.

Stockbreeding practices changed profoundly in the twentieth century, and scientific knowledge played a central role in their transformation. According to the proceedings of a 1972 symposium in honour of Jay Lush, the American pioneer of quantitative genetics, livestock breeding was finally evolving from an art into a science – a familiar trope that was used by commercial breeders and animal scientists alike at the time.[6] Agricultural policymakers and scientific experts agreed that the switch to scientific breeding was as necessary and inevitable as the ongoing process of agricultural modernization. However, the art-to-science scenario is too simplistic to do justice to the complex dynamic that characterized the transformation of the field. To illustrate this, I will focus on the circulation of knowledge and practices at the intersection between animal science and commercial breeding. As we will see, little was inevitable about the growing role of science in stockbreeding. And the idea of an inescapable modernization is not helpful in explaining how and why practical breeders were induced to embrace science-based breeding technologies.

The activities of both scientists and livestock breeders were embedded in what may be called cultures of breeding – shared convictions, beliefs, traditions, and practices – that involved scientific, technical, economic, aesthetic, normative, and commercial considerations. What needs to be explained, then, is how a culture of breeding that was dominated by the insights of commercial breeders became a culture of which science was one of the pillars. The differences in size, prolificacy, generation time, and monetary value between the various livestock breeds entailed significant differences in the breeding cultures they engendered. To reveal what was generic and what was specific to these cultures, I investigate and compare the breeding histories of five domestic species: dairy cattle, chickens, pigs, sheep, and horses.

The Dutch livestock breeds that take centre stage in this book were products of the twentieth century. Modern chickens, pigs, and horses, moreover, are hybrids, produced from parent breeds that were of equally recent origin. The methods used by the breeders to propagate and improve their stock were much older. Deliberate attempts to change the characteristics of domestic species have been undertaken since at least antiquity, and inbreeding, crossing, and selection were deployed systematically from the eighteenth century onwards. It is mainly because we know so little about earlier breeding practices that Robert Bakewell of Dishley (1725–95) has been customarily credited with pioneer status, because his work is one of the earliest well-documented examples of a sustained effort at breed improvement. Bakewell consciously used selection, inbreeding, and crossing to improve his domestic animals. By the early nineteenth century, as is evident from a treatise by John Saunders Sebright from 1809, the best breeders were fully aware of why, how, and when to use – or not use – these methods.[7] They could be varied and combined in many ways, but the fundamental methods have not changed since Bakewell's time. In the following chapters we will see how science transformed livestock breeding in the twentieth century almost beyond recognition. Still, the foundation of all breeding work continued to be selection, inbreeding, and crossing, regardless of whether it was done by practical breeders or scientists. Furthermore, I argue that genetics, the scientific study of heredity that developed in the twentieth century, has not markedly altered this situation. The "rediscovery" of Mendel's laws in 1900 and the theory of heredity built on this foundation were of little relevance to the development of scientific animal breeding. More generally, scientific breeding cannot be equated with "applied genetics."

A whole new field, informed by mathematics and statistics, formed the basis of scientific breeding practices, namely quantitative genetics. The name is somewhat misleading, as it seems to suggest that genetic theory is somehow involved. The only assumption about hereditary mechanisms that quantitative genetics makes, however, is that males and females contribute about equally to the hereditary make-up of the next generation – a presupposition that many breeders in the nineteenth century, following Bakewell and Sebright, already took for granted. Quantitative genetics is, first and foremost, about quantities: it involves measuring, weighing, counting, and calculating. Whereas genetic theory aims to explain heredity in a causal way, quantitative genetics is based on correlations and, as such, is a continuation of pre-Mendelian breeding methods. For instance, the nineteenth-century dairy-cattle breeder who picked a breeding bull on the basis of external characteristics – his conformation – made the same basic assumption as the quantitative geneticist who selects a bull on the basis of the milk-production figures of his daughters: they both reason that their selection criterion is correlated with the bull's hereditary potential for siring excellent cows. Neither of them knows which genes are responsible for milk production, nor do they need to know. For the quantitative geneticist, computing power, rather than knowledge about genes, is essential, and the advent of fast computers signalled a breakthrough for the field.

Especially after the Second World War, the role of science and scientists in Dutch breeding practices increased rapidly, as a consequence of what was called the postwar "modernization project" in agriculture, initiated by the Dutch government in the decades after the war in close cooperation with agricultural scientists from Wageningen Agricultural College (*Landbouwhogeschool*), the only institution for higher education in agriculture in the Netherlands.[8] (The graduates were called *landbouwingenieurs*, agricultural engineers – I will refer to them as agriculturalists, scientists, or experts.) To increase productivity, Dutch farmers were encouraged to scale up, mechanize, specialize, and intensify their farms, and Wageningen scientists led them through this process. As convinced advocates of modernization, the scientists presented it to the farmers as economically inevitable. The farmers, however, did not blindly follow the advice of their scientific advisers. On the contrary, they actively opposed the experts' prescriptions for modernization if they did not perceive them as serving their interests. In this respect, there were significant differences between the breeding cultures of the various livestock species. For instance, for several decades dairy-cattle breeders resisted the call to increase the productivity of their cows, insisting that it was their animals' beauty of conformation rather than their milk production that guaranteed their quality. Horse breeders effectively undermined a government plan to collectivize their sector, which they considered an unacceptable intrusion. On the other hand, chicken and pig breeders were more willing to follow their advisers in their endeavour to reform breeding practices, whereas sheep breeders saw several such attempts simply fail. Obviously, biological differences between the livestock species that constrained their amenability to science-based improvement also have to be taken into account; what worked well for one species might not work for another.

Historian Abigail Woods has noted that even recent histories of agriculture tend to present its postwar development as an almost teleological process towards more industrialized forms of agriculture, as if there was indeed something inevitable to it.[9] The history of livestock breeding provides examples galore that undermine this idea of a linear development. I show that the logic of the scientific approach or of modernization alone cannot explain the developments in animal breeding. Farmers did not follow one single logic. To understand why they embraced or rejected new approaches, their reactions to more specific pressures and the particulars of their breeding practices need to be taken into account. Put differently, it is more fruitful to analyse the transformation of livestock breeding in terms of changing cultures of breeding, taking into account not only scientific and economic, but also practical, commercial, normative, and aesthetic considerations.

Chapter 1 explores the background to each of the two major changeovers in Dutch dairy cattle breeding in the twentieth century: from breeding for production to breeding for conformation in the early twentieth century, and the return to breeding for production in the 1970s. Until about 1900, Dutch black-and-white dairy cattle were famous for their exceptional milk yields. Their reputation was seriously damaged, however, by an epidemic of bovine tuberculosis, a disease they were believed to be highly susceptible to. In reaction, breeders decided to give up selection for high milk production and switch to a long-term strategy of breeding physically robust, disease-resistant cows. As expected, production figures became more average, yet the black and whites regained their popularity, now as a reliable dual-purpose breed, providing meat and milk.

In the 1950s, however, when the breed's fame was at its height, Wageningen agricultural experts launched a sustained attack on the leading breeders. They accused them of clinging to obsolete methods and breeding for show rather than for production. The breeders rejected this criticism and defended their breeding strategy as "responsible." Even though they enthusiastically adopted artificial insemination (AI) as a new breeding technology, they did not deploy it to raise their cows' milk productivity. It was only around 1970 that farmers began to accept milk production as the principal focus of selection. They even imported high-yielding American Holstein cows to make faster progress. This turnabout was not so much an indication that they had finally been convinced by the scientific perspective, but rather a consequence of the dramatically rising costs and the stagnating prices of agricultural produce that signalled the failure of the EEC's agricultural policy in those years. The breeders felt that increasing productivity per cow was called for if they were to survive the crisis. Their new approach fit in perfectly with the scientific viewpoint, and scientists now began to play a central role in cattle breeding. The episode is customarily presented as a conflict between "art" and science in Dutch dairy cattle breeding, yet a deeper understanding is gained by interpreting it as a confrontation between differing normative views of what constituted good farming practices.

Egg production from layer hens, the subject of chapter 2, was a sideline on Dutch farms until the late nineteenth century. The agricultural crisis of the 1880s, when cheap American grain flooded the market, prompted the growth of animal husbandry in the Netherlands, and many farmers' wives took up chicken farming to supplement the family income. Wageningen agriculturalists successfully advocated purebred breeding after 1900, and poultry husbandry gradually became an important activity on the mixed farms. As its commercial importance grew, the male farmers took a more active role, focusing in particular on the production and multiplication of breeding animals. The ravages of the economic crisis of the 1930s induced the government to make purebred breeding mandatory to secure the availability of good breeding stock.

After the war, the government placed limits on the scaling-up of chicken farms to enable small farmers to continue earning part of their living from producing eggs for the table. The purebred breeding policy was also maintained until it had to be abandoned after the European Economic Community (EEC) was established in 1958. By then, hybrid breeding, a new breeding technology developed in the United States, had begun to gain a foothold in the Netherlands. The method was first developed by scientists engaged in maize breeding, and one of its main purposes was to create a "biological lock" that prevented farmers from using the seeds of their crops for breeding purposes, implying they had to buy new seeds every year. The method was hailed by geneticist as a triumph of Mendelism. We will see, however, that the method was anything but a straightforward application of Mendelian insights and should instead be seen as a new combination of older methods.

Of all Dutch livestock breeders, chicken breeders proved to be among the most receptive to scientific approaches. This is partly explained by the biological characteristics of chickens, and partly by the absence of a show tradition and of breeders' associations. In the 1960s, traditional chicken breeders were pushed out of business by an ever-smaller number of specialized commercial companies, which employed scientists to do the breeding work. The example of Hendrix Genetics, now one of the world's leading laying-hen breeding corporations, will serve to elucidate how its entrance into the sector transformed chicken breeding.

Chapter 3 examines the development of Dutch pig breeding. In the early twentieth century, most pigs belonged to a plethora of so-called Landraces that had resulted from indiscriminate crosses between various domestic and foreign breeds. To improve the sector, scientists advised the breeders to restore purity within two breeds, the Dutch Yorkshire and the Improved German Landrace, and to first and foremost select their animals for their meat production qualities. These qualities were judged on the basis of conformation, and competitive pig shows became the principal sites for the selection of breeding stock.

When the British import market for fresh meat was closed in the 1920s, the Dutch breeders responded by turning their animals, particularly the Yorkshire, into bacon pigs, for the production of salted meat. As a result, they were competing directly with Danish pig farmers, whose high-quality bacon dominated the British market. Pig breeding in Denmark had achieved a high level of organization at the time, and the breeders had established testing stations for selecting their stock. Following the recommendation of their scientific advisers, Dutch breeders copied this testing system in the early 1930s.

Commercial companies began to acquire a share of the pig-breeding market in the 1960s, and, following the logic of the chicken breeders, they deployed hybridizing techniques resulting in biological locks to protect their investments in new breeding stock. To keep up with this new competition, the traditional pig breeders' societies called in scientific expertise to help them raise the productivity of their purebred animals. Artificial insemination was introduced to speed up the process, yet this breeding technology met with a mixed reception among the farmers. While the breeders embraced it enthusiastically, the multipliers, who produced pigs in great numbers for the fatteners, initially saw no use for it, much to the dismay of their scientific advisers. Furthermore, as it turned out, the scientists' quantitative approach resulted in a type of pig that was more profitable to the butcher than to the farmer and that was still inferior, in most respects, to the hybrid pigs developed by the private companies. On the rebound, the societies also switched to hybrid breeding techniques in the 1980s. These proved particularly useful for combining traits such as growth and fertility, which were difficult to select for simultaneously in a single breed. By the 1990s, in the face of the globalization of pig breeding, the Dutch societies and private companies merged into ever-larger (international) corporations, of which only a few remain today. While pig breeding organizations, particularly in the second half of the twentieth century, increasingly adopted the rhetoric of modernization, we have to take into account the specific practical and economic contingencies that confronted the sector to understand how and why scientific innovations were, or were not, adopted by the breeders.

Sheep breeding, as we will see in chapter 4, provides an illustration of the various functions and purposes of the idea of a breed. Breeders on the Isle of Texel and on the adjacent mainland of North Holland experimented with crossing their sheep with English breeds in the nineteenth century, yet they gradually came to the conclusion that purebred breeding worked better in their situation. Once Texel sheep were established as a pure breed, their preferred conformation was spelled out in detail by the breeders' societies. Over the years, some of the Texel's characteristics were exaggerated by means of selection, particularly by the top breeders, to make their animals stand out. An example was the Texel's short, very wide face, illustrating that such features were not necessarily productive traits; rather, they served as tell-tale signs of quality – as brand features, one might say. The top breeders considered preserving such traits to be nearly as important as improving the Texel's productive qualities.

Crossbreeding of Texel sheep was reintroduced by agricultural scientists in the 1970s, and at first sheep farmers were interested in its benefits. Within a few years, however, the participants in the crossbreeding program came to the conclusion that it was too complicated in practice, and turned one of the scientists' newly created crossbreds, the Swifter, into a pure breed. As a consequence, as in the case of the Texel, a clearly defined conformation standard also became important for the Swifter breeders.

In the second half of the twentieth century, Wageningen scientists attempted to introduce index breeding and AI into the sheep sector. The breeders initially welcomed these plans, yet their concern over conformation features played an important role in the eventual failure of the scientific program: the improved rams the scientists made available to them did not live up to their conformation standards. Besides this, the small scale of the sheep sector posed a serious obstacle: in the end, gathering sufficient data for index calculation and AI proved to be the Achilles heel of the scientists' endeavour to increase productivity.

Breeders did agree with the scientists, however, that the Texel's productivity needed improvement, and when the scientific approach began to lose steam, they deployed their customary breeding method to accomplish this. What the scientists had been unable to achieve the breeders realized by means of selection on the basis of conformation, that is, by using the traditional instrument of the "breeder's eye." In doing so, they not only succeeded in improving their sheep's productivity, but also in preserving its characteristic type. The scientists thus found out the hard way that a breed's marketability depends not only on its utility, but also on its distinguishing features.

Chapter 5 discusses the most interesting episode in twentieth-century Dutch horse breeding. This began in the 1950s, when farmers set themselves the task of transforming their Warmblood working horses, which were no longer needed for farm work, into saddle horses for leisure riding and sports. There were two different types of Dutch Warmbloods: the Gelderlander and the Groninger. They were not bred purely, but as utility types, the Groninger being used for heavier work than the Gelderlander. The transformation of both types was achieved by hybridization: Thoroughbreds and Thoroughbred-crossbreds were used as sires to infuse riding-horse characteristics into the Warmbloods. It was an arduous procedure, since the result of each and every cross had to be judged on its own merits, and there was no simple rationale about how to proceed after the first generation of crossbreds had been produced. Genetics was of no help in guiding the transformation process; it basically came down to trial and error. These uncertainties notwithstanding, the first results were encouraging: many crossbreds between Warmblood mares and Thoroughbred stallions proved to be eminently suitable for both leisure riding and sports.

In the late 1970s, animal scientists became increasingly critical of the breeders' selection procedure, as it was predominantly based on the evaluation of conformation. They argued that much better results could be obtained by collectivizing the sector, replacing natural mating by artificial insemination, and by systematically recording quantitative performance data. In this way, they believed, the sector's viability, which had suffered severely from the economic stagnation of the 1970s, could be restored. The government plan to achieve these goals, which was initiated on the scientists' advice, met with strong opposition from the farmers, who felt it impinged on their autonomy. While the plan largely failed, as a result of their resistance, it did not leave the farmers unaffected. They found ways to collaborate with the scientists on their own terms, and together they succeeded in improving the selection procedure, which was revised so as to include the evaluation of breeding stock on the basis of quantitative data. Their joint effort was successful: by the late 1980s, an international market for Dutch show jumping and dressage horses had arisen, which was to grow spectacularly in the ensuing decades. This chapter thus underlines the farmers' crucial role in shaping the postwar agricultural modernization process.

The conclusion compares the breeding histories of the five farm animal species to establish differences and similarities. What motivated the choice for particular breeding methods such as purebred breeding or crossbreeding? What was the role of commercial breeding and scientific breeding in these five species, and how did breeders and scientists interact? If the "art-to-science" scenario fails to do justice to how the modernization of livestock breeding in the twentieth century came about, how then can the circulation of knowledge and practices between science and practice be characterized more fruitfully? Livestock breeding as a whole indubitably became more scientific over the course of the twentieth century, but what did that entail, and what exactly did scientists contribute? Did they provide a novel foundation for livestock breeding or, rather, did they add new instruments to existing breeding practices? And what motivated the breeders to follow, or not follow, their scientific advisers' instructions? Finally, the scientists' conviction that scientific modernization was inevitable must be addressed. It seems to fit in perfectly with the teleological trend towards industrialization wittingly or unwittingly conveyed by some general histories of modern agriculture. Yet the argument of this book is that the scientific modernization of breeding practices was a contingent process, brought about by very specific circumstances rather than driven by the logic of science and modernization. I will suggest we have to take the moral economy of modernization into account to see that there is no contradiction here.

# 1 Breeding for Nobility or for Production? Friesian Dairy Cattle

In the 1970s and 1980s, a characteristic element of the Dutch pasturelands underwent a change that may have escaped city dwellers but to the experienced eye it was dramatic. Slowly but surely, the traditional Dutch black-and-white dairy cows, known abroad as Friesians, were replaced by their American cousins, the Holsteins. Thus, a dual-purpose breed that produced milk and meat gave way to specialized dairy cattle bred purely for milk production. Remarkably, the reverse had happened half a century earlier. Until the 1910s, the Friesians had been a pure dairy breed, widely known for their exceptional yields, but in the interwar period they were turned into dual-purpose cows.

The story behind these changes offers illuminating insights into the practices of dairy cattle breeders and their interactions with the scientists who advised them. Historical studies of the Dutch dairy industry have explained the interwar switch to the dual-purpose type as a side effect of the breeders' commercial interests: bulls and cows of this type sold better on the market for breeding stock. In terms of milk production, however, the dual-purpose cows did less well: production figures even appeared to be steadily declining, and by the 1960s the breeders were supposedly trapped in a blind alley. Science is said to have come to their rescue: guided by agricultural scientists, the farmers returned to the dairy type. In the process, scientific methods gained the upper hand over the traditional methods of the breeders, and thus breeding was turned from an art into a science.[1]

This art-to-science scenario is in line with what is called the postwar modernization project in Dutch agriculture, instigated by the government in close cooperation with scientific experts. To increase productivity, Dutch farmers were induced to rationalize, scale up, mechanize, specialize, and intensify their farms. The switch to the Holsteins, the pre-eminent dairy breed, can be seen as a natural step in this process. However, despite its apparent logic, this scenario ignores important aspects of the story. For one thing, it seems to set "conservative" breeders against "progressive" scientists. In reality, however, most farmers and breeders took an active part in the rationalization of their practices and, at times, even pushed forward at a faster pace than the scientists deemed advisable. Furthermore, besides scientific and economic considerations, normative views on profitable and responsible farming were a crucial factor. For instance, the commercial success the dual-purpose type enjoyed for some time was based on its aesthetically pleasing appearance, but it was not just external qualities the buyers were interested in: beauty was seen as a reflection of inner quality; a beautiful cow was a productive and healthy cow.

As we will see, a better way to understand the turnabouts in the Dutch dairy cattle type is to interpret them in the light of changing cultures of breeding, in which scientific, practical, economic, commercial, aesthetic, and normative considerations were inextricably linked.

## The Breeders Get Organized

In the nineteenth century, the most productive Dutch dairy cattle, the black-and-white Friesians, were traditionally found on the specialized dairy farms that exploited the vast natural pastures of clay soil of the western and northern provinces, particularly Friesland and North Holland.[2] By the 1890s, however, black and whites also began to be kept by farmers in the sandy regions in the south and east. There were several reasons for this. Around the middle of the century, animal husbandry started to become more profitable as a consequence of the liberalization of the export markets in many European countries. The increased interest in animal husbandry was also helped by improvements in transportation and reinforced by the sharp drop in grain prices in the 1880s, when American grain flooded the world market.

By the end of the century, farmers on the many small mixed farms in the east and south concentrated their activities by and large on the production of milk, meat, and eggs, and they increasingly devoted their arable land to producing fodder for their animals. Concentrates also became cheaper and were being fed in growing quantities. Another major stimulus to dairy farming across the country was the establishment of cooperative dairy factories from the mid-1880s onwards. These creameries lifted a major constraint on the growth of dairy farms in that they solved the farmers' problem, especially in remote areas, of finding an outlet for their milk. While the number of dairy cows had been more or less constant until the 1880s, it rose from some 900,000 in 1890 to about 1.3 million in 1930.[3]

Meanwhile, partly as a consequence of the agricultural crisis of the 1880s, the government had given up its nineteenth-century laissez-faire attitude to agriculture and began to stimulate and support the improvement of breeding practices. A new method for assessing the quality of dairy cows was introduced in the 1890s, following the example of Danish farmers: the systematic recording of milk production. Friesland led the way in establishing milk-recording associations and would remain the province with the highest participation in milk recording. The members of these associations had their cows' milk yield carefully weighed and recorded on a regular basis. Their yearly production could thus be estimated, and the figures obtained in this way could also be used to assess the hereditary quality of both cows and bulls.[4]

In the same period, local, regional, and provincial dairy cattle breeders' associations were created in quick succession. The vast majority of the Dutch dairy farmers bred their own cows – to have replacements for the old cows, and of course because a cow must have a calf once a year to produce milk. Only a small percentage of the dairy farmers specialized in producing and selling breeding stock, particularly bulls, and only a few dozen breeders made serious money from these activities.[5] Still, since cattle reproduce slowly and are too costly to keep solely for breeding purposes, all specialist breeders were also dairy farmers. The specialists dominated the associations, but many farmers with pedigree animals were also members.

A national cattle breeders' society, the *Nederlandsch Rundvee Stamboek* (NRS), was established in 1874, and administered the herd book in which the local associations registered their animals. Five years later, breeders in Friesland decided to keep their own records and founded an independent society, the *Friesch Rundvee Stamboek* (FRS). Initially, the registers of these breeders' organizations functioned mainly as address books for buyers of breeding stock. With the advent of many smaller breeders' associations everywhere in the country, however, they began to play a leading role in giving direction to the development of the Dutch cattle breeds. Agricultural scientists educated at Wageningen Agricultural College – the only institution of its kind in the Netherlands – and veterinarians were appointed to act as advisers to milk-recording and breeders' associations and to develop educational programs for the farmers. Finally, more and more creameries provided farmers with an incentive to intensify the selection of their animals by basing payments on the butterfat content of the milk supplied, because this was important for butter and cheese manufacturing. Milk-recording data showed that the percentage of butterfat was determined to a considerable degree by heredity. Milk yield, on the other hand, while also partly heritable, was much more sensitive to environmental influences. Thus, the milk's butterfat percentage provided an excellent opportunity for selection.[6]

Articles in agricultural newspapers and weeklies, such as *Het Friesch Landbouwblad, Het Landbouw Nieuwsblad, De Veldbode,* and *De Veldpost,* testify to the growing significance attached to breeding practices after 1900. Agricultural journalists, scientists, and government animal husbandry advisers regularly exchanged views on the aims and methods of breeding in such periodicals, and more and more reports appeared on cattle shows and on the accomplishments of breeding associations and individual breeders. The interest taken in the subject by the dairy farmers themselves can be gleaned from the lively exchanges in the questions and answers section of weeklies such as *De Veldbode* and *De Veldpost.*[7]

As a result of these developments, good breeding stock and, in particular, good bulls were in high demand in the final decades of the nineteenth century, and the breeders of black-and-white Friesians experienced a golden age. Yet the proliferation of the Friesians was not without its challenges. In the early twentieth century the breeders were confronted with a serious problem.

## Type and Tuberculosis

The late-nineteenth-century black and whites in Friesland and North Holland were big, gaunt, leggy, sharp-backed, narrow-chested, and ewe-necked animals (Figure 1.1). "All milk, skin and bone," as a British commentator put it.[8] They were milking machines indeed, and it was precisely for this reason that thousands of Friesians from these provinces were exported as breeding stock in these decades. Most famously, breeders from the United States and Canada imported some 7,500 black and whites, which became the exclusive foundational stock of the premier American dairy breed, the Holstein-Friesians or Holsteins.[9]

Animal husbandry experts in the Netherlands, however, agreed that Friesians could only be profitably exploited on exceptionally fertile soils. These highly productive cows were delicate and needed high-quality food and careful management. This was not a new insight. Farmers had long known all too well that many livestock breeds could not be simply transferred to different climates or soils. The failed attempts to introduce Spanish Merino sheep in various European countries are a well-known example.[10] Careful management was required to prevent them from deteriorating under unfavourable environmental conditions. In the eighteenth century, German buyers of Friesians had learned the hard way that these Dutch dairy cattle were an exacting breed. For this reason, Friesians in the Berlin area were cared for by

Figure 1.1. Friesians in 1900. From Kuperus & Zonen, *Eenige mededeelingen*, 30.

Dutch immigrant farmers.[11] American farmers also knew how to handle their Holsteins: they were fed rich diets and on many farms they remained housed all year.[12]

Understandably, when farmers in the south and east of the Netherlands began to import black-and-white Friesians in the 1890s, many experts felt compelled to sound a cautionary note. The mixed farms on the sandy soils provided an environment that was hostile to Friesians, they contended. The farmers could not provide the high-quality foodstuffs required, and they did not have time to provide the care the animals needed. Under such less than optimal circumstances Friesians were said to become leggy looking and weak. After a few generations, they were no longer better milk producers than the local breeds. Friesians had been bred exclusively for production, wrote NRS herd-book inspector Iman van den Bosch, a respected authority on cattle breeding. This had weakened their constitution, and thus they demonstrated the wrong-headedness of the much-debated *Zucht nach Leistung* (selection for performance), promulgated by the German agriculturist Emil Pott.[13] Hendricus Kroon, professor of animal breeding at Utrecht Veterinary College, agreed that Friesians ran the risk of becoming so "overbred" that their functionality was jeopardized. Wageningen agricultural experts fully agreed, and, similarly, a government report on the improvement of animal breeding warned against the risks of one-sided breeding for production.[14]

The most damaging allegation of all was that Friesians, if not properly cared for, were highly susceptible to bovine tuberculosis, a disease that was becoming more and more problematic around 1900. A German visitor at a national show remarked that if the conformation – the external shape – of Friesian cattle was not enough to make one suspicious, the constant coughing that could be heard in their barns would not fail to do so.[15] According to the veterinarian Aryen van Leeuwen, German experts even considered Dutch cattle to be the most severely afflicted with tuberculosis worldwide. Belgian buyers also complained that Friesians were unfit for their soils and often fell victim to the disease.[16]

Before long, the black and whites came to be held in bad repute in many regions of the Netherlands too. It was claimed that seemingly healthy Friesian breeding stock "degenerated" in other provinces and then succumbed to tuberculosis. Veterinarians compared the soft-skinned and emaciated dairy type to the tuberculosis-prone *habitus phthisicus* in humans, characterized by a weak frame and an almost translucent complexion.[17] There was wide agreement that the black and whites' delicacy and exceptional productivity made them particularly vulnerable.[18]

Acting on this advice, a considerable number of farmers on the sandy soils preferred to use the Dutch red-and-white cow, traditionally found in the regions along the major rivers (the Meuse, the Rhine, and the IJssel), commonly referred to by the acronym MRIJ cattle. The red and whites were stockier and less demanding, and thus better adapted to the circumstances on small mixed farms. Their milk yield was not as high as that of the Friesians, yet they were better meat producers: they could be fattened more easily and the quality of their meat was better. Last but not least, they were claimed to be less susceptible to tuberculosis.[19]

A second alternative was a more robust type of black and white, found in the provinces of Groningen and South Holland. Thanks to the availability of agricultural waste products, fattening had traditionally been more important here than in Friesland and North Holland, resulting in a preference for heavier animals. Like MRIJ cattle, cows of this type were believed to be more resistant to tuberculosis than Friesians. In the 1910s and 1920s, a group of breeders of this variety, all living in the village of Hoornaar in South Holland, offered serious competition to the Friesian breeders of black and whites. An impression of the provincial rivalry sparked by this competition can be gleaned from the articles that one of the type's promoters, the agricultural journalist Engelbert van Muilwijk, published in *De Veldbode*. With respect to Friesian bulls he wrote, for example, that farmers should beware of using such "effeminate aristocrats" as sires, for within a few generations, tuberculosis-prone, bony offspring with a miserable constitution would be the result.[20] Animal husbandry adviser Jacques Timmermans challenged his readers to name a single Friesian bull that had done well in the southern province of Limburg. Imported Hoornaar bulls, on the other hand, he claimed, had almost without exception improved the local breed in this province.[21]

Figure 1.2 shows the most famous bull of the Hoornaar type: Dirk 4. For years, from the mid-1910s until well into the 1920s, he and his male offspring were considered to represent the ideal type of sire for dairy farmers on the lighter soils. The fact that their daughters' milk yields were lower than those of Friesian cows was acknowledged but accepted as the price to be paid for a healthy breed. As early as 1906, Inspector Van den Bosch had argued that it was better to aim for reasonable milk yields with a high butterfat percentage than to strive for record yields of milk with a low percentage of butterfat. Foreigners, he wrote, preferred cows with a sound conformation, and cows that produced milk that was almost like water were undesirable.[22] Van den Bosch had a point: English farmers in the 1910s and 1920s described the Friesians as an "irrigation breed" and as "mere water carts."[23] According to Carl Kronacher, a professor of animal breeding and a leading German expert, most German breeders preferred animals that were more solidly built than the Friesians.[24]

Nevertheless, the popularity of the Dirk 4 bloodline declined in the 1930s. Farmers may well have become dissatisfied with the even less than mediocre milk yield of this type of cow. The most important reason for its dwindling popularity, however, was that the Friesian breeders of black and whites made a rather spectacular comeback in these years. They had taken the criticism of their type to heart and had been working to improve it since the 1910s. In the 1920s, Friesian farmers also began a vigorous campaign to eradicate tuberculosis among their animals. With the help of the Friesian breeders' society, the cooperative creameries, and other provincial organizations, the first provincial animal health service in the Netherlands was established in Friesland in 1919. The other provinces would follow suit only after the Second World War. As a result, in 1950 the black and whites in Friesland would be the first to be officially declared free from bovine tuberculosis.[25]

A culmination point of the Friesian breeders' efforts to improve their black and whites was the bull Adema 197 (Figure 1.3), born in 1934 and bred by the reputed Knol Bros. in the hamlet of Hartwerd. In the eyes

Figure 1.2. Dirk 4. From Van Muilwijk, *De preferente zwartbonte N.R.S.-stieren*, 83.

Figure 1.3. Adema 197. From Strikwerda, *Een eeuw*, 310.

of the cognoscenti, this animal was the most glorious Friesian bull ever bred. Adema 197 was claimed to represent a type that adapted more easily to varying circumstances than the original Friesians. His back was broad and flat, and he was heavier, deeper, and shorter-legged than his late-nineteenth-century forebears. In contrast to the rather crude and coarse-haired Dirk 4, however, he retained the Friesian dairy type in his more elegant lines, supple skin, and fine hair. Moreover, Adema 197 exuded "nobility" (*adel*), as the breeders called it, a term borrowed from Friesian horse breeding, of which no straightforward definition can be given. It was used to denote the extra quality of conformation, or "beauty" (*schoonheid*), which distinguished the pick of the breed from animals that were merely phenotypically correct representatives. In the 1950s, the meaning and significance of the term would give rise to extensive discussions in the breeders societies' journals. Yet, whether it was a useful notion or not, no conformation expert would deny that Adema 197 was an icon of nobility.[26]

Adema 197's daughters were said to have a milk yield that was "satisfactory" – not too high, but good enough – while their milk had a high percentage of butterfat. Overall, Adema 197 thus represented an almost perfect bull according to prewar criteria. As a foundational bull for what came to be called the Modern Friesian, he was the most influential black-and-white Friesian sire for several decades. In the 1950s, there were few Friesian bulls that did not have Adema 197 in their pedigree at least once.[27]

## The Moral Economy of Breeding

The Modern Friesians, with Adema 197 as their harbinger, restored the breeders in Friesland to the respected position they had had in the late nineteenth century. In the 1950s, they experienced the heyday of their fame, nationally and internationally. The FRS, the Friesian breeders' society, flourished, the small circle of top breeders enjoyed enormous prestige, and their animals were sold for high prices. The jubilee shows organized by the FRS every five years attracted an international audience.[28] Foreign buyers were particularly impressed by the uniformity of the Friesians, and they knew full well that the breeders gave priority to quality of conformation. George Hobson, the secretary of the British Friesian Cattle Society, even stated categorically that in Holland "high milk yields [are] not sought."[29]

Two other factors contributed to the success of the black-and-white Friesians. To begin with, by the mid-1950s, bovine tuberculosis had been eradicated in all Dutch provinces.[30] Second, the differences in fertility between the heavier and lighter soils in the Netherlands had almost disappeared by that time as a result of artificial fertilizers and improved pasture management techniques, thus removing the major obstacles to the dissemination of the Friesian type.[31]

Still, the constitution of their animals continued to be one of the Friesian breeders' central concerns in the 1950s. It was their job, they argued, to safeguard the health and adaptability of the breed. While it might be argued that productivity came first for run-of-the-mill dairy farmers' cows, a different standard was needed for the breeding stock from which these animals were bred. Trade-offs between milk yield and conformation were necessary in the case of breeding stock; to strive for uniform and harmoniously built animals was no mere luxury or fancy. In the long run, well-bodied cows were profitable cows, and the nobility that distinguished the top of the breed was an extra guarantee of the quality of their progeny.[32]

Clearly, there was a normative element in the breeders' preference for the Modern Friesian. An analysis of Friesian farming practices by the rural sociologist Jan Douwe van der Ploeg helps to put this aspect into a wider perspective.[33] From the final decades of the nineteenth century onwards, according to Van der Ploeg, Friesian farmers developed an intensive style of dairying they designated as "neat" or "decent" (*kreas*, in Friesian) farming, as opposed to "rough" or "careless" (*rûch*) farming. The latter style had been dominant during parts of the eighteenth century, when floods and epidemics such as rinderpest were regular occurrences. Under such circumstances, farmers were reluctant to invest in their animals. They preferred an extensive farming style that aimed for quick profits with minimal investments of capital and labour. Food costs were kept as low as possible. The cows were housed only under severe weather conditions, and the young animals in particular were reared on sparing diets. Resources such as hay and manure were sold when market prices were favourable. Production was maximized by milking as many cows as was feasible and by keeping their dry period as short as possible. There was little or no interest in breed improvement and stockbreeding.

In the second half of the nineteenth century, however, when epidemic diseases were reasonably under control and economic prospects were better thanks to the opening of new markets, dairy farmers began to invest more in their animals and land, and to aim for long-term improvement. Central to this new style of farming was the idea of pursuing a perfect balance of resources within a closed system that produced only milk and meat as commodities. Hay and grains were no longer sold but fed to the animals as winter feed. Manure was used only to fertilize the farmers' own fields. The best calves were kept and reared on good food, either to replace the oldest cows or to be sold. In the first half of the twentieth century, this style of farming had become synonymous with good farming, according to Van der Ploeg. The farmers' own designation of their dairying style as neat or decent clearly indicates its normative character. Wageningen agricultural experts saw this intensive style as a model for the improvement of dairying practices in the Netherlands as a whole.

Friesian farmers' breeding practices and their perception of the ideal type of cow fit perfectly into this style of *kreas* farming. The increasing demand for breeding stock towards the end of the nineteenth century is in itself an illustration of the rise of an intensive farming style characterized by long-term planning and improvement. The fact that the farmers became more concerned with the quality of their products and aimed their selection efforts at raising the butterfat percentage of the milk points in the same direction. Another example is provided by the breeders' reaction to the problem of tuberculosis in the early decades of the twentieth century. Instead of resorting to *rûch* farming, as had been customary in earlier times, breeders faced the disease by modifying their animals to decrease the risk of infection: they turned the weedy Friesians into a sturdier type of cow. In the process, they sacrificed their extraordinary yields: maintaining a careful balance between constitution and production was believed to be the best option in the long run. The conviction that it was unwise to aim for record yields can thus be seen as an integral part of the *kreas* style of farming.

To a considerable extent, the same can be said of the high value attached to aesthetically pleasing cows, since many breeders considered beauty and constitution to be intimately related: beauty was an indication of the extra quality of constitution that was needed for breeding stock. Thus, striving for beauty was not necessarily a tell-tale sign of breeding for show. The beauty of a breeder's animals indicated his high standards of farming and breeding. From his customers' perspective, this was also the attraction of buying and owning such animals: if beautiful cows were good cows, beautiful animals contributed to the status of their owners as good farmers; such animals had the extra benefit of lending prestige. In this way, the aesthetic element gained its own momentum as a conspicuous breed characteristic of the Friesians, yet this does not alter the fact that, initially, this type of cow had been bred not just to please the eye but for reasons connected to what was considered to be good farming practice by breeders and buyers alike.

Seen from this perspective, it might be argued that the term *dubbeldoelkoe*, a literal translation of the English term dual-purpose cow, which gained currency in the 1950s, was a misnomer, as far as the Friesians were concerned. Before 1900, Friesian dairy farmers kept cows for their milk. It was the milk that earned them the bulk of their money; the meat was a by-product. The breeding of beefier animals, after 1900, was never intended to produce more meat. Nor were beefier animals believed to be more profitable. On the contrary, it was accepted that such animals might possibly be even less profitable in the short run than the pure dairy-type Friesians. The reason they were preferred was that stock of this type was believed to be more resilient and more profitable in the long run, over the generations. Considerations of this kind were at the heart of *kreas* farming, and thus the farmers' dairy cows were *kreas* animals rather than dual-purpose animals. The Modern Friesian, in summary, was as much a product of the moral as of the political economy of dairy farming.

## Bloodlines and Purity

The American cattle traders who bought thousands of Dutch Friesians in the 1870s and 1880s provided an incentive for organized breeding in the Netherlands by directly stimulating the establishment of breeders' societies. An American importer, Holstein pioneer Solomon Hoxie, acted as an adviser to the founders of the Friesian society FRS, and he and several other American buyers became founding members.[34] There is a pattern here, as Margaret Derry has shown: the establishment of breeders' societies and herd books is indicative of a rising international market.[35] The guarantees on paper provided by the societies' herd books were especially important for American buyers. Whereas a Dutch farmer would never buy a cow he had not inspected himself, North American geographical distances meant that the farmers had to rely on catalogues and certified pedigrees.

What pedigrees had to prove was purity. In the case of Arabian horses, for instance, purity was ascribed only to an animal all of whose ancestors descended from horses that had been bred, literally, in the desert. In Shorthorn cattle, purity referred to descent from the breeding stock of a very limited number of British breeders.[36] Likewise, a pedigree Friesian could be trusted to have descended from black-and-white ancestors bred in the province of Friesland. The Dutch national cattle breeders' society, the NRS, registered dairy cattle belonging to what was then called the Dutch Lowland Breed, mainly comprising the black and whites, the red and whites (MRIJ cattle), and the Groningen Whitehead (*blaarkop* in Dutch).[37] To safeguard the exclusivity of their black and whites, the FRS did not accept black and whites from other provinces to be registered in its herd book.[38]

The concept of purity was an ambiguous and contested one.[39] For instance, the nineteenth-century notion of constancy of a pure race (*Konstanztheorie*), propagated by the German horse expert Johann Justinus, was based on the conviction that purity resided in an inborn potential of a true race to pass down its defining characteristics consistently and unchangingly over generations, regardless of the circumstances under which the animals were kept.[40] Many nineteenth-century livestock breeders knew from experience, however, that the purity of their breeds could not be so strictly defined. Friesian breeders were well aware that the purity of their black and whites needed maintenance even under stable environmental circumstances. This was demonstrated, for instance, by the irregular occurrence of red-and-white calves born from black-and-white parents. In its early years, the FRS was happy to register such calves and other off-coloured animals. They would soon be relegated to separate registers, however, to please the American buyers, for whom a pure Friesian had to be black and white.[41]

Still, Friesian breeders did believe that their animals represented a very old purebred breed that had been native to Friesland since prehistoric times.[42] Crossing different breeds, which was still common in other provinces at the time, was supposed to have been the exception in Friesland, and a "pure" core of Friesians was claimed to have been preserved in the province through the ages.[43] Accordingly, the most stringent requirement for a Friesian to be accepted for registration in the herd book concerned geographical provenance: the animal should be descended from ancestors bred by Friesian breeders. In this way, the notion of purity functioned exactly as intended, namely to protect the commercial interests of breeders in Friesland and their buyers.

After 1900, geneticists would translate purity into Mendelian terms: purity meant homozygosity of the genes responsible for the breed's characteristics. Yet the purity concept had connotations of exclusivity and quality that Mendelism could not capture. An example is provided by a veritable cause célèbre in Dutch cattle breeding, the so-called coloured spots problem (*vlekjeskwestie*). In the middle of the nineteenth century, a number of Shorthorn bulls were imported into the Netherlands from the UK. Some agricultural experts believed that they might be able to improve the beef quality of the Dutch dairy cows.[44] The experiment was soon terminated, however, because the milk yields of the crossbreds turned out to be disappointingly low. Traces of Shorthorn influence remained visible for some time in the coloration of the experimental herds, but these progressively disappeared over the course of several generations. However, the idea took hold, among breeders and farmers alike, that isolated coloured spots on the lower legs were an indication of lingering Shorthorn influence. Such spots were therefore considered to be flaws, and highly undesirable. In the 1920s, animals with spots on their phalanges were even excluded from registration by the FRS.[45]

Until well into the twentieth century, scientists and animal husbandry advisers would spill gallons of ink trying to convince the breeders' organizations that excellent animals were, for no good reason, being kept out of breeding programs in this way. In their view, there was no evidence that the coloured spots derived from Shorthorns, while, more important, a cow's productivity was in no way affected by their presence.[46] It was to no avail, however. In 1912, the breeder Arie Groneman wrote that while the experts might well be right, breeders had different concerns: buyers, especially foreign traders, wanted purebred black and whites, and pure animals were not supposed to have spots.[47] The breeders' organizations acted accordingly and did not change their policy. Clearly, purity referred to a breed standard that could not be compromised, regardless of whether a deviation from the standard was functionally significant or not. What was at issue here was not genetics but marketability.[48]

To maintain the desirable qualities of their herds, Dutch breeders employed methods that, as Roger Wood and Vítězslav Orel have shown, had been common practice among experienced breeders since the late eighteenth century.[49] Breeders knew that the best strategy to maintain the defining characteristics of their stock was to breed the animals among themselves.In its strictest form, this amounted to inbreeding, which was indeed practised by all experienced breeders of Friesians.[50] Even parent-offspring and sibling matings were not shunned. Adema 197, to give but one example, was the product of a mating between siblings. He had only one grandfather, and his grandmothers were related, as aunt and niece.[51] The risks of inbreeding were well known. Defective offspring had to be culled carefully and some outbreeding was unavoidable once in a while. Still, the ideal of a uniform herd, in the breeders' opinion, could only be realized by means of close inbreeding. The top breeders created their own "bloodlines" in this way which were considered to buttress the quality of the breed as a whole.[52]

An additional advantage of breeding in bloodlines was that the herds of the top breeders were not only very uniform; there were also slight differences between them. This was the result of minor variations in conformation, present in each herd, that had been consolidated through inbreeding. This enabled farmers to tell the bloodlines apart, and thus helped the breeders to enhance the exclusivity of their stock. For instance, breeders in North Holland produced black and whites of a larger and milkier type than those in Friesland. Experienced buyers had no difficulty distinguishing between them on the basis of their conformation.[53]

Agricultural exhibitions and conformation shows were the breeders' principal instrument to demonstrate the conformation quality of their stock. They had been introduced around 1850 to raise interest in breed improvement, but they began to play a prominent role only in the early twentieth century. The increase in the number of regional, provincial, and national shows that breeders and farmers associations organized after 1900 testifies to the growing popularity of purebred breeding. Commercial interests were an important driver, for, as indicated, show prizes earned breeders money. After a successful show, sales of their stock would immediately pick up.

Several other instruments were employed by breeders' organizations and the government to rationalize the methods used by farmers to improve their herds. The new insights provided by Mendel's theory of inheritance, "rediscovered" in 1900, were among them.

## Scientific Breeding

For the Dutch botanist Hugo de Vries, one of the "rediscoverers," the improvement of plant breeding and agriculture had been the principal motive for investigating hereditary phenomena, and he considered Mendel's laws to be directly relevant for breeding agricultural varieties.[54] While the possible implications of Mendelism for agriculture had thus been pointed out from the start, Dutch animal breeding experts were more hesitant in confronting their field with Mendelian genetics. The subject only began to receive serious consideration in the 1910s, when Mendel's laws were explained in several monographs and articles.[55] Even then, the authors took most of their examples from botany; examples from livestock breeding merely involved simple Mendelian phenomena, such as the inheritance of coat colour in farm animals.

The veterinarian Aryen van Leeuwen, the stockbreeding expert of *De Veldbode*, expressed his reservations about the general validity of the theory. He enquired among his readers about the possibility of a black-and-white cow being bred from red-and-white parents. Black and whites were known to occasionally produce a red-and-white calf, but was the reverse also possible? A group of farmers responded that they had never come across such an anomaly; only a single farmer believed that he had. Van Leeuwen concluded that although alternative explanations could not be ruled out, this was indeed supporting evidence for interpreting the red colour as resulting from a Mendelian recessive trait.[56] The presence or absence of horns appeared to fall into the same category, and the more difficult example of coat colour in horses also turned out to be amenable to a Mendelian explanation.

In 1910, the geneticist Arend Hagedoorn, a pupil of Hugo de Vries and Jacques Loeb, was invited by the Holland Agricultural Society to help design breeding strategies for the improvement of Texel sheep.[57] Breeders had been hybridizing the Texel with English races, such as the Lincoln and the Wensleydale, for several decades. Aiming for a uniform new type, they were struggling to get rid of unwanted fleece and nose colours. Hagedoorn tried to help them by devising breeding schemes along Mendelian lines. As we will see in the chapter on sheep breeding, the project was discontinued after some time, probably because of the complexity and rising costs of test-mating and culling.[58] This example illustrates the problems inherent in applying a Mendelian approach to livestock breeding compared to plant breeding. As the Wageningen animal husbandry professor Jan Reimers pointed out in 1916, experimenting with plants was easier because they could be self-fertilized, were cheap, and could easily be obtained as well as dispensed with in large quantities. Individual animals, on the other hand, especially the larger farm animals, represented a significant economic value and produced far fewer descendants. The costs of experiments therefore quickly became prohibitive.[59] Deliberately trying to produce even a single red-and-white calf, for instance, was not something a breeder of Friesians would readily do for experimental reasons. And he would certainly not be prepared to experiment with more than one detrimental recessive factor.

Moreover, until now, we have only been discussing qualitative characteristics such as coat colour, which are based on a single or a small number of Mendelian factors. Economically, the most important characteristics of livestock, such as milk and meat production, are of the quantitative kind. Even scientists who were convinced that such characteristics could also be explained in Mendelian terms had to admit that in this case the practical application of Mendelian theory was virtually impossible. According to Reimers, a quantitative characteristic such as milk yield might be accounted for by assuming that a group of Mendelian factors with additive effect was responsible for the trait. Yet, even if a Mendelian breeding scheme based on this assumption could be devised to improve milk yields, the complexity and costs of such a program presented insurmountable difficulties. In the same vein, Hagedoorn remarked that breeders of farm animals, unlike plant breeders, would learn nothing of practical use from a visit to the leading agricultural experiment station in Svalöf, in Sweden.[60]

Hagedoorn would become a widely known expert in animal breeding and genetics, yet he confined his experiments to small laboratory animals such as mice and farm animals that were inexpensive, could be kept in large numbers, and produced reasonable numbers of offspring, such as chickens and rabbits. He entertained no doubts that Mendelian theory provided the basis to decide on the rationality of traditional cattle-breeding methods, yet he was well aware that a Mendelian reform of breeding strategies was an entirely different matter. The genes responsible for quantitative characteristics such as milk yield and egg production were unknown, so they could not be analysed by Mendelian crossing schemes. Consequently, traditional breeding methods would be indispensable for a long time to come. In 1927, Hagedoorn stated that the influence of genetic theory on cattle breeding practices had been negligible. In his well-known *Animal Breeding* (1939), he even wrote that it had been the other way around: geneticists had learned a lot from the best breeders. What geneticists had to offer to the breeders of large farm animals was different: "The geneticists' main contribution to animal breeding is not an analysis of genes, but an analysis of breeding methods."[61] This view was widely shared among animal breeding experts at the time.[62]

What did the assistance geneticists might give consist of, according to Hagedoorn and his scientific colleagues? To begin with, geneticists and animal husbandry experts concurred with the breeders that inbreeding was a rational strategy. The haphazard crossing of breeds that had been customary among small farmers until the late nineteenth century had resulted in motley collections of animals with unpredictable and widely varying characteristics.[63] Improvement was impossible on such as basis, and the board of the NRS had been wise, in 1906, to have formally subdivided the Dutch Lowland Breed into three clearly delineated breeds: the black-and-white Friesian, the red-and-white MRIJ, and the Groningen Whitehead.[64] Still, even stock improvement within narrowly defined breeds would remain something of a lottery as long as bulls of different provenance were used every few years. The scientists agreed with the top breeders that it was much better to start from a group of excellent animals and to consolidate their qualities in a closely inbred herd. Purity, translated into Mendelian terms, meant homozygosity, and inbreeding increased the degree of homozygosity. Therefore, inbreeding was a rational strategy of breed improvement, provided it was accompanied by scrupulous culling of animals with unwanted recessive traits. Scientists explicitly advised against needless outbreeding with unrelated animals. A bull from an unrelated herd with a long history of its own was bound to be genetically different, in many characteristics. Recombination would bring these differences to expression in the second generation, thus possibly undoing the accomplishments of years of careful inbreeding and selecting. Moreover, animals imported from other regions might not adapt well to local circumstances, as illustrated by the example discussed earlier of Friesians deteriorating on poor soil.[65]

At the same time, however, scientists warned breeders not to overestimate the value of pedigrees. Obviously, the productivity of his ancestors should play a role in the choice of a bull, but it was of little use to study more than a few generations of an animal's ancestry. From a Mendelian perspective, it was more instructive to look at a bull's brothers and sisters, since they provided more reliable insights into his genetic strengths and weaknesses than remote ancestors, whose contributions to his genes were insignificant.[66]

It is hard to say whether commercial breeders heeded this advice. Yet even a cursory survey of breeding journals and histories of cattle breeding suffices to conclude that, as far as the market for breeding stock was concerned, the preoccupation with pedigrees continued at least as long as inbreeding remained the principal breeding method and a breeder's reputation was inseparably bound up with the reputation of his bloodlines. For instance, until well after the Second World War, journal articles on individual breeders invariably included detailed information on the pedigrees of the foundational animals of their herds. The NRS published several illustrated genealogies of the most prestigious bloodlines, and a detailed description of bloodlines constituted the pièce de résistance of historical works on the breeders' societies.[67] The top breeders, Knol Bros., even had the history of their stock farm and bloodlines privately published.[68] Again, pedigree, like purity, was not merely about genes. Famous ancestors, however remote, continued to lend prestige to their bloodline; a herd's history guaranteed its quality and distinction. There is an obvious contrast here with the Mendelian interpretation of purity: as soon as a breed becomes pure in Mendelian terms, i.e., homozygous, its history becomes irrelevant. In a sense, the point of Mendelian breeding could be said to be the elimination of a herd's history.

Another frequently heard scientific critique of breeders' practices was that the breeders' organizations were attuned to their members' commercial interests rather than to cattle improvement. Herd books, it was argued, might serve as invaluable tools. For instance, much might be learned about hereditary diseases if all descendants of pedigree animals were registered and if their genetic peculiarities were also recorded.[69] It takes no stretch of the imagination, however, to realize that breeders could muster up little enthusiasm for such a suggestion. To begin with, they were charged for registering their animals, so they offered only the best ones for inspection.[70] Second, for obvious reasons, many breeders preferred any malformed progeny of their prize-winning animals to disappear without a trace. Officials of the breeders' societies feared that they would lose all their members if complete registration became compulsory, and scientists conceded that they had a point.[71] Thus, in the period before the Second World War, the herd books did not develop into the instruments for rational breeding that scientists would have liked them to become.

Finally, scientists agreed that rational breeding should be based on progeny testing. Conformation and pedigrees were helpful for finding a promising young bull, yet, ultimately, it was the performance of his daughters as dairy cows that determined the true value of a sire. Therefore, breed improvement required the systematic use of tested bulls. Incidentally, this was not a new insight. It was hinted at in the well-known biblical phrase "the tree is known by its fruit," and some breeders in antiquity were certainly aware that the value of breeding stock could be gauged from their offspring. The methods of eighteenth-century breeders such as Robert Bakewell also reflect this principle.[72] From the early decades of the twentieth century onwards, Hagedoorn in particular campaigned in agricultural weeklies for progeny testing, and he relentlessly repeated the message in his scientific and popular publications. Ideally, he added, several promising young bulls should be tested on a limited number of cows, and only the best ones should then be widely used as sires.[73]

In this case, there is no evidence that the breeders disagreed in principle. Yet again, however, meeting this demand in practice was a different matter. The ideal situation, as sketched by Hagedoorn, was impracticable in every respect until the 1940s.[74] Farms in the Netherlands were small and very few farmers milked more than ten cows. For instance, in 1920, the 953 members of breeding associations in the province of Limburg owned a total of 2,990 cows. In the Netherlands as a whole, an average number of ten cows per farm would only be reached in the 1950s.[75] Bulls were costly to maintain, and bull calves increased in value only until their second or third year. As a rule, farmers who could afford a bull of their own bought a young bull calf, used it for a year or two, and then sold it for slaughtering.[76] Thus, by the time their daughters began to give milk and their real worth became apparent, most bulls were dead.

Since the late eighteenth century, small farmers in many regions of the Netherlands had traditionally shared a bull, purchased with municipal support. There were fine animals among them, yet poor ones too.[77] After 1890, more and more farmers joined breeders' associations, which enabled them to buy and share better bulls. Government premiums helped them to keep the good ones for a longer period.[78] While some of these associations flourished and managed to improve their members' stock in this way, others fared less well and were discontinued after a number of years. There were many obstacles to overcome: farmers had to agree on the type of bull to be purchased; after several years of use, father-daughter inbreeding became unavoidable; a shared bull might spread venereal diseases; older bulls might become dangerous or too fat to perform; and the progeny even of an expensive bull could turn out to be disappointing.[79] On the other hand, once a breeding association had acquired a certain reputation, its members might be tempted to buy or rear a bull of their own to get a share in the breeding market.[80]

Farmers might also use an excellent sire owned by a breeder. Yet, even if distance and the difficulty of transportation did not preclude such an option, the prices that breeders charged for insemination put many farmers off. Around 1910, prices varied between 25 cents and 20 guilders, and the breeder Florentius Groneman found that most small farmers were not prepared to pay the 2 guilders he charged for an insemination by his service bull.[81]

Besides such complications, the number of cows inseminated by a bull exploited by a top breeder or an association was still small. In many cases, a reliable assessment of a bull's productive qualities, for which a substantial number of lactating daughters was required, was possible only after his death. Most bulls that earned the coveted title of *preferentschap*, indicating proven hereditary excellence, were no longer around to receive the honours or at best were near the end of their period of service.[82] The ideal situation as envisaged by Hagedoorn, in which a fair number of young bulls were tested before the best of them – by that time having reached the age of five or six years – seriously began their tour of duty, was beyond the means, financially and practically, of even the most prosperous breeding associations. In 1941, after Hagedoorn had once again underlined the importance of systematic progeny testing in a public lecture, H.W. Kuhn, the NRS president, commented that Hagedoorn was apparently ignorant of commercial cattle breeding: breeders could not possibly implement such a system, for both practical and economic reasons.[83] The animal husbandry adviser Reinder Anema even predicted that current practices would probably not change for a hundred years.[84]

Kuhn and Anema's assessment of the prewar situation was correct, yet with respect to the future it turned out to have been premature. Progeny testing became feasible after the introduction of artificial insemination in the early 1940s, and its implementation went hand in hand with drastic changes in the organizational structure as well as in the moral economy of dairy cattle breeding. In the process, scientists took the lead in breeding matters, while the breeders were slowly but surely relegated to the sidelines. This transformation did not take place overnight; it took several decades, and it was accompanied by a prolonged and heated debate over which qualities were essential for good breeding stock. The first impetus to the eventual changeover in breeding culture was given when Dutch agricultural policy was reoriented after the Second World War.

## Nobility or Production?

In the Netherlands, the first two decades after the war were years of vigorous growth – of the population, the economy, and of agricultural production. In the late 1940s, the Dutch government's agricultural policy took a new approach. Mindful of the crisis of the 1930s, which had heavily taxed the farmers, and of the famine during the last winter of the war, Minister of Agriculture Sicco Mansholt, later to become the first EEC commissioner for agriculture, set himself the dual task of stepping up agricultural production to feed the rapidly growing population and ensuring the farmers a reasonable income. In the early decades of the century, the profusion of small farms that characterized Dutch agriculture had been supported by the government in various ways. Small farming, it was reasoned in those years, could earn a great many households a decent livelihood. By the end of the 1940s, however, this was no longer deemed rational. Productivity per worker on small farms was too low, compared with that of industrial workers, and prospects for increasing it seemed dim. Mansholt decided that his ministry should redirect its support towards farms that were large enough to offer opportunities for increasing both production and efficiency.

Thus, around 1950 the agricultural "modernization project" was begun, whose principal objectives were to scale up, mechanize, specialize, and further intensify farming. The government took an active part by establishing price protection measures and by investing in research, education, and advice. The agricultural advisory service was expanded, and besides giving technical advice the advisers now also evaluated individual farms from an economic perspective, to determine whether it was rational to keep the farm going and what it would take to do so successfully. The guaranteed prices that farmers were paid for their products were based on such analyses of viability. Thus, in the 1950s, many farmers modernized their holdings in the sense envisaged by Mansholt, and they managed to earn an income that more or less kept up with industrial wages. Others gave up their farms: between 1950 and 1960, the number of dairy farmers decreased from 208,000 to 183,000.[85]

The policy to help increase productivity found ready support among the Wageningen agricultural experts. Wageningen Agricultural College was unique in that it was not responsible to the Ministry of Education, like the universities, but to the Ministry of Agriculture. During the greater part of the twentieth century, the ties between Wageningen and the Ministry were very close. Historian Harro Maat has characterized the alliance between agricultural science and the government as a "discourse coalition" in which problems were commonly defined and also solved through close interaction.[86] As a rule, the heads of the ministerial Directorate of Animal Husbandry and Dairying were recruited from the Wageningen corps of agriculturalists, as were most governmental animal husbandry and dairy advisers.[87] Conversely, the activities of the Wageningen animal husbandry department reflected the ministerial objectives. According to Wageningen's leading postwar cattle-breeding expert, Rommert Politiek, dairy farmers should not just scale up their holdings but also pay much more attention to the productivity of individual cows: as he phrased it, "more *better* cows per farmer" should be their motto.[88]

In line with the government's new policy, the average Dutch dairy farm was scaled up and intensified in the number of cows per farm and per hectare. Between 1950 and 1974, numbers rose from 7.1 to 22.7 cows per farm and from 1.15 to 1.69 cows per hectare.[89] Yet where the productivity of individual cows was concerned, animal husbandry specialists felt that the farmers were doing much less well. While participation in milk-recording associations grew from some 20 per cent of all dairy farmers before the war to almost 70 per cent in the 1960s, milk yields were increasing much too slowly in their view. In 1950, the average yearly production of milk-recorded black and whites was 4,054 kg; in 1960, it was 4,378 kg and in 1970 the figure had risen to 4,652 kg (Figure 1.4). Milk yields in Friesland hardly increased at all during this period.[90]

Insufficiently intense selection for production, particularly of the breeding bulls, was targeted as the main reason for these disappointing results. Looking at a sample of 166 breeding bulls, the agricultural scientist Bertus Geessink concluded in 1956 that 27 per cent of them had caused a stagnation and 38 per cent a decline in milk yields.[91] In 1964, less than 3 per cent of all sires were found to be excellent in terms of both milk yield and the milk's butterfat and protein percentages.[92] Considering the improvement of fodder production and pasture management techniques in the postwar years, experts suspected that the bulls' hereditary potential for production might actually be declining. This was all the more frustrating, they felt, because the main tool for

Figure 1.4. Milk recording around 1950. From the archives of the cattle breeders' journal *Veeteelt*. © Veeteelt (CRV Holding BV).

systematic improvement of milk yields, artificial insemination, had been widely available since the 1940s.[93]

AI was introduced in cattle breeding in western countries in the mid-1930s. In the Netherlands, the veterinarian Jan Siebenga was the first to investigate the technique. In collaboration with the British AI pioneer John Hammond, he produced the first "international calf" by sending a vial containing fresh semen across the Channel to Cambridge, where a cow was successfully inseminated with it. Interestingly, the technique was initially developed as a solution to the problem of infectious genital diseases, which caused sterility and abortions and had become a serious threat to many herds in the interwar period. The first Dutch AI association was established in 1939 to fight such infections.[94]

Yet the technique's potential for breeding purposes was recognized from the start. Milk recording provided the farmer with information about the productivity of his individual cows, yet breed improvement via the selection of the best cows was a slow process, as each had only a single calf per year. The bull, however, was half the herd, as the saying went: he contributed 50 per cent of the next generation's genetic make-up. Besides allowing for hygienic exploitation of a sire, AI enabled a bull of high genetic merit to impregnate many more cows. Depending on the quality of his semen, several hundred (later up to several thousand) cows could be inseminated with diluted portions of a single ejaculate. Moreover, as it was no longer the animals themselves, but only the sire's sperm that did the travelling, the geographical range of action of a good bull was vastly expanded. Last but not least, AI facilitated the progeny tests needed to find good bulls in an efficient manner. Before the war, without AI, progeny testing had been virtually impossible.

The geneticist Hagedoorn, for instance, strongly recommended the use of AI for breed improvement in his *Animal Breeding*. Directly after the war he was joined by the Utrecht animal scientist Gerard van der Plank, who explained how American and Scandinavian breeders were beginning to exploit the possibilities of AI for improving their animals' hereditary potential for milk production.[95] As we will see, however, the scientists' high expectations of the use of AI for breed improvement were not to be realized until about 1970.

While the number of AI associations in the Netherlands began to grow rapidly in the 1940s, the initial reactions of the breeders' societies to the new technique were dismissive. They had been established in the late nineteenth century to protect the interests of commercial breeders, and it was obvious that fewer bulls would be needed if AI became a success. The Friesian FRS, which counted some of the country's best breeders among its ranks, therefore prescribed that its members refrain from using AI. The national NRS similarly declared it would not help advance a technique that undermined its members' incentive for breeding. Yet before long, the rapid expansion of AI forced the societies to reconsider their ban. By 1946, when national regulations for AI were drawn up, they accepted calves produced through AI in their registers.[96]

The rapid spread of AI was due entirely to its effectiveness in preventing venereal infections, not to its potential as a tool for increasing milk yields. Much to the scientists' dismay, breeders, farmers, and also some of the animal husbandry advisers clung to the ideas they had developed in the decades before the war about how to breed dairy cattle and what the characteristics of such animals should be. The heart of the matter was that, for breeders and farmers, a good sire was not necessarily an animal that had performed well in a progeny test that established his hereditary potential for milk production. In their view, a good bull, like a good cow, was an animal that won prizes for conformation at cattle shows, because quality of conformation was a reflection of inner quality, particularly of the animal's constitution. And as the problems with the Friesians in the early twentieth century had shown, priority in selecting breeding stock should be given to constitution rather than milk production. *Kreas* (decent) farming, which was aimed at long-term improvement, required that a watchful eye be kept on the breed's robustness, even if this entailed a sacrifice in milk production. Even such details as the shape of an animal's head and the fineness of the horns were tell-tale signs to the experienced breeder: "The head," said breeder and FRS chairman Sijtze Kingma, "reveals the very nature of breeding stock [because] behind a fine head there is always a good breeding cow."[97] One-sided selection for milk production might yield remarkable short-term results, yet in the long run well-bodied cows were more low-maintenance and disease-resistant – and therefore more profitable.

As numerous comments in cattle breeding journals reveal, the breeders believed that scientific rationality would never be able to displace their intuitive and subjective evaluation of a bull or cow's qualities. According to IJsbrandus van Popta, the editor of the Friesian cattle breeding journal *De Friese Veefokkerij*, breeding was more than math, and breeders' intuition and practical insights should always take precedence over dead production numbers. The "creative potential" to safeguard quality of conformation, he wrote, was not to be found "in the minds of biologists, geneticists, inspectors or administrators, but in the mind of the breeder who loves his animals and for that very reason understands their nature."[98] And did the booming market for Friesians not demonstrate that the breeders had got their priorities right?[99] The editors of the NRS breeding journal *De Keurstamboeker* conveyed the same message in equally confident terms: "We are absolutely convinced that [our international reputation] is partly due to our system of evaluating conformation."[100]

Conformation was also important for the breeders from a purely commercial perspective. The Modern Friesian enjoyed immense popularity in the 1950s, and both the pedigree breeders and the leading breeders' societies experienced a heyday (Figure 1.5). Membership of the societies grew to unprecedented heights: in the early 1960s about a third of all dairy farmers had joined the FRS or the NRS, and with its 58,000 members the NRS claimed to be the biggest cattle breeders' society in the world.[101] Black-and-white breeding stock was sold to more than forty countries in Europe, South America, Africa, and Asia, and the best animals were sold for record prices of up to 250,000 guilders. Obviously, besides long-term profitability, good conformation also indicated marketability. As Theo Kees Rijssenbeek, the animal husbandry director of the Ministry of Agriculture, conceded in 1956, while it was hard to say whether the Modern Friesian represented a more profitable type for the farmer, it definitely sold better than the old milkier type.[102]

This acknowledgement did not prevent agriculturalists and veterinarians from launching a sustained attack on the role of shows in breeding

Figure 1.5. Crowd at a cattle show in Leeuwarden (Friesland) in 1953. From the archives of the cattle breeders' journal *Veeteelt*. © Veeteelt (CRV Holding BV).

practices in the late 1950s. In their view, the focus on conformation was becoming a serious impediment to the improvement of productivity. While data from the milk-recording services showed that milk yields had hardly increased since the war, the bulls and cows themselves were definitely changing: they were becoming smaller, bulkier, shorter-legged, and beefier. True, the Dutch dairy cow produced milk and meat, but the greater part of the profit came from the milk, and the breeders were overemphasizing their animals' disposition for meat production. Considering the many prizes such stocky animals were awarded at shows, it seemed as if breeders were unwittingly turning the Dutch dairy cow into a hobby breed unfit for its main economic purpose.

Even the breeders' societies were puzzled by the loss in withers height of the black and whites: NRS official Klaas Stapel speculated that smaller cows, while producing less, were easier to maintain in the years of crisis before the Second World War.[103] Wieger de Jong, professor of animal husbandry at Wageningen Agricultural College had argued more plausibly as early as 1943 that the decrease in size was a side effect of breeding for shows. In terms of procreation, the fate of a bull was decided on at an early age. According to De Jong, animals that matured early, i.e., acquired adult proportions rapidly and fattened easily, were preferred by herd book inspectors and judges at bull shows. As it happened, such qualities were more often found in relatively small bulls than in larger ones, which looked rather gawky in their younger years. De Jong concluded that since small bulls won the prizes at shows, they had been systematically preferred as sires, and in the long run this had resulted in a decrease in size of the breed as a whole.[104]

De Jong occupied the middle ground in the rising debate over breeding practices in the 1940s and 1950s. He had risen from the ranks in both practical and scientific circles. The son of a dairy farmer and a Wageningen graduate, he had worked as a provincial animal husbandry adviser and herd-book inspector before being appointed president of the NRS in 1947 and, in the same year, professor of animal husbandry at Wageningen.[105] In these capacities, De Jong represented both the Wageningen scientists and the organized breeders, and he carefully weighed the arguments from both sides against each other.

First, he pointed to the difficulties inherent in the notion of constitution. Unquestionably, a healthy constitution was important, yet how were constitution and conformation related? Were short legs stronger, did a weedy frame affect longevity, were sturdy-looking animals really healthier? Only comparative studies could decide on such matters, he argued, and these had yet to be undertaken. Nevertheless, De Jong sympathized with breeders who strove for beauty of conformation. Even hobby breeding should not be rejected out of hand, as for many farmers the joy of breeding was bound up with their competitive efforts to create the perfect animal. Conformation shows provided the sporting ground to assess the level of their achievement, and breeding would lose much of its attraction without these incentives.[106]

While sympathetic towards the breeders' concerns, De Jong was no less worried about the productivity of the black and whites than his scientific colleagues. As early as 1943, he had shown that there was no correlation between the overall scores for conformation that animals were allotted by herd-book inspectors and their milk yield. As to the different parts of the body, only the points for udder quality were correlated with productivity.[107]

According to the more outspoken Piet Hoekstra, professor of animal breeding at Utrecht University, the notion of nobility contributed nothing tangible to the functionality of the black and whites. Hoekstra argued that selecting for nobility was damaging to the breed's principal purpose, because productivity in terms of milk yield was showing stagnation. Like Hagedoorn before the war, Hoekstra accused the top breeders of breeding for show and of turning cattle shows into sporting events. Nobility, he noted scornfully, merely helped breeders to get better prices for their bulls.[108]

The Wageningen animal husbandry lecturer Rommert Politiek pointed to the equally deplorable fact that show practices hampered the implementation of progeny testing, for the breeders' focus on conformation was shared by the executive committees of the cooperative AI associations. The bulls that were most sought after by these committees were the ones that had won prizes at important shows, not the ones that had proved to be of high genetic merit for milk production. Thus it was no rare occurrence that an expensive prize bull's daughters turned out to be poor milk producers. A radical change of strategy was required, Politiek and other experts argued. AI associations should stop buying show champions (or their sons) and switch to bull calves from parents with excellent milk-production credentials. And they should first put these young bulls to the test and use only the best ones as breeding bulls.[109]

The AI associations ignored this advice and continued to give priority to conformation. This is reflected in their organization: until the late 1960s they would remain too small to be capable of performing effective progeny tests. An association had to have a minimum size to be able, practically as well as financially, to perform adequate progeny tests on promising bulls. It was a laborious procedure that entailed the following steps. A number of young test bulls had to be bought and mated to a restricted number of cows. The bulls then had to enter a waiting period of several years until their daughters' milk production performance was known. Then one or several of them – depending on the preferred intensity of selection – could be selected to become breeding bulls. Politiek calculated in 1969 that the costs involved in raising a reasonably good proven bull amounted to 80,000 guilders, a sum manageable only for the larger AI associations. Practically speaking, according to Politiek, an association's bulls had to service at least 50,000 cows a year to maintain an effective progeny-testing program. Only a single association in the Netherlands had reached this size in 1969. There were ninety-three AI associations at that time – far too many, in the scientists' view – and the average association performed only just over 12,000 inseminations annually.[110]

From the farmers' perspective, however, this large number of small AI associations made perfect sense. Many of the associations were direct descendants of the numerous local associations for breed improvement that had existed before the war. The introduction of AI had merely changed the modus operandi of the breeding bulls, so to speak, not that of the association as a whole. Bulls were chosen after long deliberation, and the smaller an association was the more influence its members had on the choice. The details of a bull's conformation reflected the aims the members set themselves for breed improvement. The bulls were quite literally the AI associations' showpieces, as they competed with each other in the show ring. Sharing good bulls or merging associations to enable progeny testing was contrary to the spirit of competition that dominated the relations between associations. In the late 1950s, the national AI supervisory committee regretfully noted that their exclusivity even prevented associations from cooperating with their direct neighbours. Inseminations with semen obtained from other associations accounted for barely 0.5 per cent of the total number of inseminations performed by all associations in a year.[111]

Technically speaking, there were no obstacles to merging AI associations into larger units. As long as fresh semen was used, it was the range of action of the inseminators – the geographical area they could cover in a day – that set practical limits on the size of an association. Sperm preservation by freezing, developed in the United Kingdom in 1952 and introduced in the Netherlands in 1954, enabled associations to store and use their semen for years.[112] Transportation was facilitated by the techniques of packing semen in tablets or straws. Thus good bulls could be exploited on an unprecedented scale. Yet the freezing technique remained of only marginal importance in the Netherlands until the late sixties. In 1964, ten years after its introduction, frozen sperm accounted for less than 1 per cent of all inseminations.[113] In other words, the AI associations remained small enough to manage with short-lived live sperm, and felt little need to exchange sperm with other associations at a distance. Likewise, the possibilities of international exchange remained virtually unexplored.

In the mid-1960s, Politiek and his scientific colleagues had a list of complaints they regularly put before the AI associations. They were said to disregard the advantages of collaboration and of the use of frozen sperm, and to continue to use show bulls whose hereditary capacity for milk production was unknown. Even when attempts at progeny testing were made, these could not yield trustworthy results: the associations were simply too small to perform reliable tests, as data from the milk-recording services amply confirmed.[114] Moreover, good sires – in terms of milk production – were sometimes refused the official title of proven sire by the breeders' societies because their offspring's quality of conformation was considered insufficient. Conversely, beautiful daughters that were below-average producers regularly earned their father the coveted title.[115] All in all, the experts concluded, it was hardly surprising that progress in improving milk production was slow. According to the 1965 yearly report of the national AI supervisory committee, it was high time for the AI associations to overcome their wariness of merging and to adopt a more businesslike approach.[116]

Clearly, conflicting views on which characteristics made for a profitable breed, and should therefore be most intensively selected for, were at the basis of the disagreement between scientists and breeders. The scientific experts focused on milk production per cow and accordingly emphasized the importance of progeny testing. Breeders and farmers concentrated on excellence of conformation, which in their view guaranteed the robustness of the breed and was at the basis of the Modern Friesian's commercial success.[117]

The breeders' viewpoint was to remain dominant in breeding practices until the late 1960s, yet the stagnation of the growth of milk production did not leave them altogether indifferent. In 1963, the breeders in Friesland were unnerved by the news that the cows in most other provinces were now more productive than theirs. The FRS suggested that the explanation was to be found in management differences, not in the quality of the cows.[118] Still, as the 1960s progressed, the breeders and their organizations increasingly turned their attention to production figures. For instance, in 1965 the NRS decided that young bulls from Friesland, to be admitted for registration by the NRS, should have fathers that met minimum productivity requirements.[119] In 1966, after more than eighty years of isolation, the FRS dropped the requirement that a pedigree black and white had to have Friesland-born parents.[120] This enabled its members to buy black and whites elsewhere, particularly in North Holland, where many farmers produced milk for consumption and yields had always been slightly higher.[121]

The late 1960s witnessed the beginning of a growing willingness to change course. In 1968, a respected spokesman for the breeders acknowledged that their autocracy was a thing of the past; science had begun to play a role that could no longer be ignored. More and more, Politiek noted with satisfaction, breeding policy decisions were taken by the AI associations rather than by the traditional breeders. In 1969, Piet Scheer, secretary of the provincial union of AI associations in Friesland, was convinced that a breakthrough was imminent.[122] The main impetus for this turnabout, I would suggest, was provided by a looming economic crisis in the late 1960s.

**Entrepreneurship**

As we saw earlier, Sicco Mansholt, the first postwar Dutch minister of agriculture, used price protection as a means of guaranteeing the farmers an income that was on par with industrial wages.[123] This worked fairly well in the 1950s, when the Dutch government succeeded in keeping wages within bounds. When he became commissioner for agriculture of the European Economic Community in 1958, Mansholt again focused on price protection as the basic tool of the joint agricultural policy of the member states. Yet by then the economy was growing too fast for the labour market to handle. Worker demands in the 1960s were more and more successful, until wages virtually exploded in the early 1970s. For farmers, the rising wage costs meant rising production costs, driving their incomes steadily back compared with those in other sectors. Meanwhile, the long years of unprecedented economic growth were coming to an end; 1973 witnessed the first oil crisis, and by 1974 a recession had set in. On top of this, accumulating EEC dairy surpluses put the system of guaranteed prices under increasing pressure. By the end of the 1960s, the infamous milk lake and butter mountain, which had been building up virtually since the establishment of the EEC in 1958, began to put a disproportionate strain on the EEC budget. By 1975, price intervention in agriculture would use up as much as 70 per cent of the EEC budget.[124] Mansholt's expectation that price protection based on the needs of viable modern farms would suffice to keep total production within bounds – without the help of additional measures such as production quotas – had proved to be far too optimistic. Among the reasons for the surpluses was the rapid growth of production in the less highly developed agricultural regions within the EEC.

When the surpluses threatened to go completely out of control, Mansholt took the initiative to try and stem the tide. According to the notorious Mansholt Plan of 1968, it was no longer justifiable to uphold the price protection system. Drastic structural changes aimed at cost reduction were required if European farmers were to survive the competition in the global market. The future, Mansholt now believed, was in industrial farming. Some 5 million farmers in the EEC countries would have to go. Those who remained should scale up by merging their holdings and make another leap forward in efficiency of production by further mechanizing and intensifying.

Although the strong agricultural lobbies in the member states would succeed in watering down the Mansholt Plan to a "mini-plan" from which all drastic measures had been removed, the original plan's revisionary outlook did set the tone for the early 1970s and added significantly to growing unrest among the farmers. Arduous EEC meetings in which agricultural prices were negotiated were accompanied by massive demonstrations. In March 1971, a demonstration in Brussels by some 80,000 farmers demanding better prices became so unruly that a farmer was killed. Mansholt was accused of aiming for a voluntary collectivization of agriculture. Dutch farmers, who had always seen him as one of their own – Mansholt was a farmer's son – now felt that he had betrayed them. German farmers called him a "Bauernkiller" (killer of farmers).

An extra difficulty for Dutch dairy farmers was that throwing in the towel, as many had already done – the number of dairy farms had dropped from 183,000 to 116,000 between 1960 and 1970 – became an even less attractive option in the early 1970s, when unemployment in industry began to rise. It is indicative of the farmers' predicament that, nevertheless, the number of holdings would be further reduced to 67,000 by 1980. Meanwhile, the average number of cows per farm would continue to increase, from twenty in the early 1970s to forty in the early 1980s.[125] Expanding their herds presented the farmers with another challenge: their traditional barns, in which the cows were lined up in rows, were too small and had to be replaced by more spacious and labour-saving accommodations in which the animals were loose-housed.[126]

To the Dutch Ministry of Agriculture and Wageningen scientists it was a given that only farmers who used all available means to increase efficiency of production would have a chance of survival. Further growth of the number of cows per farm and of their individual capacity for production, combined with unremitting mechanization and rationalization, were indispensable for survival, insisted Bertus Geessink, director of the Department of Animal Husbandry.[127] Farming was no different than running a business and farmers had to become entrepreneurs. Striving for continuity and to make ends meet would no longer do; the new watchwords were now growth and profitability. "The times of the peaceful peasant are over, the future is for the dynamic agricultural entrepreneur," an analyst from the *Landbouw Economisch Instituut*, the government institute for agricultural economics, wrote in 1970.[128]

Thus, in the years around 1970, an atmosphere of urgency, if not of crisis, hung over agricultural circles, and it was in this period that the scientists' pleas that breeding stock should be selected for milk production began to find widespread acceptance. From 1969 onwards, the yearly reports of the AI supervisory committee indicate that more and more AI associations were entering into partnerships with their neighbours. Collaboration was initially preferred over merging, yet before long larger units also began to be formed. The number of associations dropped from 93 in 1969 to 48 in 1980, yet collaboration agreements had by then reduced the number of actual breeding units of black and whites to 27.[129] A decade later, 95 per cent of all inseminations of all dairy breeds would be done by nine associations that collaborated in three regional breeding units. Ultimately, in 1996, these units would merge into a single cooperative, Holland Genetics, which in its turn would merge with the breeders' societies in 1998 into a single organization, CR Delta (*Coöperatie Rundveeverbetering Delta*). In 2002, after a merger with a Belgian partner (VRV), CR Delta became CRV Holding BV. Along with US-based companies such as World Wide Sires, Alta/CRI, and ABS Global, it is now one of the major suppliers of Holstein genetics worldwide.[130]

In the early 1970s, all AI associations set up progeny-testing programs. The Friesian associations decided to introduce systematic testing in 1969, and the Mansholt Plan was mentioned explicitly as underlining the necessity of this decision.[131] To bear up against rising costs, which the guaranteed milk prices could no longer compensate for, "our policy has to be directed at increasing the productivity of our cows," chairman Wieger Bosma, of the union of Friesian AI associations, stated. It was a seemingly innocuous statement, yet it was rife with meaning for the pedigree breeders, because it signalled the end of selecting breeding stock for conformation.[132]

In line with the new course, sires of known genetic merit for milk production were increasingly preferred over untested show bulls, and the influence of the top breeders, particularly those in Friesland, steadily waned. In the 1970s, for the first time since the war, Friesian breeding bulls lost their hegemony to the more productive bulls from North Holland.[133] A clear indication of the growing willingness among AI associations to collaborate was the rise of the use of frozen sperm, which lifted the restraints on the growth of associations and enabled long-distance exchange. From 3.5 per cent in 1968, inseminations with frozen sperm shot up to 25.5 per cent in 1970, 72.2 per cent in 1975, and 86.4 per cent in 1980.[134] Meanwhile, sperm exchanges between associations increased from 2.5 per cent of all inseminations in 1965 to 21.4 per cent in 1980.[135] In 1974, a ministerial committee set up to evaluate the AI organizations' breeding policy noted that, while there was still a long way to go, the necessity of collaborating and scaling up to increase efficiency of production was now generally accepted. Breeding for conformation had been replaced by breeding for milk production.[136]

The acceptance of the new breeding policy was marked as well as reinforced by the growing number of veterinarians and agriculturalists employed by AI associations. When, for instance, the associations in the provinces of South Holland and Zeeland decided to cooperate and to introduce systematic progeny testing in the late 1960s, they appointed the veterinarian Hans Uwland as their breeding adviser. This new breeding unit was the first example of large-scale collaboration, and under Uwland's supervision it switched to the exclusive use of frozen sperm. In Friesland, the Wageningen-trained agricultural scientist Piet Scheer was the driving force behind the introduction of progeny testing. Over the course of the 1970s, most other associations would follow suit in employing academically trained experts. The three breeding units that remained in the 1980s had Wageningen graduates as directors.[137]

Understandably, the transition to selecting bulls for milk production was hard for the traditional breeders to stomach. Tensions between breeders and the cattle breeders' societies on the one hand and the farmers' AI associations on the other sometimes ran high. In October 1970, the board of the FRS was confronted by a protest action from a group of young farmers who felt that the officials' continuing defence of the breeders' interests obstructed the reforms aimed at improving their animals' milk production capacity.[138] In this period, Scheer, one of the instigators of the reforms, received anonymous threats, presumably from breeders, and for some time would not visit breeders' meetings unaccompanied.[139]

The new focus on the productivity of individual cows required a change in the culture of breeding that affected the breeders' commercial interests as well as their deepest convictions. While formerly the secret of successful breeding had rested in their unique skills and experience, the emphasis on milk production displaced them from their leading position. In fact, any farmer who participated in official milk recording might now contribute to breed improvement if he owned an exceptionally productive cow that might produce promising young test bulls. What had previously been decided in the show ring was now determined by AI associations on the basis of quantitative data gathered by the milk-recording services.

A certain disdain for this "breeding on paper" and for the "scientific calculators" that processed the milk-recording data would linger for years. Former NRS herd-book inspector Cees Kroon deplored the disregard of the breeders' intuition in modern practices and felt that breeding was becoming a shallow affair. Commenting on the use of computers to process milk-recording data, a farmer said: "That's all very well, but a computer can't look at my cows."[140] Yet others felt no qualms about identifying with their new role as entrepreneurs. Breeder P.J. Koster was quoted as saying: "There's no room for pet cows in modern farming. [My breeding work] is aimed at ... the commercial farmers, the dairymen who earn their money by producing milk." And farmer Henny Heemskerk succinctly stated his convictions as follows: "More science, more numbers, less tradition, less emotion and no mysticism."[141]

A survey among young farmers in the province of Drenthe in 1979 revealed that conformation no longer played a decisive role in bull choice for them. Only functional characteristics, such as the udder and the hooves, were considered important. Interviews with farmers in the province of Gelderland in the same year can be summarized by quoting a comment made by one of the interviewees: "Our job is to milk, not to put up a show." For the traditional breeder, good looks had been an indication of profitability, yet for farmer Boyen de Boer it was the other way round: "A profitable cow is, for that very reason, a beautiful cow."[142]

## Indexes

The decision by the farmers and their associations to give priority to breeding for production enabled the Wageningen agricultural experts to move to the centre of breeding practices and to make one of their most significant contributions to dairy-cattle breeding, the development of milk production indexes.

Quantitative studies of milk production were taken up systematically by Rommert Politiek in the 1960s.[143] Politiek, a farmer's son born in 1926, had devoted his PhD dissertation to a quantitative analysis of protein percentages in the milk of Friesian cows.[144] He was appointed lecturer in Wageningen in 1960 and became full professor and chair of the department of animal husbandry in 1968. In Wageningen, he chose quantitative genetics as his special field. An autodidact in quantitative methods, he sent several of his students to experts abroad, such as Ivar Johansson at the Swedish Royal Agricultural College in Uppsala and Harald Skjervold at the Agricultural University of Norway in Ås, to acquire more advanced mathematical skills.[145] Together, Politiek and his pupils would develop a series of indexes that enabled Dutch farmers to evaluate and compare animals on the basis of their production records.

The basic principles of the index concept were very simple. The only assumptions it required about the mechanisms of heredity were that both parents contribute equally to the hereditary make-up of their offspring and that the offspring's characteristics (in this case their milk yield and the quality of the milk) are determined by both hereditary factors and the environment. Incidentally, these assumptions represented about as much as could be said at all about the genetics of a quantitative character because nothing was known about the genes involved. Only their effects could be measured, quantitatively, which was the very reason the field was called quantitative genetics rather than population genetics. Nor was such knowledge needed for the quantitative, statistical analyses of milk production through the generations. Neither the principle of progeny testing nor its effective implementation is predicated on a specific theory of heredity.[146]

An elementary index for the butterfat percentage of milk, for instance, can be devised by taking a sire's daughters and their mothers as a basis for comparison. The daughters' average butterfat percentage ($D$) must be halfway between the sire's genetic merit for butterfat production ($S$) and the average butterfat percentage of the daughters' mothers ($M$). So $D = ½(S + M)$ and $S = 2D - M$. As $D$ and $M$ can be calculated on the basis of measurements, bulls can thus be ranked on the basis of index $S$. Indexes for milk yield or the protein percentage of milk can be constructed in the same way.

As can easily be imagined, the practical application of these elementary principles was fraught with difficulties. Many decisions had to be taken. How should yields be measured, how often, and for how long? Cows' lactation periods differ, between individuals and from year to year, and a cow's age has a considerable effect on her production level. Biases had to be allowed for – for example, that bulls might have been tested on herds of unequal quality. Most important, seasonal differences and differences in feeding and management, which heavily influenced production levels, had to be dealt with. Finally, the means and methods to obtain, collect, and process great quantities of data had to be developed and their reliability assessed.

The index concept was not new. It was one of the instruments developed by the American pioneer of quantitative genetics Jay L. Lush and his school between the 1930s and 1950s.[147] As early as the 1930s, experiments with index breeding in dairy cattle had, for instance, been conducted by E. Parmalee Prentice, on Mount Hope, his farm in Massachusetts.[148] The main task facing the Wageningen agricultural scientists was to develop indexes that were tailor-made for the Dutch situation. While initially rather crude and unreliable, they were gradually refined and made more robust.

In the early 1960s, Politiek and his collaborator Theo Vos developed the first Dutch indexes for milk yield and for butterfat and protein content on the basis of mother-daughter comparisons.[149] As expected, the index for milk yield proved highly sensitive to environmental influences. For instance, a survey sampling done among Friesian cows in the mid-1950s revealed that only 35 per cent of the observed variation in the animals' milk yields could be accounted for by hereditary factors.[150] Comparing mothers and daughters of the same age (necessitated by the relation between age and production level) implied that yields obtained in different years had to be compared, which seriously affected the reliability of the results.[151] To avoid this problem, the evaluation was later based on the so-called daughter-contemporaries comparison, again adapted to Dutch circumstances by Politiek's collaborator Jan Dommerholt, in which the heifers sired by a particular bull were compared with all Dutch heifers that had calved in the same year and month. Thus seasonal influences were more or less excluded.[152]

Milk-recording data were stored and processed electronically from 1968 onwards.[153] The daughter-contemporaries method would hardly have been possible without the use of computers. This was even truer for its successor, the bull index, introduced by Dommerholt in the early 1980s. Most quantitative traits, such as milk and egg production, have a low heritability; they are highly sensitive to environmental factors such as feed and management. This problem was tackled by Lush's student Charles R. Henderson, who developed the BLUP – best linear unbiased prediction – method in the 1950s and 1960s. This statistical tool enabled index calculations to be corrected for various environmental influences and it would become the international standard for the evaluation of sires.[154] Dommerholt's bull index weighted several additional factors, such as genetic differences between the test bulls' herds of origin and genetic improvement from generation to generation.[155] The possibility of processing ever-growing quantities of data facilitated the development of more and more indexes – such as, for instance, the cow index, which gave an estimate of a cow's genetic merit for milk production, or the lactation index, which predicted a cow's production curve in its next lactation period.

Two further efforts to increase the possibilities for comparison, also emanating from earlier work done by Lush's pupils, were of particular importance.[156] The first of these, aimed at direct economic comparison, was again undertaken by Dommerholt in the late 1970s. As already indicated, Dutch farmers were paid for the butterfat percentage of the milk. Since the late 1960s, they had also been paid for the protein percentage. Dommerholt developed a production index that represented the net gain or loss in Dutch guilders to be expected from using a particular bull as a sire.[157] For this, current production costs as well as producers' prices were included in the index calculations. Apart from providing direct economic information, the advantage of Dommerholt's net milk money index or Inet, as it was called, was that it solved the difficulties involved in interpreting a bull's production figures. To give an example: Was a bull with a very high index for milk yield more or less profitable than a bull with a lower milk index but with higher butterfat or protein indexes? Inet weighted the current prices of milk, butterfat, and protein, and thus supplied the answer. Economic comparison of bulls became even more important in the mid-1970s, when dairy factories began to charge farmers for processing their milk.[158]

Second, production records were made internationally comparable. Traditionally, different countries had widely varying milk-recording and data-processing practices, so that indexes had different meanings and could not be compared between countries. By the early 1980s, however, conversion programs had been developed that enabled comparisons between the Dutch indexes and those of the most important breeding organizations abroad.[159] Both the Inet index and the opportunity to compare bulls internationally would play a central role in the Holsteinization process, to which we must now turn.

## Holsteinization

Serious interest in the North American Holsteins arose in the late 1960s, when AI associations began to switch to breeding for production. Dutch breeders had always kept an eye on the development of Holstein breeding, if only because the Holsteins were originally of Dutch black-and-white parentage. Yet whereas the Dutch, for reasons discussed above, had turned their Friesians into a dual-purpose breed after 1900, American breeders had continued to breed their imported Friesians as a pure dairy type. Most Holstein farmers in the United States and Canada produced milk for consumption. Moreover, there were separate breeds for meat production in North America, an option the Dutch, in their small and densely populated country, did not have because of the vast expanses of cheap land it required.[160]

Until well into the 1960s, Dutch breeders and farmers, and even Wageningen scientists, saw no reason to fundamentally change their Modern Friesians, as meat prices were excellent in the decades after the war and the dual-purpose type was believed to best suit the Dutch circumstances.[161] The majority of dairy farmers produced milk for the manufacture of butter and cheese, which put a premium on high percentages of fat and protein. Holstein milk had a prescribed minimum butterfat percentage, but American farmers were not paid for higher percentages and did not select for them. Thus Holstein milk, like that of their nineteenth-century Friesian forebears, was watery. Also, the feeding regime in North America was different. Especially in the western states of the US, herds were kept inside year round and were fed ample quantities of grains. In the Netherlands, dairying was based on grazing. The cows were housed only in the cold months, during which their diet consisted mainly of hay and grass silage. Feeding great quantities of concentrates was considered to be uneconomical: besides the fact that the fertile Dutch fields provided a much cheaper alternative, the prices of concentrates were considerably higher in the Netherlands than in North America. Finally, while the best Holsteins might produce impressive yields, Dutch dairy cows had always had a higher average yield than their American counterparts. That was still the case in the 1960s. So there was no reason to think the Holsteins were better overall.[162]

Or was there? To put the matter beyond doubt, a direct comparison between Holsteins and Friesians under Dutch circumstances was required, and this had never been done. The Holsteins in America were reported to produce rapidly increasing yields: towards the end of the 1960s, Holsteins whose milk yield was recorded produced a yearly average of more than 5,500 kg of milk – well over 1,000 kg more than the Dutch cows for which records were kept. Even the black and whites in Sweden were said to surpass the Friesians by that time.[163]

In the disconcerting economic climate of those years, the matter was deemed important enough to be investigated. NRS and FRS officials and breeders made several trips to the United States and Canada and reported their findings in the journals of the breeders' societies. Their conclusions were predominantly negative. American black and whites still looked much like the nineteenth-century Friesians, with all their supposed defects: they were big, leggy, sharp-backed, and narrow-chested (Figure 1.6).

After a visit to a show, farmer Anne Oosterbaan ruefully noted that he liked the American breeders' showmanship better than their cows.[164] On many farms, milk yields were excellent, to be sure, but this was no surprise considering the different feeding regime. Visitors from North Holland were not convinced that the Holsteins surpassed the Dutch Friesians in hereditary potential. As expected, butterfat percentages were low, and protein content was not even recorded. The

Figure 1.6. Breeder Siem Moeyes, visiting the United States, inspects a Holstein bull. From the archives of the cattle breeders' journal *Veeteelt*. © Veeteelt (CRV Holding BV).

officials noted approvingly, however, that on many farms the cows had well-formed udders and strong hooves. Obviously, Holstein breeders kept an eye on functional characteristics rather than on overall quality of conformation.[165] The visitors perceived a clear difference in dairying culture, especially in the West: "[The Californian farm] breathes professionalism; factors such as capacity, quality and know-how are discussed in terms of their monetary value. [The farmers] may well love their animals and their farm, but it doesn't show, and they don't talk about it; this is quite different from the situation in the Netherlands."[166]

The reports concluded that the best Holsteins might help improve the functionality of the Dutch type, but whether they would also contribute positively to milk yield was not clear. Therefore, the breeders' societies warned against uncontrolled experimenting by breeders or farmers as long as it remained uncertain whether the Holsteins would do more harm than good to the Friesians.[167]

Meanwhile, a controlled experiment was under way.[168] In 1968, a group of researchers from several government and academic institutions, Rommert Politiek and his assistant Henk Vos among them, formed a working group that aimed to put the Holsteins to the test, under Dutch circumstances, in a series of comparative experiments. Several farmers were invited to participate in the experiments, which began in 1970 after a period of preparation.[169]

The principal dairy types involved were black and whites from Friesland and North Holland and Holsteins from the United States and Canada.[170] Three questions were investigated. Was there really a hereditary difference in performance between bulls from North Holland and bulls from Friesland, as many breeders suspected? How did purebred Dutch Friesians compare to purebred Holsteins? And how did crossbreds between Holsteins and Dutch black and whites perform?

It took several years for the comparative scientific experiments to yield their first results. Meanwhile, in spite of the negative advice from the cattle breeders' societies, "wild" experiments were started by several AI associations. The farmers involved were indeed becoming entrepreneurs, for obviously their motive for not awaiting Politiek's results was that they might have an edge if his conclusions turned out to be positive. In 1970, the AI associations in Friesland, led by Piet Scheer, took the plunge and began to import Holstein semen, first on a small scale and later in greater quantities.[171] Scheer had been impressed by the Holsteins' productivity after visiting Holstein farms in Israel in the mid-1960s.[172] At his instigation, the Friesian union of AI associations entered into a contract with one of the major American AI organizations, World Wide Sires, for the exclusive distribution of Holstein semen in the Netherlands.[173] In 1972, the collaborating AI associations in the southwest of the Netherlands, led by veterinarian Hans Uwland, became the first to import four live Holstein bulls from the United States. In the same year, a young Wageningen graduate, Pieter ter Veer, started a new breeding farm with the express aim of achieving complete Holsteinization through the exclusive use of Holstein semen. In 1974, Ter Veer and farmer Jan Maat set up a study club of like-minded, mostly young, farmers that advertised the use of Holsteins by way of a newsletter and demonstration shows of daughter groups.[174] Ter Veer was probably the first to predict that the Dutch dual-purpose type would be outcompeted by the Holsteins.[175]

Not surprisingly, the top breeders of Friesians took a dim view of these developments. To underline that their faith in the Dutch black and whites remained unshaken, a group of Friesian breeders publicly vowed that they would refrain from using Holsteins for at least eight years.[176] As it turned out, however, only one of the vow-takers would keep the promise. Pedigree breeders in North Holland, another stronghold of the Dutch black and whites, had an additional reason to cling to their own bloodlines in the 1970s: Politiek's comparative breeding experiments showed that North Holland bulls performed 10 per cent better than bulls from Friesland.[177] Finally, the breeders' societies demonstrated their worries about what Holstein bulls might do to the Friesians' proverbial excellence of conformation by putting up barriers to the acceptance of Holsteins and crossbreds in their registers.[178] Within a few years they had to come around, however, as the numbers of crossbreds continued to grow. Still, as late as 1978 a (failed) attempt was made to block the election of a candidate for membership of the FRS board who entertained Holstein sympathies.[179] The last demonstration of dissent came in 1983, when the NRS refused the title of proven sire to a Holstein bull because of his below-standard conformation, even though his daughters had proved to be exceptional producers. Holstein adepts considered this an outrage.[180]

In the mid-1970s, however, it seemed that the breeders' associations' warnings not to throw caution to the wind had been fully justified. When the results of the comparative experiments came in, the Holstein pioneers had no cause for celebration. To be sure, mating a Holstein bull with Friesian cows resulted in daughters that produced higher milk yields than purebred Friesians. The yields of purebred Holsteins were higher still. The catch, however, was that the crossbreds turned out to be only marginally more profitable than purebred Friesians, whereas the purebred Holsteins were not more profitable at all. The reasons were the higher feeding costs of the bigger and heavier Holsteins and their crossbreds, the lower butterfat and protein percentages of their milk, and the lower quality of the meat of (crossbred) Holsteins and their calves.[181] On the basis of an investigation of beef production and beef prices, breeding expert Theo Vos concluded that for the majority of the farmers the dual-purpose cow was still the best option. Only a very few of them would be able to reduce their costs in such a way that milking the highly specialized Holsteins would become more profitable.[182] The general conclusion reached by Politiek and his collaborators was that no advantages were to be expected from replacing the Friesians by Holsteins. American bulls might perhaps be used occasionally to help improve udders and hooves, but otherwise the Friesians were not inferior to their American relatives.

The alternative of using the slightly better crossbreds was never seriously considered, then and in later years. As in hybrid-corn breeding, hybrid vigour, the phenomenon that crossbreds between pure breeds tend to do better than their parents, was surmised to be partly responsible for the crossbreds' better yields. Yet cows are not corn plants, countless hybrids of which can be obtained from purebred lines at relatively modest cost. Cows reproduce too slowly and are much more costly, and the advantages of the crossbreds would be offset by the need to rear, maintain, and milk many purebreds to obtain them.[183] Another option was to create a new breed from the best crossbreds, yet this would take years of careful breeding and selection. The discussion would never get this far however; the farmers made a different choice.

In the second half of the 1970s, although the NRS and the FRS felt vindicated by the comparative experiments and even Holstein pioneer Piet Scheer was sounding a cautionary note, the farmers stayed the course of Holsteinization by systematically using Holstein bulls as sires.[184] They chose their Holsteins carefully, however. As the comparative investigations had shown, the Holsteins' higher milk yields did not automatically make them more profitable, as their milk was often watery. But what if Holstein bulls with better credentials for butterfat and protein could be found? Whether Holsteins were better than Friesians was the wrong question to ask, according to Jacob Chardon, a rare Holstein enthusiast among the NRS inspectors. The pertinent question was whether *any* Holstein bulls might be found that were more profitable.[185]

That such animals did indeed exist became evident when the production figures of Mowry-C. Bootmaker Bill, one of the American bulls imported by the southwestern AI associations, were published. His daughters' net butterfat and protein production surpassed that of the progeny of all available Dutch bulls at the time. His star immediately began to rise and by 1978 he was the most frequently used sire in the Netherlands.[186] Thus he paved the way for many more American bulls with respectable butterfat and protein indexes and with equally ornate names, such as Tops Monitor Legend and Gardenia Chief Astronaut. Over the years, a group of collaborating AI associations would import 161 of such Holstein bulls.[187] In addition to live bulls, semen was imported, reaching a peak of almost a million straws (each containing the dose for a single insemination) in 1982 and 1983. From the early 1980s onwards, AI associations also cooperated to import Holstein embryos.[188] Thus, the average percentage of Holstein genes carried by the Dutch herds increased rapidly, in some years by more than 10 per cent. Milk yields increased accordingly, from 4,652 kg in 1970 to 5,502 kg in 1980 and 7,204 kg in 1990. It should be added, though, that part of the increase was due to the fact that concentrates became cheaper in the 1970s and were fed in greater quantities.[189]

Another boost to the genetic displacement of the Dutch black and whites by Holsteins was given by an international comparative experiment conducted in Poland, started in the mid-1970s under the auspices of the FAO, the Food and Agriculture Organization of the United Nations, which included Holstein and Dutch Friesian bulls from ten different countries. As it turned out, in the early 1980s, the Friesians' daughters had performed disappointingly on the Polish farms. In terms of milk production they were near the bottom of the list, with only the Polish cows behind them. Holsteins from the United States, New Zealand, and Israel were at the top. For most Dutch farmers, the results allowed for no other conclusion than that the Dutch Friesians were obsolete and that the future belonged to the Holsteins.[190]

Two further developments illustrate the extent to which the new course of breeding for production had taken hold within Dutch cattle breeding. The first of these was the Holsteinization, quite unexpectedly, of the second Dutch dairy breed, the red-and-white Maas-Rijn-IJssel cattle or MRIJ. As mentioned earlier, the red and whites had served as a model for the improvement of the Friesians in the interwar years. They were a less exacting breed, adapted to the more sober feeding and management regimes of mixed farms on sandy soils. While their milk yield was lower than that of the black and whites, this was compensated for by the production of more and better meat: the calves, in particular, brought better prices. They were thus a genuine dual-purpose breed. On balance, the MRIJs were about as profitable as the Friesians in the 1970s.[191]

One might think that breeding for higher milk yields was less urgent in the case of the MRIJs. Indeed, Politiek and other agriculturalists repeatedly stressed that improving the red and whites' milk yield should not come at the expense of beef production, which enabled the MRIJs to hold their own against the black and whites.[192] Ironically, however, it was the economic comparison made possible by the Inet index developed by the same experts that initiated the MRIJs' undoing as a dual-purpose breed. Around 1980, when the admixture of Holstein genes resulted in steadily increasing yields in the black and whites, doubts began to arise as to whether the MRIJ would be able to keep up, economically speaking. An estimate using the Inet index showed that in ten years the black and whites might be producing an additional 450 guilders' worth of milk; it seemed doubtful that the MRIJs would be able to match this, even if both their milk and meat production increased.[193]

Experts feared that without special measures the MRIJs would indeed lose out. Considering that a substantial part of Dutch beef production was intended for the national market and that the Netherlands would have to import beef if the dual-purpose breeds were to disappear, scientists from Wageningen and other institutions, Politiek among them, agreed that the MRIJs' value for the national economy warranted a rescue operation.[194] In 1981, a committee of breeders and agricultural experts was established to investigate the possibilities of restricted use of a sub-breed of the American Holsteins, the Red Holsteins, and several other foreign red-and-white breeds to improve the MRIJs' milk yield. They also decided to develop a meat index to speed up the improvement of the MRIJs' genetic merit for beef production.[195]

As expected, the committee found that using Red Holsteins as sires for MRIJ cows resulted in significantly higher yields. It proved more difficult to develop a workable meat index, but in the end the committee successfully completed this task too.[196] It was to no avail, however, for after about 1985 the major MRIJ associations lost their faith in the breed. It seemed pointless to them to preserve the MRIJ as a dual-purpose breed when Holsteinization seemed to promise even better results with less effort.[197] Or, as Jan Goossens, director of an MRIJ association, put it: "It's not my job to preserve a breed but to keep the farmer in business."[198] Repeated assertions from scientific experts that the MRIJs were still competitive left the farmers unmoved.[199] By the mid-1990s, the red and whites carried more Red Holstein than MRIJ genes.[200] The purebred MRIJ, like the purebred Friesian, was becoming a rare breed.

An additional factor played a role in the Holsteinization of both Dutch dairy breeds: the long-expected proclamation of a milk production quota by the European Community in 1984. Up to that point, the general feeling had been that a production quota would benefit the dual-purpose breeds, particularly the MRIJs.[201] Actually, however, the quota precipitated their demise, because the farmers' response to this new challenge was to step up their efforts to increase their cows' milk yield. The quest for increases in total milk production having been curtailed, they now aimed to fill their quota with the lowest possible number of cows. As a result, the number of dairy cows in the Netherlands would drop by 20 per cent in five years.[202]

By and large, the Holsteinization of the Dutch black and whites was completed in the late 1990s, when the portion of Holstein genes in the Dutch herds had come close to 100 per cent.[203] The Dutch dairy cow had lost much of her international reputation in the 1980s, particularly after the results of the experiment in Poland had been published. By the mid-1990s however, Dutch breeding organizations had regained their international competitiveness and had a share in the worldwide Holstein semen market. Exports of breeding stock also recovered and reached new postwar heights.[204] The Dutch-bred bull Sunny Boy set a record of more than 2 million semen straws produced, a feat that earned him an obituary in *Time* magazine when he passed away in 1997.[205]

**Market and Moral Economy**

Before the Second World War, Dutch cattle breeders and their scientific advisers entertained compatible views on the best methods for breeding dairy cattle, even though some of the scientific experts criticized the breeders for attaching too much importance to conformation and pedigrees. Where their opinions diverged, aesthetic and commercial considerations on the breeders' part were often involved. For instance, while certain details of conformation, such as coloured spots on the lower legs, might not be demonstrably relevant for milk yield, they did make a difference in the market for breeding stock.

Scientists readily acknowledged that the insights Mendelian theory provided into hereditary mechanisms were of little practical use to breeders of livestock. The new genetics was considered helpful mainly for assessing the value of the breeders' traditional methods. For instance, striving for purity by means of sustained inbreeding and breeding in bloodlines was deemed to be perfectly rational, since it was consistent with Mendelian theory. Yet, as we have seen, the terms "purity" and "bloodline" had different connotations for scientists and commercial breeders. For the former, such notions referred to the homozygosity of the relevant genetic factors; for the latter, they buttressed the constancy and consistent quality of a commercial breed. Consequently, breeders set great store by the history of their bloodlines, while Mendelian geneticists may be said to have aimed at making such histories superfluous.

In the interwar period, livestock breeders and their scientific advisers agreed that selecting animals purely for production was ill-advised. Agricultural experts considered the extreme dairy type to be too costly to maintain on poorer soils, and veterinarians warned that cows of this type were prone to diseases, particularly bovine tuberculosis. These concerns were at the basis of the development of the Modern Friesian. In response to the problems with the original black and whites, breeders and farmers developed an ethos of "decent" breeding and farming of which the Modern Friesians' solid build and nobility were the hallmark. Their reasoning was that conformation mirrored constitution and that well-balanced cows were low maintenance and good producers: a beautiful cow was a profitable cow.

For the breeders among the farmers, purely commercial considerations were also important. In the 1950s, the Modern Friesians' quality of conformation contributed greatly to the international success of the breed. Conformation shows were the scene of ongoing competition between the top breeders before an audience of potential buyers. After a major show, points and prizes for conformation were translated into cash. Accusations by scientific experts that breeding for nobility was becoming a fad could easily be parried by the breeders: from their perspective, the booming market for Modern Friesians vindicated their approach. Thus, as Margaret Derry has also found in her analysis of dog and horse breeding, the breeders' aesthetic preferences and their commercial interests were intimately connected.[206] Similarly, while the Holsteins had been derided as ugly ducklings by the Dutch farmers when they were first imported in the Netherlands, they soon grew into graceful swans in the eyes of the Holstein enthusiasts.[207]

After 1945, scientists seriously began to question the breeders' view that conformation should come first. They argued that there was no hard evidence that conformation was related to constitution and that only the quality of functionally important outward characteristics merited attention. While they saw it as their task to assist farmers in rationalizing the search for animals of high genetic merit, the scientists' principal loyalty was to the Ministry of Agriculture, or to what scientists and government administrators jointly conceived of as matters of national interest, which did not always coincide with the interests of the farmers.

Scientists had advocated the use of proven sires from the early twentieth century onwards. In the Netherlands, however, practical realities set severe limits to the implementation of progeny testing. Systematic testing became feasible only after the introduction of artificial insemination in the 1940s, a technique originally developed to fight infertility caused by infections. The use of AI rapidly increased, but to the dismay of the scientific experts, the technique was not deployed to facilitate progeny testing. Only in about 1970, after a long period of debate, would the farmers come around and switch to progeny testing and breeding for production.

Commentators wrote that the art of breeding was finally being turned into a science. There is something to be said for this interpretation, which seems to suggest that the debate was essentially about the best methods for breeding profitable dairy cows. The contestants' rhetoric seems to point in this direction too: scientists spoke of subjective versus objective approaches, and breeders contrasted their creativity with the number crunching of computers. As we have seen, however, a more fundamental, normative issue was at stake: should breeding stock be selected for quality of conformation or for milk yield? Breeders and farmers aimed for a long-term strategy of breed improvement, whereas Wageningen scientists advocated the more direct approach of selecting breeding stock on the basis of production figures. The methods preferred by breeders and scientists derived from their breeding strategies. Breeding for quality of conformation required the breeders' subjective judgment, while breeding for milk production depended on quantitative data.

Furthermore, the breeders did not object to quantitative approaches as such or to input from science and technology more generally. Their stance may be called pragmatic: they accepted what suited their purposes, and if the stakes were high enough they were prepared to give up deeply held convictions. A few examples may illustrate this. Quantitative milk recording was introduced in the late nineteenth century, and many farmers adopted the procedure. Before the 1970s, however, they used it mainly to increase the butterfat percentage of the milk, rather than to increase milk yield. Similarly, the technique of AI was welcomed as a remedy for genital infections but not as a tool for breeding for higher milk yields; accordingly, frozen sperm technology was at first ignored. While breeders in the first half of the twentieth century maintained that they judged a cow's merits intuitively, they had long been using detailed point systems to objectify (and monetize) their verdicts. Finally, after 1970, once the farmers had endorsed selection for production, they sometimes even surpassed the scientists in basing their breeding decisions on quantitative data. A case in point is the scientists' (failed) attempt to prevent the Holsteinization of the red and whites because of this breed's importance for the national beef supply. Remarkably, Wageningen agricultural scientists felt compelled, in this case, to argue against the ongoing specialization of production envisaged by the modernization project.

There is a strong sense of economic necessity in historical works on the postwar modernization project in Dutch agriculture and its effects on cattle breeding. Market pressures were of course of principal importance in instigating the changes in breeding strategy that we have described. Yet the suggestion that the changes were inevitable overlooks the uncertainty and contingency of essential elements of the process. To give an example: while the Wageningen agricultural scientists contended that there was no evidence that the Modern Friesian was more profitable than the older, more specialized nineteenth-century type, the reverse was also true: in the 1950s and 1960s, there was no concrete evidence that cows with a higher genetic capacity for milk production would actually do better. Interestingly, Politiek's colleague Theo Vos suggested in the early 1970s that the breeders of the 1950s might well have been right after all: the feeding regime of those years had perhaps been too austere to enable even the fairly undemanding, dual-purpose Friesians to exploit their capacity for milk production to the full. Therefore, it would not have made sense to replace them with dairy specialists, because their higher genetic potential would have remained unused.[208] This was a speculative argument, precisely because economic comparisons of different types of cows had not been available in the 1950s, yet it highlights the uncertainties breeders as well as scientists had to deal with.

Van der Ploeg has argued that the postwar modernization project, far from being dictated by economic necessity, was in fact a scenario for the future imposed on the farmers by what he calls the "expert system" of policymakers and scientists.[209] Van der Ploeg rightly emphasizes the scientists' central role in giving shape to the modernization project. For instance, the guaranteed prices the farmers received were based on what the scientific experts considered to be the needs of "viable" farms – that is, farms with sufficient potential for "modernization." Where cattle breeding is concerned, however, Van der Ploeg underestimates the agency of the farmers. As we saw, scientists proved unable to change the farmers' preference for breeding for conformation until the late 1960s. When the farmers came around, by 1970, this was not because they finally gave in to the pressure exerted by the expert system. Economic pressure was crucial, for it was the farmers' rising costs and diminishing returns that induced them to reconsider their strategy. Moreover, scientists and policymakers had neither planned nor hoped for this particular pressure to occur, for the farmers' predicament was a consequence of the expert system losing control: price protection had failed, surpluses were getting out of hand, and the economy was coming to a grinding halt. Furthermore, it is illustrative of the farmers' active role in the process that, once they had adopted breeding for production, it was they who effectuated the replacement of the Dutch breeds by Holsteins, even against the advice of the scientists. Van der Ploeg deplores the fact that alternative visions of the future of agriculture, such as a return to small-scale farming, were never seriously considered by the expert system. But the same can be said about the vast majority of the farmers. By the 1970s, they too had endorsed the principles of the modernization project and believed that their options were restricted to either increasing their production efficiency or giving up farming.

The shift in Dutch cattle breeding that resulted in the Holsteinization of the Friesians was neither an intended nor an inevitable outcome of the modernization project in Dutch agriculture. Cattle breeding was guided by an amalgam of considerations, as diverse as they were disputable, pertaining to practical experience, methods, scientific insights and technologies, ideas about responsible farming, aesthetic preferences, commercial interests, economic circumstances, and government policies. To put it differently: stockbreeding practices were embedded in cultures of breeding that on closer inspection show up the uncertainties, inconsistencies, and contingencies that are germane to the dynamics of any culture.

# 2 "The Most Efficient Chickens in the World"

In a recent interview in the weekly magazine *De Groene Amsterdammer*, Frans van Sambeek, head of research of the chicken division of Hendrix Genetics, is quoted as saying: "If you get off a plane anywhere on the globe and buy an egg, there's a 50 per cent chance that the egg was laid by a hen whose parents were produced by us." Hendrix's laying hens are "the most efficient chickens in the world," according to Van Sambeek: they produce maximum output for minimal costs of production. Hendrix Genetics is an international livestock breeding company that has its home base in Boxmeer, in the south of the Netherlands. Its main competitor is Erich Wesjohann Gruppe in Germany, which controls roughly the other half of the global market for laying-hen breeding stock.[1]

Around 1900, chickens produced an average of eighty-five eggs per year. This number had more than doubled by the 1950s, and today's chickens can produce more than 300 eggs per year.[2] Scientific and technical developments in the fields of housing, feedstuffs, disease prevention, and breeding were crucial for this increase. I will zoom in on breeding methods and also on the role of private business, because its entrance into the field entailed major changes in breeding methods. A sketch of the development of the laying-hen division at Hendrix Genetics will serve as an example.

It is not surprising that scientists played a major role in the development of chicken breeding. In comparison with other farm animals, chickens are inexpensive and manageable, and they reproduce rapidly and in ample numbers. For these reasons, chickens were perfectly amenable to the kind of breeding methods that scientific experts would develop over the course of the twentieth century. Furthermore, the scientific approach to breeding was readily accepted by most commercial breeders in the Netherlands. The tensions between farmers and scientists that we encountered in dairy cattle breeding had no parallel in the chicken breeding world.

The government had a pivotal role in the development of the Dutch chicken industry. Whereas postwar agricultural policies were generally aimed at expansion and specialization, the government curtailed the growth of chicken farms for a number of years, hoping to create a niche for small farmers who lacked the means to expand their holdings. This policy also affected breeding practices. In the 1960s, however, the agricultural policy of the EEC became the guiding principle and the restrictions on the sector's growth were lifted. Before long, scientific experts were given ample scope for shaping breeding practices according to their insights.

## From Side Business to Mainstay

For the vast majority of Dutch farmers, chickens were of marginal importance as a source of income until the early twentieth century, and on many farms they would continue to play only a small role until the 1950s.[3] Before 1900, few farmers had more than 10 to 20 laying hens, and there were no chicken runs that counted more than 500. The introduction of industrial milk processing in the 1890s took away part of women's work on the farm, and many farmers' wives turned to chicken husbandry to supplement the family income (Figure 2.1).[4] Being a sideline, its status was low. There was no equivalent in rural chicken husbandry to the elaborate culture involving breeders' societies, shows, and prize contests that the dairy farmers had by then established. There were no poultry flock books or chicken farmers' associations, and barnyard chickens were an indiscriminate mixture of Landraces and foreign breeds.

The grain crisis of the 1880s stimulated the development of all branches of animal husbandry. Feedstuffs became cheaper, while the price of animal products was affected much less by the crisis. In addition, Dutch poultry farmers profited from growing export markets in Germany and England. From 1907 onwards, the Netherlands had an export surplus for eggs, and production continued to increase rapidly. At one of the major auction houses, in the city of Roermond, 0.8 million eggs were offered for sale in 1905, 13.6 million in 1910, and 40.8 million in 1915. Exports increased from 4,000 to 20,000 to 33,000 tons in these years.[5] The introduction of incubators in the early 1900s in which eggs were hatched artificially facilitated the increase of production as well as specialization. In the following decades, some farmers became specialist breeders, focusing on the improvement of their stock. They sold a proportion of their animals to the multipliers, who produced laying hens in the numbers required by the third party in the chain, the farmers who no longer bred their own animals but concentrated

Figure 2.1. Chickens on a mixed farm in the province of Drenthe, around 1910. From Schot et al., eds., *Techniek in Nederland*, vol. 3, 156.

on producing eggs for consumption. In addition, specialized hatcheries arose in the 1920s, and after the Second World War raising chicks to maturity became the task of specialized growers. This division of labour came about only gradually; until the 1950s, many farmers still combined several tasks.[6]

During the interwar years, layer hen poultry farming spread to virtually all mixed farms on the sandy soils. The smaller farms had 40 to 50 hens, the larger ones about 100. Thus, as agricultural historian Marijn Knibbe has shown, chicken husbandry, while still a sideline for most farmers, slowly but surely developed into one of the cornerstones of Dutch agriculture.[7] Women would continue to do the daily work of feeding the chickens and harvesting eggs on many farms. As soon as the more commercial approach to chicken farming emerged, however, more men began to take an active part in it – most breeders and multipliers were men, for instance. Chicken breeding continued to be a sideline, however, and the lack of a breeding culture comparable to that in dairy farming may partly explain the absence of conflicts between farmers and scientists of the kind we encountered in cattle breeding. Whereas dairy cattle breeders and scientists became increasingly divided over the importance of conformation in evaluating breeding stock, commercial chicken breeders and their scientific advisers were agreed that conformation was important only to the extent that it affected production. There was no noticeable opposition to a scientific approach to chicken breeding.

Wageningen agricultural scientists were appointed as the farmers' animal husbandry advisers after the Dutch government had given up its laissez-faire policy for agriculture in the late nineteenth century. A journal for chicken breeders was founded in 1900, in 1910 a special adviser for poultry farming was appointed, and a description of the utility breeds was published in 1912. The government also supported the sector by subsidizing the establishment of breeding stations for the production of high-quality breeding stock, which was made available to the farmers. From 1921 onwards, all aspects of chicken husbandry were studied at the national agricultural experiment station, *Het Spelderholt*.[8]

The scientific advisers, in close collaboration with a growing number of farming organizations across the country, first directed their efforts at the promotion of purebred breeding, which they saw as a prerequisite for improving egg production. As long as chickens were of marginal importance, farmers cared little for breed purity, and as a consequence the barnyard chicken was a mix of local and foreign varieties. In the second half of the nineteenth century, amateur chicken fanciers who bred their animals for beauty or production, or both, had imported various foreign breeds such as Cochins, Brahmas, and Leghorns.[9] Such animals, which competed for prizes at fancy poultry shows, regularly found their way to the farms for breeding purposes, thus adding to the mix of breeds. After the turn of the century, however, when commercial egg production on the farm became more important, the fancy breeders and the farmers increasingly went their separate ways, the fanciers focusing on breeding for beauty, whereas on the farm, the production of eggs and – to a lesser extent – meat was all that mattered.[10] Reliable commercial production required a focus on purebreds, according to the farmers' advisers. Mendelian genetics confirmed the rationality of this approach, because it explained why haphazard crossbreeding was bound to result in undesirable genetic variability.

In the nineteenth century, most Dutch farm chicken varieties laid small eggs. The pure breeds that became popular after the turn of the century produced not only bigger, but also more eggs. The best known among these were the Dutch-bred Barnevelder and Welsumer; the White Leghorn, originally from Italy; and the American Rhode Island

Red. The Barnevelder was created by crossbreeding and selection of a number of local varieties and foreign breeds such as Cochins, Brahmas, and Orpingtons. Selection for a consistent type began early in the twentieth century and resulted in a robust breed that laid dark-brown eggs, which were very popular in England. The Welsumer, Rhode Island Red, and the White Leghorn similarly originated from crossbreeding in combination with selection. Before long, the White Leghorn would become dominant as the most productive breed, even though its eggs were white and the cockerels and spent hens were of little value as meat producers. This created a niche for the meatier Rhode Island Red, despite its lower production and smaller eggs.[11]

Besides advising farmers to switch to more productive purebreds, scientists stimulated sustained selection for egg production within the breeds. For this purpose, they performed experiments with trap nests – nest boxes that closed automatically after a hen entered them, enabling the researchers to assess the laying capacity of individual animals. Beginning in 1919, laying contests were organized throughout the country to raise the farmers' interest in breeding better layers.[12] Geneticist Arend Hagedoorn repeatedly warned his colleagues that laying contests were based on the principle of mass selection – the aim was to find the best egg layers in the population – and therefore unreliable. The reason was that the best layers were not necessarily the best animals for breeding purposes, because their high production might be the result of non-hereditary factors, such as feed and management. So a hen that was mediocre, genetically speaking, might produce more eggs in a laying contest than a genetically superior one. Put differently, laying contests selected hens on the basis of phenotype, not genotype. It would help, according to Hagedoorn, if a number of hens were picked randomly from each flock, instead of being chosen by the breeders themselves, as was customary. For it was the genetic merit of their flock as a whole that breeders should be interested in, not the performance of outstanding individuals.[13]

A much more effective approach, in Hagedoorn's view, was to concentrate selection on the cockerels, because they contributed 50 per cent of the genes of the flock's next generation. Superior males could be found by recording the productivity of their daughters under controlled, uniform conditions. Hagedoorn was referring, of course, to the progeny test, propagated by Robert Bakewell in the late eighteenth century. As in cattle breeding, practical implementation of the test was problematic, however, as flocks were small and the procedure was more laborious and time-consuming than mass selection. In the 1900s, Raymond Pearl experimented with progeny testing in chickens at the Maine Experiment

Station, yet his approach was too complicated – theoretically as well as practically – for the average farmer to copy.[14] It was not until chicken breeding had become more organized that effective progeny testing became feasible on a significant scale. In the Netherlands, this only happened after the Second World War.

The focus on breed purity in Dutch poultry breeding was reinforced by the economic depression of the 1930s. Egg prices dropped sharply, and exports went down from more than 1 billion eggs in 1931 to 700 million in 1933. The government intervened by establishing guaranteed prices for eggs and by regulating the sector. There were about 200 breeders at the time, and some 200,000 poultry farmers. In 1934, the government issued a regulation, the *Teeltregeling*, which curbed the growth of production. Breeding became a licensed activity, and the breeding season was shortened to prevent overproduction. Only purebreds were to be used for breeding, to make sure that the inevitable shrinking of the sector would not also annul the qualitative progress that had been made in the preceding decades.[15]

This mandatory scheme was not only maintained during the war, it also provided the backbone of the government's policy in the postwar reconstruction years, when grain and currency shortages stood in the way of the sector's renewed growth. After the situation had normalized around 1950, an ambivalent aspect of Dutch agricultural policy became apparent. As we saw earlier, Minister of Agriculture Sicco Mansholt had made both increased production and increased productivity the prime objective of his campaign for the modernization of agriculture. The many small farms that characterized Dutch agriculture were no longer deemed efficient, and the Ministry directed its support measures at what were called viable farms of sufficient size. Technological and economic developments pushed more and more holdings towards the edge of viability, however, and the government recurrently struggled with what was called *het kleine-boerenvraagstuk*, the smallholders dilemma.[16] To give a sizable proportion of the farmers who lacked the means to expand a chance to survive, the Ministry decided to put a cap on the growth of poultry farms and to preserve the small-scale character of the sector. There were some 300,000 poultry farms in the early 1950s, most of them small, mixed, and concentrated in the sandy regions of the country. Mansholt planned to keep it this way and in 1953 issued a regulation (the *Pluimveeregeling*) that connected the number of chickens a farmer was permitted to keep to the size of his holding and that required him to grow part of the chicken feed on his own farm. A maximum of 50 chickens were allocated to farms smaller than 0.25 hectare; farms between 0.25 and 20 hectares could have more, depending on their size, up to a maximum of 600. To ensure a high standard of quality, the prewar regulations that only a restricted number of pure breeds were to be used and that crossing was prohibited were maintained. These restrictions notwithstanding, the Netherlands became the world's leading egg-exporting country in 1953.[17]

As a consequence of the *Pluimveeregeling*, the introduction of a new breeding method was delayed in the Netherlands for some time. This method, hybrid breeding, had been developed in the United States in the interwar years, and it had brought about a remarkable increase in the productivity of laying hens.

## Hybrid Breeding

Hybrid breeding was commercially developed in the 1920s by the American corn-breeding industry. Henry A. Wallace's Hi-Bred (later Pioneer Hi-Bred) Corn Company, established in 1926, was among the first to bring hybrid-corn seed successfully to the market. Before long, the company decided to try and extend the breeding method to chickens. Let us first take a look at how the method worked with corn.[18]

The productivity of hybrid corn is based on hybrid vigour, or heterosis, the effect that the crossbred offspring of two breeds, or of two genetically distinct lines within breeds, are more productive than expected on the basis of the productivity of the parents. This effect had been known among breeders for a long time. Sooner or later, breeding with purebreds inevitably entails inbreeding, as the number of animals within a breed is finite and they are bound to become genetically closer over time. Moreover, breeders in the nineteenth century routinely used inbreeding, in combination with selection, to create or "purify" a breed, that is, to fix its desirable characteristics. The risks of inbreeding were well known. For instance, the experienced breeder John Saunders Sebright had pointed out in 1809 that inbreeding, while indispensable to obtain a stable breed, could also fix undesirable characteristics and thereby weaken the breed. To prevent this, sharp selection was needed, as well as an occasional outcross with an unrelated individual, which quickly restored the breed's vitality. Charles Darwin described the phenomenon on the basis of experiments with corn: inbred corn tended to grow weaker, whereas an outcross brought back its vitality.[19]

Nineteenth-century breeders deliberately used the beneficial effect of crossing to obtain better results. In his breeding handbook, William B. Tegetmeier, Darwin's adviser on poultry breeding, recommended crossbreeding as the best way to produce good meat chickens. In the second half of the century, crossing with foreign, particularly Asian breeds, became routine among poultry and pig breeders, and American breeders began to cross corn varieties for the same reason.[20] The best breeders were perfectly aware that crossed animals were unfit for further breeding, as the heterosis effect rapidly disappeared in the following generations. Moreover, the offspring of first-generation crossbreds tended to display a wide variability in appearance and production. As Darwin noted, a cross between two breeds resulted in first-generation animals that were fairly uniform, yet this uniformity disappeared if these animals were used to produce the second generation.[21] Mendel's theory explains this on the basis of independent assortment and recombination of alleles, but experienced breeders did not need this theoretical insight to convince them that breeding from crossbred animals would not work out well. This is not to say that it did not happen in practice. Barnyard chickens were rarely bred according to plan in the nineteenth century and were an indiscriminate mix as a result.

Only the most accomplished breeders, endeavouring to create a new breed in which the desirable characteristics of two (or more) breeds were brought together, knew how to effectively use sustained crossing for a number of generations, combined with inbreeding and selection. In the late nineteenth century, new corn varieties were developed in this manner in the United States, as were the Barnevelder and the Welsumer chicken breeds in the Netherlands.

As indicated, a single cross between unrelated parents was required if the heterosis effect was the objective. In this case, the first-generation crossbreds were the end product. The term heterosis was coined in 1914 by the American geneticist George Shull. Together with the geneticist Edward East, Shull investigated strongly inbred and thus nearly pure (homozygous) corn strains. Heterosis, he hypothesized, was due to heterozygosity.[22] His corn strains, having become (nearly) homozygous pure lines through inbreeding, were likely to produce highly heterozygous offspring if they were crossed with other such lines, provided they were sufficiently unrelated. For instance, crossing a pure line homozygous for characteristic A (designated as AA in Mendelian notation) with a pure line homozygous for a (aa) would result in uniformly heterozygous offspring Aa. If the heterosis effect appeared, the heterozygote Aa performed better, on average, than both homozygotes AA and aa. From a Mendelian perspective, however, it is not at all self-evident why this is so. Shull and later researchers suggested a variety of possible explanations.[23]

One of these was the hypothesis of overdominance: a phenotypic characteristic is expressed better or more strongly if it is brought about by a heterozygous combination of alleles instead of by a homozygous combination. Obviously, this explanation is not complete, because the mechanism that brings about the overdominance effect remains unclear, and Mendelism provides no clue as to what it might be. Additional hypotheses are required to suggest how the alleles might interact in such a situation.

An alternative explanation for hybrid vigour suggested that the effect was due to the elimination of deleterious allele combinations. Suppose the recessive allele a is less beneficial for the organism than the dominant allele A, implying that an organism with aa is clearly disadvantaged. Inbreeding can increase the frequency of aa, resulting in a strain that becomes weaker and weaker – a well-known consequence of sustained inbreeding. Crossing aa with AA will reinvigorate the strain. This explanation is not entirely satisfactory either, however. If it were correct, one would expect individuals with AA to do better, or at least as well as Aa, implying that there is in fact no point in crossing.[24]

Yet another explanation for heterosis assumed that epistasis occurs, the phenomenon that genes on different loci on the chromosome may depend on each other to bring about a certain phenotypic effect; if such genes happen to be brought together by crossing, the effect will occur. Yet again, this is a hypothesis that begs the question of the mechanism that causes the effect.

It remained controversial among geneticists whether one of these hypotheses, or a combination of them, provided the correct explanation of heterosis, and the matter is still unresolved today. Hybrid vigour is a well-confirmed empirical fact, and it provided the foundation for the hybrid-corn industry, yet there is no satisfactory Mendelian account of the effect.[25]

Nonetheless, Shull's assumption that heterozygosity was somehow involved in heterosis did imply that it made sense to cross unrelated, heavily inbred pure lines, because this would strongly increase the chances of heterozygous combinations of alleles in the first generation. This is indeed what Shull and East did, yet there was a complication: the inbred lines were very weak and their fertility was seriously impaired. When crossed, they did produce vital hybrid progeny, yet their number was very small – too small to be commercially interesting. Moreover, they found that a cross between two inbred lines did not unfailingly produce offspring that were superior to both parents. The chances of the heterosis effect occurring were in fact quite small, and a great many inbred lines and crossing tests were required to find, by trial and error, the occasional superior hybrid. The main disadvantage of the method followed directly from this: it was so time-consuming and costly that it was beyond the means of the farmers.

A bonus of the hybridizing method was that first-generation hybrids were often very uniform, phenotypically speaking, which made for easy harvesting of the mature plants. All in all, however, it seemed that the disadvantages outweighed the benefits. On top of this, as we will see, it soon became clear that the heterosis effect could also be taken advantage of without prior inbreeding. Nevertheless, seed companies remained interested in the method. What motivated them was not so much their trust in the scientific soundness of the approach, but its commercial potential. Farmers who bought hybrid-corn seeds had to return to the seed company every year for new seeds, as hybrids could not be bred from without losing both the heterosis effect and the plants' uniformity. Seed companies could thus make sure they would receive an adequate return on their investments. It might well have been possible, as critics of the hybrid-corn industry have pointed out, to produce highly productive plants on the basis of purebred breeding. The farmers would have benefitted from such an approach, as purebreds can be propagated from seeds. Yet then the question arises as to who would have been prepared to invest in the creation of a product that could be sold only once, because there was no patent system for living organisms.[26] The hybrid-corn method functioned as a "biological lock" that prevented other parties from reaping the rewards of a company's investments.

East and Shull's research on hybrid corn soon piqued the interest of other researchers. The most pressing problem to be solved was the reduced fertility of the inbred strains. In 1917, Donald F. Jones, at the Connecticut Agricultural Experiment Station, succeeded in overcoming this complication by developing an approach that was to become the standard method of the hybrid-corn industry: the four-way cross. Jones's solution to the fertility problem was the result of tinkering and luck in equal measure. Sheer curiosity induced him to cross two different first-generation hybrids and, by mere chance, the offspring turned out to be superior to both their parents. Thus the principle of the four-way cross was established: inbred lines A and B are combined in hybrid X, and X is then crossed with hybrid Y, where Y is the combination of inbred lines C and D. The end product Z, the result of crossing X and Y, can be sold as seeds to the farmer. The reason for the double cross was that X and Y, unlike their parents, were both viable and fertile, and produced offspring in sufficient numbers for commercial purposes. Furthermore, by using four inbred strains that were different in many characteristic, the heterosis effect was kept virtually intact.

As indicated, Jones was lucky to come across a superior double cross right away, Normally, many crosses with inbred lines are needed to find promising combinations, especially when the inbred strains are produced by "blind" inbreeding only. Researchers realized, however, that they could increase their chance of obtaining good results by selecting the inbred lines for desirable qualities, which, provided they had a genetic basis, would predictably reappear in the hybrids. Predicting the quality of the final result remained difficult, however, as corn hybrids appeared very sensitive to environmental circumstances; their productivity was strongly dependent on soil and climate conditions. All in all, hybrid-corn breeding required long-term commitment and ample funds. Besides commercial companies with capital, the American government also made substantial investments in the new method. To perform the complex crossing schemes, both the companies and the government employed geneticists. Wallace's Hi-Bred Corn Company brought hybrid-corn seeds to market in 1926. Other companies, such as Funk Brothers and Dekalb followed suit, and the market share of hybrid corn increased steadily. By 1959, hybrid corn accounted for more than 95 per cent of the United States' corn acreage, and production had doubled since 1929.[27]

The fact remained, however, that producing hybrid seeds was cumbersome and costly. This was even truer for hybrid-chicken breeding, which was developed by Henry A. Wallace and his son Henry B., among others, in the mid-1930s, after the method had proved fruitful in the corn business. To begin with, creating pure lines in chickens is even more laborious, because, unlike corn, chickens are not self-fertilizing. In addition, chickens turned out to be more sensitive to the adverse effects of inbreeding than corn. Sooner or later, a considerable part of the newly created inbred chicken lines succumbed to all kinds of defects. Therefore, researchers soon turned their attention to possible alternatives. One of these, developed in the late 1940s, was reciprocal recurrent selection (RRS). This method was also based on hybridizing, yet it avoided heavy inbreeding.

American poultry breeder Arthur Heisdorf of H&N Farms was the first to market a laying-hen strain that was obtained through RRS: the Nick Chick, which still exists. The method entails a specific form of progeny testing, in which the performance of the offspring is used to assess the merits of the parents as breeding animals. The offspring, in this case, are hybrids of different parent breeds (or separate lines within breeds) that have not been inbred and thus are genetically variable. Each new hybrid generation is created by choosing animals from only those parental strains that produced the best crossbreds in previous combinations. Assuming that hybrid vigour is somehow caused by heterozygosity, repeating this procedure for generations will result in parental strains that become more and more different from each other and thus produce hybrids that are increasingly heterozygous. There is no need for the complicated double cross in this case, because no inbred lines with impaired viability are involved. RRS was to be regularly used in chicken breeding from the 1960s onwards. The double-cross method, which many companies had heavily invested in, also remained in use, but breeding systems based on intense inbreeding would gradually become less common.[28]

Geneticist Hagedoorn suggested another alternative, which became known as the nucleus system. A nucleus of breeding stock was created by focusing selection on the cockerels. First, several hen groups, each with a single cockerel, were formed. The progeny of these groups were compared, and only the best group of sons and daughters was kept. The daughters were then divided into groups again, and the hens within each group were mated to one of their half-brothers. The offspring of these groups were treated in similar fashion, the best performing siblings being bred among themselves. This was continued for several generations. The repeated sister–half-brother matings resulted in the cockerels becoming more and more homozygous for the characteristics they were selected for, according to Hagedoorn, and they would ultimately become pure lines that performed optimally.[29] Critics were quick to point out, however, that Hagedoorn ignored the adverse effects of sustained inbreeding and underestimated the number of genes involved in production properties such as egg laying, implying that it was much harder to attain purity than Hagedoorn imagined. Dutch poultry experts also rejected the system for its excessive reliance on inbreeding.[30]

Yet another alternative for the double cross was selection for vitality among the inbred lines. In this way, parental lines were obtained that produced a satisfactory number of healthy first-generation hybrids, so that a second cross was no longer needed.[31] The last method to be mentioned here, which would become particularly important for the production of chicken meat, was also based on selection in the parental lines. Some traits, such as efficient feed conversion and rapid growth, tend to have a negative effect on egg production; in other words, growth and fertility are antagonistic; they cannot be simultaneously selected for in a single line. This difficulty was circumvented, as far as possible, by combining a cockerel from a strain selected for growth with a hen from a strain selected for fertility: the hybrids of such parents showed a combination of growth and fertility that would have been impossible to attain in a single line.[32] Pig breeders, as we will see later, deployed the same principle.

These examples of further developments in hybrid breeding show that, as in the case of the original double cross, selection was a vital element of the methods used. Shull and his colleagues propagated the hybrid-corn breeding method as the rational, Mendelian alternative to traditional mass selection, yet in practice breeders could not do without the latter. This was especially true for animal breeders, as animals took worse to inbreeding than plants.[33]

Among the most important contributions by scientists to hybrid breeding methodology, and to animal breeding in general, was the development of mathematical models and statistical tools to rationalize breeding practices. In 1942, for instance, George F. Sprague and Loyd A. Tatum introduced a method for estimating the potential of two strains to combine well in a cross – their combining or "nicking" ability – which enabled a considerable reduction in the number of test crossings needed to find good combinations.[34] As we saw in the previous chapter, Jay Lush and his school laid out the principles of quantitative genetics between the 1930s and 1950s, and the calculation of indexes was an important aspect of this quantitative approach. As in dairy cattle, a cockerel's hereditary capacity to transmit his productive traits can be expressed in an index, for instance by comparing the egg production of his daughters to that of the average production of other cockerels' daughters. More advanced indexes allowed for the correction for environmental influences (BLUP) or for the selection of a weighted combination of traits, their relative weight being determined by their economic value. Optimum use of such tools had to await the advent of computers. The BLUP method was introduced in Dutch cattle breeding in the 1970s; it was not used in chicken breeding until the 1990s.[35]

In dairy cattle breeding, the effective use of statistical tools was predicated on the widespread adoption of artificial insemination by both breeders and farmers, which vastly increased the number of inseminations per bull and thus multiplied the data available for determining his breeding value. In chickens the role of AI was more limited and confined to the breeding sector. Whereas AI made the reproduction of dairy cattle more efficient, it was too labour-intensive to produce the millions of chickens required for meat and egg production. In stockbreeding, however, it was important to have reliable data on the individual descent of breeding animals. The use of AI, combined with individual housing in battery cages, ensured the reliability of such data. Furthermore, as in cattle breeding, AI helped to prevent contagious diseases.[36]

## Hy-Line and Hendrix Genetics

Father and son Wallace of the Pioneer Hi-Bred Corn Company founded Hy-Line Poultry Farms in 1936 to create a hybrid laying hen using the hybrid-corn method.[37] In 1940, they began to market a hybrid chicken named Hy-Line: a double cross with a brand name. Its development had been a laborious and tedious process. Inbred lines were formed from Leghorn and White Minorca stock by means of five to nine generations of brother-sister matings. As in corn, the lines were not made haphazardly; they were selected carefully for egg production, egg quality, vitality, early maturity, low incidence of broodiness, and other relevant properties. Harmful recessives were eliminated whenever possible. Due to the sharpness of selection and the losses caused by inbreeding, more than 90 per cent of the lines had to be discarded. In the end, however, the commercial success of the hybrid laying hens compensated for the high costs incurred in their production. In the United States, 17 million Hy-Line chicks were sold in 1951, 31 million in 1954, and 70 million in 1959.[38]

A significant factor in the success of Hy-Line Poultry Farms was that they did not simply sell chicks, but offered a service package that included management and animal care advice. The extra service was not only a marketing tool, it was also intended to prevent negative publicity from farmers insufficiently aware of what was needed to make Hy-Lines realize their full potential for egg production. The importance of these aspects was underlined by *Wallace's Farmer*, an agricultural magazine established by Henry A. Wallace's grandfather: "Poor managers can't make money on any kind of chickens. Top managers may be able to do as well with standard-breds as with hybrids. What really counts, after all, is what happens in your own hen house."[39]

The Hy-Line's fame spread rapidly, and despite the regulations privileging purebred breeding, Dutch experts began to take an interest in the opportunities provided by crossing different breeds and the hybrid-corn method. As early as 1932, Hagedoorn had reminded the breeding experts that they should not rely exclusively on purebred breeding, as it had long been known that first-generation crossbreds often excelled in vitality and productivity.[40] Some scientific crossbreeding experiments were conducted in the interwar years, but it was not until the late 1940s that farmers began to take an interest. This was probably because the principal egg-laying breed, the Leghorn, was believed to have suffered from too much inbreeding during the war, when its population was very small. Once begun, the popularity of crossbreeding rose quickly: from a few per cent in 1948, by 1953 about 60 per cent of egg-laying hens were crossbreds. The parents of these crossbreds were purebreds, and the multipliers, who performed the crosses, had to obtain permission to apply the method. There were as yet no inbred hybrids produced by the hybrid-corn method in the Netherlands.[41]

At the beginning of the 1950s, several Dutch poultry experts made a trip to the United States to learn more about hybrid-breeding methodology.

Agricultural expert K. Bos of *De Schothorst*, the national experiment station for feed research, reported that hybrid chickens were kept on a large scale in the Midwest, with excellent results. Considering the high costs involved, however, Bos doubted whether this breeding system would be suitable for Dutch breeders. He also expressed his concern about the heavy inbreeding that was part and parcel of the method and suggested that reciprocal recurrent selection might be a more promising approach.[42] Bos's colleague Gerard van der Plank, professor of animal science at Utrecht University, saw no future for hybrid chickens in the Netherlands either. The system was too expensive, and the hard-won purity of the Dutch breeds might go to waste if breeders were unwise enough to use first-generation hybrids as breeding animals. Van der Plank also recommended breeding methods that were less dependent on inbreeding, adding, however, that it would take extensive collaboration between specialists and breeders to make systems such as reciprocal recurrent selection work in the Netherlands.[43] The professional poultry journal *De Bedrijfspluimveehouder* concurred with Van der Plank and also concluded that the costs of the hybrid-corn method were prohibitive for Dutch chicken breeders.[44]

Hendrix Industries N.V. in Boxmeer had few such reservations. The company did not have a breeding division at the time; its core business was the production of compound feed for cattle, pigs, and chickens. Customers of Hendrix were given access to several other services provided by the company, such as its veterinary service, which provided them with vaccines from Nobilis (now MSD), founded by Hendrix in 1949. Hendrix also ran a slaughterhouse, and the farmers who purchased its products and services were entitled to receive a slaughter premium.[45] So, like Hy-Line Poultry Farms in the US, Hendrix sold their products as packages, including information and other services.

Guust P.A. van den Eynden, a Wageningen graduate working as a corn geneticist at a Dutch plant breeding cooperative was the first to see business opportunities in hybrid chicken breeding. Early in 1951, he contacted Hy-Line Poultry Farms headquarters in Des Moines, Iowa for information about the method, and then discussed the option of selling Hy-Lines in the Netherlands with Wim Hendrix, president of Hendrix Industries. Considering that selling highly productive hybrid chickens might increase feed sales, as did the veterinary and other services his firm provided, Wim Hendrix was definitely interested.[46]

Van den Eynden approached Henry B. Wallace about the option and enquired whether he might be sent a batch of fertilized Hy-Line eggs for practical testing under Dutch conditions. After some correspondence, Wallace consented.[47] Importing the test eggs proved more difficult than expected, however. The Dutch Poultry and Eggs Board, representing the interests of both employers and employees in the sector, refused to sanction the transaction. Besides competitive considerations, they feared that importing Hy-Line hybrids might ultimately result in the Dutch poultry industry becoming dependent on American breeding technologies.[48]

Wim Hendrix found a way to bypass the Board, however. His pharmaceutical company Nobilis was licensed to import eggs for vaccine production, and on 16 April 1951, he requested permission from the Ministry of Agriculture to import 720 Hy-Line eggs for a test program to improve a vaccine against smallpox and diphtheria. Permission was granted, and the eggs, taken from eight different inbred strains, arrived a couple of weeks later. On 29 April they found themselves in an incubator in St Anthonis, a village in the vicinity of Boxmeer.[49]

There are two different versions of what happened next, yet in both of them the Poultry and Egg Board got wind of Hendrix's scheme and ordered him to destroy the eggs. Hendrix ignored the order and secretly rushed the eggs (or the chicks, according to the alternative story) to a monastery near the Dutch-Belgian border, whence the chicks were smuggled out of the country, to be raised in Belgium.[50]

The mature chickens proved to be excellent egg layers, and Hendrix Industries signed a contract with Hy-Line Poultry Farms to take one of the hybrids to the European market. The parental lines needed to produce them arrived in Belgium in 1952. The hybrids themselves participated in their own marketing campaign: they competed in laying contests in Belgium, Germany, and the Netherlands, and won all of them. Even before the Hy-Lines were available in the Netherlands, Hendrix had ads and advertorials published in the agricultural press and issued a brochure to promote the Hy-Lines that was designed to look exactly like the company's feed brochures.[51]

Meanwhile, Hendrix began negotiations with the Dutch government to obtain permission for some form of commercial exploitation of hybrid chicken breeding in the Netherlands. Like the Poultry Board, the government at first prohibited the import of fertilized eggs, as this would make Dutch farmers dependent on regular deliveries from the United States, which, moreover, would have to be paid for in dollars, an expensive currency. By 1953, however, the government was prepared to condone the exploitation of the complete hybrid breeding program in the Netherlands. This implied that Hendrix would become a franchise, with a permit to be registered as a breeding company in the Netherlands. It was also stipulated that production would have to be for export only, although this restriction was lifted two years later.[52]

Negotiations with the Americans over the franchise option took quite a while. Initially, Hy-Line Poultry Farms was not interested in having a European franchise partner, as they had their hands full managing the rapid growth of Hy-Line sales in the United States. Yet after Henry B. Wallace and Wim Hendrix had visited each other in Des Moines and Boxmeer, an agreement was finally drafted in 1954, which licensed Hendrix to sell Hy-Lines bred in Boxmeer from the American parental lines.[53] The breeding program was transferred to a newly founded subsidiary of Hendrix Feed Industries, Euribrid, which also incorporated the breeding program for broilers the company had started in 1953. Hendrix Industries employed Guust van den Eynden to supervise the program.[54]

In 1957, *De Bedrijfspluimveehouder* published an overview of the performance of the Hy-Lines from 351 farms in Belgium, comprising 94,500 hens that were born in 1953, started to produce eggs in 1954, and were monitored until the summer of 1955. Their production was better and losses due to sickness and death were lower than the averages obtained with White Leghorns as well as with crossbreds in the Netherlands.[55] The figures did not fail to impress the Dutch poultry farmers. In 1956–7, when Hy-Line chickens entered the Dutch market for the first time, some 600,000 layers were sold. A year later their number had grown to 2.4 million. In the 1956–7 season, the average Dutch chicken produced 237 eggs in 18 months; the Hy-Lines outdid them, producing 279 eggs in 18.5 months. Of the Hy-Lines, 22.3 per cent died or had to be culled; in Dutch crossbreds it was 34.6 per cent. Marketing strategy also played an important role in the Hy-Lines' rise in popularity. The chicks were born at special Hy-Line hatcheries, and each one was marked with a wing tag and delivered with a certificate guaranteeing its origin. Euribrid thus provided the same package of information and services traditionally provided by Hendrix's feed division.[56]

The Hy-Lines were more expensive than Dutch chickens, yet the expectations of their performance were high. In an advertisement from 1957, a farmer shared his experience, saying: "You can quote us on this ... we're happy to tell anyone that Hy-Lines may be more expensive, yet they made up for this even before they began to lay eggs. They need little feed, and their laying potential is enormous. They're a fine flock, our Hy-Lines" (Figure 2.2).[57]

The first chicks brought to market rapidly sold out by subscription. "The Hylines are coming," announced an article in *De Bedrijfspluimveehouder*, and the Dutch breeders, who were only working with purebreds and their first-generation crosses, realized the hybrids were going to provide strong competition for their animals.[58]

Figure 2.2. A Euribrid advertisement. From *De Bedrijfspluimveehouder* 35, no. 19 (1957): 11.

## From Purebreds to First-Generation Crossbreds

After the government licensed the production of crossbreds from purebred parents, their market share increased rapidly, to 70 per cent in 1955.[59] The multipliers, who performed the crosses, used various breeds for the purpose. Usually, they had little or no information about the origin of the particular strains they deployed. As a consequence, the results were highly variable and often disappointing. Advisers from Hendrix Industries drew attention to American research that had demonstrated the importance of the combining ability of the parents, which might be improved by reciprocal recurrent selection. To make this work, however, farmers would have to provide the breeders with feedback on the productivity of their crossbreds, which they did not routinely do at the time.[60]

*De Bedrijfspluimveehouder* urged farmers to explore this possibility,[61] and poultry expert D.C. Heijboer felt that combining ability tests and organized strain selection were indispensable for the survival of the small-scale breeding sector. Breeders and multipliers could no longer work in isolation but had to collaborate. Heijboer calculated that a viable parent strain consisted of between 750 and 1,000 hens, and that a breeder needed a fair number of such strains for a fruitful investigation of their combining ability. To make this a realistic option, breeders would have to collaborate and exchange strains. This was a sensitive issue, Heijboer acknowledged, yet for individual small breeders their chances of survival were grim, unless they were prepared to work together.[62]

To help the breeders cooperate, the poultry sector instituted a foundation, Stifo (*Stichting voor het Fokkerijwezen bij de Pluimveehouderij*), of which Heijboer became secretary. A testing station was built in Putten to evaluate the laying capacity of the first-generation crossbreds.[63] As many breeders had imported foreign breeds after the war, there was no shortage of experimental animals, and strains of different origin within the breeds were also available. The latter were preferred by breeders who still had reservations about giving up purebred breeding. Stifo enabled breeders to register their strains, and within a year after its establishment, the foundation had registered 240 strains from 130 breeders. The test results obtained in Putten were published in *De Bedrijfspluimveehouder*, and breeders began to use them for advertising purposes.[64]

While many small breeders were at first hesitant about collaborating with colleagues who were also their competitors, they appeared even more apprehensive about the growing competition offered by Euribrid.[65] In 1955, a group of some twenty small breeders established a cooperative, the *Coöperatief Pluimvee Instituut* (CPI), with a breeding and testing station in the village of Nuland. The first director of CPI, K. Bos, former poultry expert at *De Schothorst* experiment station, had a clear view of the task ahead: finding and improving strains that combined well together. Most breeders were unable to do this on their own, as developments in the United States had shown, where most small companies had disappeared. American enterprises had a population of 50,000 to 300,000 hens, and they employed scientific staff to supervise their breeding program. By 1957, some fifty breeders had joined CPI. Chicks were marketed under the CPI trademark, and the influence of individual members on the breeding program was limited.[66] In the same year, CPI joined forces with a Belgian partner, and they founded

Hypeco, a breeding company for both laying hens and broilers.[67] Hypeco would provide effective competition for Euribrid.[68]

The third company to achieve a competitive position was Bovans, the first private breeders' combination, established in 1956 by four Dutch breeders. Bovans maintained the strains of five different breeds, comprising 200 flocks and about 15,000 animals and marketed all cross-breds under the brand name Bovans.[69]

## Industrialization

The establishment of the European Economic Community put the Dutch poultry sector under extraordinary pressure. To even out the differences in cost prices between the countries that opened their borders to each other, a system of export taxes was implemented that turned out to be very unfavourable to the Dutch breeders. Exporting eggs became much more expensive, and exports to Germany, the most important buyer, dropped alarmingly, from 3.087 billion eggs in 1961 to 763 million in 1967. Exports to other countries also dwindled, partly because American hybrid chickens were claiming a growing share of the market. Before long, Dutch poultry farmers were forced to cut back on production.[70]

As a result, competition became more cut-throat. Poultry farming was still mainly in the hands of the mixed farmers on the sandy soils in the early 1960s, as expressly intended by the government. In 1961, 84 per cent of the holdings had fewer than 200 laying hens, and less than 1 per cent had more than 1,000.[71] After the EEC had been established, the government regulations curtailing the growth of the sector were relaxed under international pressure and ultimately abolished in 1961.[72]

Whereas there were intervention prices for milk and pork, the European market for eggs was practically free, with only a modicum of protection against cheap imports from non-EEC countries.[73] Realizing that they would have to increase their productivity if they were to survive the competition, and believing that intensification, mechanization, and scaling-up were the instruments to achieve this, more and more Dutch poultry farmers began to keep their laying hens in battery cages from the mid-1960s onwards (Figure 2.3). The battery cage was also an important innovation for the breeders, as it facilitated controlled fertilization and the recording of feed conversion and individual production – thus, trap nests were no longer needed. By the mid-1970s, about 80 per cent of all laying hens were kept in cages. Ten years later this figure had risen to 95 per cent.[74] Poultry farming became concentrated in the provinces of Gelderland, Brabant, and Limburg, and the holdings continued to increase in size and became more and more specialized.

Figure 2.3. A battery cage in the 1960s. From *De Bedrijfspluimveehouder* 43, no. 22 (1965).

The broiler industry, which had been insignificant in the Netherlands until the 1950s, became a separate sector that expanded rapidly.[75]

What was true for animal husbandry in general was also true for poultry farming, according to agricultural economist C. Zwetsloot: "Poultry farmers will have to become entrepreneurs, and they will have to make a choice: either they industrialize, or they will have to give up their farms."[76] The days of the smallholders, who had dominated the sector until then, were said to be over. In 1960, there were 199,000 poultry farms in the Netherlands, 53,000 in 1970, 8,000 in 1980, and 4,000 in 2000. Of the 2,000 remaining in 2015, 1,100 were laying-hen farms, with an average of 35,000 animals.[77]

The companies in the chain, from breeders to egg producers, including the feed industries, egg traders, and slaughter plants, became mutually dependent. Chain integration was intended to reduce the risks of this interdependence and to guarantee the quality of consumer eggs: the farmers in a chain kept hens of the same origin that were fed the same food and treated in the same way. Some chains were cooperatives, others were private. Vertical integration was also stimulated by the growing importance of the Dutch national market, after exports had imploded in the early 1960s. The retailers, representing consumer preferences, became salient players at the national level. Supermarket chain Albert Heijn was the first company from outside the sector to participate in vertical integration. Hendrix Industries did the same to market its egg brand "Golden Farm."[78]

Even though most breeders preferred to stay independent because their market area was becoming increasingly global, vertical integration did affect their breeding goals, because they had to pay more attention to consumer preferences. Traditionally, breeders sold their eggs to the hatcheries, meaning that egg quality was largely determined by hatch rates. The success of integrations, however, depended on the marketability of the end product, the egg for the table. Hence, breeders also had to select for traits such as weight and eggshell quality, and the absence of blood spots.[79]

The Dutch poultry sector faced increasing competition from the American poultry industry. The scale of the American companies was unheard of in the Netherlands. In the early 1960s, Kimber Farms, for instance, employed five geneticists, twenty staff members, and a veterinarian; they sold 100 million laying hens from a single hybrid line in four years.[80] In large parts of Europe, more and more of the remaining breeding companies were taken over by American enterprises. The Netherlands was among the few countries that managed to maintain a poultry breeding industry of some substance.[81]

Opportunities were limited, however. There were seventy breeders left in 1964, many of whom struggled to earn a decent income. Three breeders controlled 30 per cent of the market, and the top 19 had a market share of 75 per cent.[82] The larger companies began to explore new markets abroad, in the EEC and beyond. Euribrid established subsidiaries in nine countries in Western Europe and also sold its products directly to Eastern Europe, the Middle East, Africa, East Asia, and the Americas.[83] Bovans was the first to start a subsidiary outside of Europe, in Argentina, in 1965.[84] Before long, however, the owners felt the company was getting the better of them, and they sold it to CPI's Hypeco. "I'm a chicken farmer and a country boy, and I know nothing about contracts," one of them gave as the reason for this step.[85]

The decision of many breeders to end their business was motivated mainly by the rapidly increasing costs of research and development and of marketing. Besides quality, commercial acumen was crucial, according to the president of the national organization of poultry breeders, Euribrid's Guust van den Eyden.[86] The Dutch Poultry and Eggs Board concurred: "It is no exaggeration to say that more than half of the remaining breeding companies lack adequate sales organizations and research programs."[87] At a breeders' meeting in 1965, it was estimated that a yearly production of about 20 million laying-hen chicks was needed for a company to compete successfully at the global scale.[88]

After Bovans had been taken over, only two major breeding companies remained in the Netherlands: Euribrid, owned by Hendrix Feed Industries, and CPI-Hypeco-Bovans, a cooperative. The latter went bankrupt in 1991 and was bought by the chicken farmer and entrepreneur Thijs Hendrix – no relation to Wim Hendrix of Hendrix Feed Industries. The cooperative's failure was partly due to breeding decisions that did not turn out well. Substantial investments were made, for instance, in the development of the *Zwartje*, a robust type of laying hen that was fairly resistant to one of the major poultry afflictions, Marek's disease. Soon after the introduction of the new type, however, a vaccine against the disease became available, and since the *Zwartje* needed more feed and produced fewer eggs than the White Leghorn, its popularity was short-lived. The war in Iraq was also a factor, because countries in the Middle East made up an important part of the cooperative's export market. The sudden occurrence of a disease in a newly developed line of laying hens for the American market dealt the final blow to CPI-Hypeco-Bovans.[89]

In the 1970s and 1980s, many poultry breeding companies were taken over by large (vertically integrated) veterinary-pharmaceutical, feed, animal housing, and slaughtering industries. For the pharmaceutical companies, the expansion of their vaccine sales was an important motive. Another incentive for investments in animal breeding was the expectation that developments in genetics, particularly in the field of genetic modification, might bring about a biotechnological revolution. By the 1990s, however, many breeding companies were being sold again. Euribrid illustrates the trend. Its owner, Hendrix Feed Industries, was taken over by BP Nutrition – later Nutreco – in 1979. After Thijs Hendrix had acquired Hypeco-Bovans in 1991, he negotiated a merger with the laying-hen division of Euribrid. When the combination planned to expand by merging with the French laying-hen breeding company ISA in 2005, Nutreco rejected the plan and soon thereafter decided to discard the relatively small unit and its 400 employees altogether. According to Euribrid's director of innovation, Gerard Albers, the reason for this was easy to understand: "At the end of the day it appears that the breeding business requires stamina; it is a field where only the experts really know how it works as a business. Companies in other fields have difficulties understanding this, and ultimately the partnership goes sour."[90] Frans van Sambeek put it in similar terms: the breeding divisions were resold because the companies that owned them "only look at the spreadsheets for next month, and breeding does not fit into such a regime. Animals die, there are losses, all sorts of things can happen."[91]

Thijs Hendrix took over the breeding company from Nutreco, finalized the merger with ISA, and continued the new combination as Hendrix Genetics. After a number of additional mergers, Hendrix Genetics is now one of two breeding businesses – the other one being the German Wesjohann Gruppe – that dominate poultry breeding worldwide. Hendrix Genetic's laying-hen division (now called ISA) has 350 employees, 17 of whom are academics – veterinarians, biologists, and agriculturalists – for basic breeding work and research.

## Developments in Breeding

Several systems were used to create new chicken hybrids. Inbreeding in combination with selection was the preferred method at Euribrid. Brother-to-sister mating was followed by backcrossing the progeny with the parents, a procedure that was continued for several generations. The vitality of the offspring rapidly decreased over the generations – 70 to 80 per cent had to be discarded – but it was a fast route towards purity. A great number of such homozygous lines were then tested in various crosses to find the best hybrid combinations.[92]

A successful outcome was not guaranteed. When European customers began to prefer brown eggs in the mid-1960s, Hy-Line was unable to meet this demand, as there was little interest in brown eggs in the United States. Euribrid therefore decided to create a new breed that produced brown-shelled eggs. The first attempt resulted in Hy-Line 844, a hybrid created by means of the customary inbreeding and crossing scheme. It soon became clear, however, that their performance lacked consistency. Breeding director Van den Eynden then decided to try his hand at a different method, using stock from a friend, the American breeder Jimmy J. Warren, whose chickens laid brown eggs. Van den Eyden developed his parent lines purely on the basis of selection, without the use of inbreeding, and finally succeeded in making lines that combined well. The final hybrids were autosexing, meaning that male and female chicks could be sexed on the basis of differences in appearance. Van den Eynden suggested the hybrid be called Hysex. The Hy-Line company vetoed the name, however, and Van den Eynden had to settle for Hisex (pronounced he-sex) Brown.[93]

Another instructive example of the breeding techniques used at Euribrid is the new hybrid that was introduced in 1970, after the franchise contract with Wallace's Hy-Line Poultry Farms had expired. The white Hy-Line chickens' performance had by then become rather inconsistent, and they were less suited for being kept in barns because they were "flighty." Although batteries had become the preferred housing system in the United States, many European farmers still kept their chickens in barns. Furthermore, the Hy-Line was susceptible to Marek's disease, and a vaccine was not yet available. Van den Eyden thus faced the task of developing a new white laying hen that Euribrid might put on the market in 1970, when the company would have to rely on its own breeding program.[94]

It was a delicate matter, however, for two reasons. First, Euribrid was prohibited from developing alternatives to the white Hy-Line while under contract with Hy-Line Poultry Farms. Van den Eynden therefore conducted his breeding experiments "unofficially," at a different location. Second, firms were very secretive about the grandparental lines they used to produce their double-cross hybrids. They were never sold, for the obvious reason that the biological lock created by crossing them was predicated on their not being available to competitors. The only way to obtain such lines was either by developing them from scratch, or by buying an entire breeding company. The only legal way, that is – trade secrets were difficult to protect completely, and theft was not uncommon in the chicken-breeding world. A geneticist at a major breeding company even described the poultry business as "an industry of thieves."[95]

Van den Eynden did not have to start from scratch, nor did he need to have recourse to actions that were downright illegal. Because of his long experience in the breeding business and his personal relations with many breeders, he had a clear idea of which grandparental lines would be suitable for the new four-way cross he had in mind. The difficult part was to acquire both sexes of each of these lines. Breeders had no qualms about selling a single sex of a grandparental line to other breeders because, obviously, both sexes were needed to reproduce the line. But a single sex was all that Van den Eynden needed. He knew that various grandparental hen and cockerel lines, available from different breeders, had descended from the same heavily inbred original stock, and might therefore be expected to be not too different genetically. In this way he succeeded in finding suitable hens and cockerels for two of his four grandparental lines. The other two lines could not be acquired as easily as this, and here Van den Eynden resorted to simply trying his luck. Selling chickens of a single sex required them to be sexed, and even though chicken sexers were experts, they occasionally made mistakes. Van den Eynden bought large numbers of supposedly single-sex animals from the breeding lines he was interested in, and scrutinized them for accidental other-sex individuals. He thus succeeded in obtaining both sexes of the two remaining lines he needed.

Once Van den Eynden had multiplied the animals of each line in sufficient numbers, he crossed and double-crossed them in various combinations, and the end result was a new hybrid, the Hisex White, as it was ultimately to be called. To test its performance, Euribrid sent it to the testing station at Putten under a cover name, Hy-Line 11, because of the contract with Hy-Line Poultry Farms. The new white laying hen turned out to be superior to all the other lines tested in Putten, and Van den Eynden was confident that he had accomplished his mission to find a replacement for the white Hy-Line after the American contract ended.[96]

Reciprocal recurrent selection, which takes the performance of the progeny as the basis for selection within the parental lines, was introduced by CPI in the early 1960s. Euribrid only used heavily inbred lines at the time. As a result, CPI laying hens were more robust than the hens of most other breeders. Indexes were not yet calculated in the sixties, and neither CPI nor Euribrid used a computer. At Euribrid, "someone was locked in a room with all the data for two days" to make sense of them.[97] When the company made a start with reciprocal recurrent selection in 1973, calculations were still being done by hand. Van den Eynden did not favour the use of computers, which he thought were too expensive. Powerful computers only made their entrance in 1983, two years after his death, and were used not only for index calculations but also for recording and processing the breeding program data. Developing a good software program for this automation process took considerable effort, but Euribrid benefitted from its relations with Wageningen University, where scientists had routinely been calculating indexes for the dairy cattle breeders since the early 1970s. In the 1990s, Euribrid came to rely even more on computers when it adopted the BLUP method for calculating breeding values.[98]

The first genetic maps based on DNA data were published in the 1990s. Wageningen University took part in this development, using mainly Euribrid chickens for their research.[99] The prospect that a complete map of the chicken genome would soon be available induced geneticists to think about how to identify the genes responsible for quantitative properties, such as egg and meat production. Many genes were involved in the expression of quantitative characteristics, and they were surmised to have a small and additive effect. It seemed plausible, however, that some genes had a more substantial effect than others. These were obviously the most interesting from a breeding perspective. To locate such genes, geneticists developed a method that involved the identification of regions on the genome where they might be found with a certain probability. Such regions were called quantitative trait loci (QTL).[100]

These investigations were conducted by scientists at scientific institutions, but breeding companies monitored their progress closely, and some of them became interested in participating. In 1986, Euribrid was the first poultry breeding company in the Netherlands to set up a partnership with the universities of Wageningen and Utrecht, mainly "as an insurance that we would not miss out on anything," according to director of innovation Gerard Albers. The investigations of quantitative trait loci did not produce any practically useful results, however. The DNA regions containing the interesting genes turned out to be too large to be useful for selection purposes. Nevertheless, the partnership with the universities was important, in Albers' view: "We built up a relationship in this way that proved to be useful at a later stage, when practical results did come within view." Albers was referring to genomic selection here.[101]

Genomic selection is not based on estimates of the location of genes that are important for quantitative traits. Its high-tech character notwithstanding, the method does not differ from other breeding methods in its basic principle, which is finding correlations. Whereas older methods were predicated on correlations between performance and conformation or pedigree, genomic selection is based on correlations between performance and DNA structure. The technology involves the use of a large number of so-called markers, spread widely across the DNA, that represent small variations called single nucleotide polymorphisms (SNPs). In a group of breeding animals that serves as a reference population, correlations are calculated between the structure of their DNA in terms of markers on the one hand, and their economically important phenotypic properties such as egg or milk production on the other. These correlations enable the identification of potentially superior breeding animals even before they have reached sexual maturity: by assessing the specific constellation of their DNA markers, their phenotypic characteristics, including their productive qualities, can be predicted. Whereas traditional breeders tried to predict the performance of their animals on the basis of conformation, in genomic selection breeders use the "conformation" of the DNA to make such predictions. In both cases, the relevant genes themselves are unknown. The partnership with Wageningen University began to bear fruit for Euribrid in 2004, when genomic selection was introduced into their breeding program.[102]

## Chickens Are Not Peas[103]

Being cheap, manageable, and prolific, chickens lent themselves more easily than the larger livestock species to the rational breeding practices that scientists began to propagate in the early twentieth century. By the end of the century, egg production had almost quadrupled, hybrids had replaced the initially preferred purebred races, and the breeding business had come into the hands of a few globally operating companies. There appears to have been little resistance to the increasing role of science in chicken breeding in the Netherlands. This can be explained in part by the marginal position of poultry farming until the early twentieth century and the absence of flock books and breeders' societies for the utility breeds; there was no culture of breeding that might have conflicted with the scientists' approach, as in dairy cattle breeding. In her investigations of chicken breeding in North America, Margaret Derry has found considerably more tension between chicken breeders and scientists in the United States in the early decades of the twentieth century. She explains this by the fact that the United States was fairly unique at the time in that many of the agricultural experiment stations employed academically trained geneticists, whose views on rational breeding were not always received well by commercial breeders. We have seen several examples of how, in the Netherlands, the geneticist Hagedoorn was similarly rebuffed by both practical breeders and their agricultural advisers when he proffered suggestions for what he considered to be more scientific breeding methods. However, there were only a handful of geneticists at the Dutch universities in the first half of the century, and only Hagedoorn occasionally addressed the breeders directly.

The poultry farmers' regular advisers on breeding methods were the more practically oriented agricultural scientists from Wageningen Agricultural College, and they met with little resistance.[104]

Chicken breeding was based on principles that had been in use since at least the late eighteenth century: inbreeding, crossing, selection for purity, and selection for performance. In corn breeding, however, a new method was developed in the 1920s that scientists as well as historians have claimed to be a direct application of the new Mendelian genetics. Geneticists characterized the hybrid-corn method as "the greatest success story of genetics," and historians have argued that the hybrid-corn geneticists transformed Mendelism "from an analytical tool into a breeding method," and thus into an "applied science."[105] This would also be true, then, for the early phases of hybrid chicken breeding, in which the same approach was followed.

Recently, however, historians have become more sceptical of such claims.[106] Even in the case of qualitative, mono-factorial traits such as those of Mendel's peas, whose (re)appearance in the next generation can be predicted, in principle, numerically, Mendelism turns out to have been of little use in practice. Unlike laboratory geneticists, plant breeders were rarely interested in just one or a few qualitative properties of their plants. They usually selected them for multiple traits at the same time, meaning that, in practice, Mendelian crossing schemes were too unwieldy and too costly because of the rapidly increasing number of possible recombinants when multiple factors are selected for. Commercial plant breeders could not do without the traditional method of mass selection of phenotypic traits. In some cases, Mendel's rules provided an explanation for phenomena that breeders had long known from experience, such as the loss of uniformity in the progeny of two crossbreds, or the disappearance and reappearance of some traits in consecutive generations. For practical purposes, however, Mendelian factor analysis was too complicated for the breeders.

In the case of quantitative characteristics, to which the productive qualities of livestock animals belonged, factor analysis was simply impossible. How then did Mendelism work as a "method" in hybrid-corn breeding? According to geneticists such as George Shull, Mendelism replaced mass selection and provided a recipe for rational breeding on the basis of hybrid vigour.[107] The benefits of inbreeding, purity, and hybrid vigour had been known since the nineteenth century, yet the Mendelian notions of homozygosity and heterozygosity explained the nature of these phenomena scientifically, and the hybrid-corn method followed from this explanation: the aim was to achieve optimal hybrid vigour by first creating and then crossing pure lines.

Mendelism did indeed lend some plausibility to the procedure, yet it cannot be said to have really explained or justified it. The supposition that hybrid vigour arises from heterozygosity cannot be inferred from Mendelian principles. Similarly, the suggestion that hybrid-corn breeding was "applied Mendelism" has a ring of predictability about it that the method did not have, because finding pure lines that produced superior progeny when crossed boiled down to trial and error. Furthermore, breeders did not abandon mass selection; their pure lines were not created by indiscriminate inbreeding, but by inbreeding accompanied by conventional selection for desirable phenotypical traits. In short, even though there was some kind of dialectic between the hybrid-corn method and Mendelism, the latter cannot be said to have functioned as a method or an applied science in this context. Finally, it should not be forgotten that the success of hybrid corn was primarily commercially driven. Only companies with ample means could make the necessary investments, and what drove them was that the procedure entailed the creation of a biological lock that tied their customers to their business.

In chickens, the hybrid-breeding technique had such adverse effects on the animals' vitality and prolificacy that breeders soon went in search of less intrusive alternatives, such as selecting lines for vitality, followed by a single cross, or reciprocal recurrent selection. Selection and crossing were also used, particularly in broiler chickens, to overcome the problem of antagonistic traits, such as growth and fertility, which could not be simultaneously selected for in the same breed or strain. All these alternatives were new variations of the breeders' traditional selection methods, namely selection on the basis of individual performance and selection on the basis of progeny.

Of more practical import than Mendel's rules were the statistical instruments quantitative geneticists developed from the 1930s onwards, although their effective use required the processing power of computers, which would become available only several decades later. This was especially true of advanced index calculations and instruments such as BLUP. Like the traditional breeding methods, quantitative genetics is based on correlations, not on specific information on genes or hereditary mechanisms. Even though the most recent innovation in livestock breeding, genomic selection, deploys specific information about DNA structure, it is still based on correlation; the relevant genes remain unknown.

Hybrid breeding became dominant in poultry breeding in the twentieth century, first in the United States and then in Europe. In the Netherlands, the protectionist measures of the Dutch government to preserve the small-scale nature of the sector had to be revoked in the early 1960s when the EEC opened its internal borders. In most other

European countries, poultry breeding had been taken over by foreign companies by then. The Dutch breeders had been able to hold out just a little longer, thanks to the government's protectionism. It is mainly due to Thijs Hendrix's personal interest in chicken breeding, which induced him to acquire Euribrid, that the Netherlands still has a player on the world market for chicken breeding stock.

The magazine interview with the geneticists at Euribrid cited at the beginning of this chapter underlines the importance of this personal commitment. The industrialization of poultry farming may seem to have left little room for attachment to the animals, yet in the interview Frans van Sambeek emphasizes that, while this may be true for egg producers without a farming background, breeders need to have a special affinity for chickens to be successful. Both Thijs Hendrix and the scientists who work for him are proud to be farmers' children, and it was their early familiarity with chickens that drew them to breeding, according to Van Sambeek.[108] Historian Margaret Derry provides a quote in a similar vein, from Donald Shaver of Shaver Poultry Breeding Farms in Canada, formerly one of the largest breeding companies in the world and now part of Hendrix Genetics: "The poultry industry has been good to me. There are many reasons for this, but chief among them, I believe, is the fact that I've always liked chickens and had a natural "feel" for them."[109] So however great the differences in culture between the chicken and dairy cattle industries, there is still a similarity in that leading breeders in these sectors consider their affinity with their animals an essential ingredient of their success.

# 3 Breeding a Pig for All Parties

In 1968, prospects looked bright for Rommert Politiek. In that year, he became full professor of animal science at Wageningen Agricultural University. Besides this official recognition of his authority in the field of livestock breeding, there were clear indications that the non-academic breeding world had also endorsed his scientific outlook on the field. As we saw, the tide had turned in dairy cattle breeding: bull selection on the basis of conformation was being replaced by selection for milk production. Within a few years, the breeding indexes calculated by Politiek and his Wageningen staff would become the AI associations' principal tool for selecting their bulls. In 1967, another call for assistance had come from the umbrella organization of the Dutch pig breeding societies, the CBV (*Centraal Bureau voor de Varkensfokkerij*), inviting Politiek and his collaborators to screen their breeding program for efficiency. As in cattle breeding, the advice on improvement that resulted from this investigation would lead to a major revision in the way pig breeders had been selecting their breeding stock for some forty years.

Yet in the case of pig breeding, the new approach recommended by the agricultural scientists proved unsuccessful. It was criticized by the farmers from the beginning, and after a number of years even the experts acknowledged that the scientific tools that had revolutionized dairy cattle breeding did not deliver the hoped for results in pig breeding. An analysis of this failure will show that it was not so much the tools themselves that were to blame – they performed up to expectations – but rather an underestimation of the complexity of the pig sector's predicament in the early 1970s. The attempt to reduce the multiplicity of political, economic, and technical-scientific factors involved in pig breeding to a scientific issue was doomed in the end. Pig breeders may be said to have put too much trust in science in this case: building on a history of over half a century of fruitful collaboration with Wageningen experts, they assumed that a scientific overhaul might suffice to adapt their selection practices to the rapidly changing circumstances of pig husbandry at the time. Both scientists and breeders were soon to find out, however, that what was rational from a scientific point of view was not necessarily in the farmers' best interest.

The concrete question put to Politiek in 1967 was whether the so-called *selectiemesterijen* (progeny testing stations), which screened the productive qualities of potential breeding stock, were still fulfilling their task effectively. These testing stations had been established in various places in the country in the early 1930s, and a sketch of their backgrounds will show how agricultural experts had been involved in the rise of the Dutch pig husbandry sector since the early decades of the twentieth century.

## Testing for Productive Traits

When the Dutch government began to invest in the development of agriculture in the late 1890s and early 1900s, leading pig breeders and their scientific advisers agreed that their first objective should be to bring more uniformity into the mixture of breeds and their various crosses that constituted the rapidly growing Dutch pig population. The situation was similar to that in chicken breeding: in the second half of the nineteenth century, and especially after the agricultural crisis of the 1880s, pig farming had become more profitable and had developed from an unimportant sideline into a serious economic activity of many mixed farms, particularly on the sandy soils in the south and east of the Netherlands. Cheap grains and the seemingly insatiable London meat market induced many smallholders in these regions to take up commercial pig farming.[1]

Continuing a long-standing practice, farmers in the late nineteenth century bred their pigs from whatever promising stock they had access to. Dutch and German Landraces were used, as well as British breeds such as the Berkshire and the Large White, which in turn had been crossed with various Asian breeds.[2] Many farmers preferred to fatten pigs that were crosses of two or more breeds, because, as in chicken breeding, first-generation crosses had long been known to do better than the progeny of purebreds – the phenomenon known as hybrid vigour or heterosis. Yet the advice of experienced breeders that crossed animals should not be bred from, because it would result in highly variable second-generation offspring, was often ignored by smallholders. Most farmers kept only a few pigs and it was too cumbersome for them to maintain separate breeds for crossing purposes. Thus, by 1900, the

Dutch pig population was an amalgam of animals of different types that produced offspring of unpredictable quality in which the benefits of hybrid vigour had largely been lost.[3] As a consequence, the different breed names that were in use referred to geographical provenance rather than to any standard that detailed a breed's bodily characteristics.

Dutch pig breeders began to organize themselves in local and provincial associations in the early 1900s. Many of these were not single-breed associations; they registered several breeds or local types in their herd books. The animal husbandry advisers appointed by the government urged them to restrict their breeding program to a limited number of distinct breeds, such as the Dutch Yorkshire (Figure 3.1) and the Improved German Landrace (*Veredeld Duits Landvarken*). These breeds were to be kept pure and used for the production of first-generation crossbreds. This was how Danish pig breeding was organized, and Denmark's leading export position proved that it worked well.[4] Yet despite the advisers' efforts, implementing the system in the Netherlands turned out to be an impossible task. Pig breeding was under government control in Denmark, whereas Dutch breeders cooperated voluntarily. While the Danish breeders had been able to make rapid progress by concentrating on two carefully selected breeds, the Dutch associations clung to the various breeds and types they had traditionally worked with.[5] Moreover, the associations proved unable to prevent their members from using crossbred animals for breeding purposes. Consequently, as a breeder remarked in 1914: "Our Dutch pig population is still a colourful mishmash."[6]

After the First World War, breeding experts therefore abandoned their ambition to emulate the Danish example and reverted to the strategy that had proved effective in cattle and chicken husbandry: purebred breeding. "The highest stage of perfection in breeding is complete uniformity," veterinarian Aryen van Leeuwen wrote in *De Veldbode*. In the same journal, animal husbandry adviser Jacques Timmermans set the benefits of purebred breeding against the uncertainties of the "hotchpotch approach to breeding."[7] The breeding associations concurred that, since the organization and discipline needed for successful hybrid breeding was lacking, purebred breeding was the best option. The most reputable pig breeders, who were also the most vocal ones in the farming magazines and breeding journals, began to propagate purity with a zeal comparable to that of the dairy cattle breeders. For instance, in the mid-1920s, the accusation that a breeding association had used a crossbred boar as a sire created quite a scandal in the farming press.[8] Mendelian theory was brought into the discussion by the breeders themselves to explain the dangers of crossbreeding.[9] Another example is provided by the top breeder C.R. van Vloten, who strongly

Figure 3.1. A Dutch Yorkshire sow. From Löhnis, *Varkenshouderij.*

protested against the decision of the provincial breeding association in Groningen to allow the registration of Danish pigs in their herd book. He entertained serious doubts about the purity of these animals and sarcastically suggested that the association might want to change its name into "German-Danish-English Hotchpotch Association."[10]

The closure of the British market for fresh meat in 1926 provided a strong incentive to improve the national pig herd. The official reason for banning fresh meat was to protect the UK from foot-and-mouth infections that might be introduced via continental meat imports, but the Dutch considered it a protectionist measure.[11] Whatever the reason, pig farmers in the Netherlands were seriously affected, because they fattened their pigs for the British market: *Londensche biggen* (London piglets) of about 50 kg, slaughtered in the Netherlands and shipped to Smithfield Market in London the next day, were an important source of income for many farmers. When the overseas market closed, there was an obvious alternative, however. The ban did not include salted meat such as bacon, so farmers immediately began to investigate the possibilities of turning their animals into more typical bacon pigs. The Yorkshire proved to be the most suitable breed for this purpose.[12]

A serious complication arose, however: the London bacon market was dominated by the Danish farmers. And with good reason, as the Dutch breeders had to acknowledge: Danish bacon was of better quality and commanded a higher price.[13] Unlike Dutch farmers, Danish breeders did not select their animals merely on the basis of individual merit. In collaboration with the Danish government, the breeders had established progeny testing stations that assessed fattening performance in piglets to determine their parents' hereditary predisposition to produce high-quality bacon. To see this system in operation for themselves, Wieger de Jong, director of the CBV (the breeding associations' umbrella organization) and animal husbandry adviser Henri Leignes Bakhoven made a study trip to Denmark in 1929, and they reported their findings with unfeigned enthusiasm. In the Danish system, four siblings – two brothers and two sisters – produced by promising parents were sent to one of the five progeny testing stations spread throughout the country and fed and weighed according to a strict schedule for a number of months to assess their growth and feed conversion. Then they were slaughtered to evaluate their carcass quality (graded on the basis of factors such as weight, length of the back, and the percentages of fat, lean meat, and bone) and meat quality (based on criteria such as texture, colour and leanness).[14] The results were communicated to the breeding associations, who used them to evaluate the hereditary qualities of the piglets' parents. Leignes Bakhoven and De Jong ventured that this scheme of selecting for productive traits would be a "rational addition" to the Dutch selection method.[15]

On the basis of this report, the CBV decided to adopt the Danish system: potential breeding stock was henceforth to be tested at *selectiemesterijen* (progeny testing stations).[16] Parents whose external qualities were found to be excellent could earn the distinction "elite" on the basis of their progeny's performance at the stations. Most Dutch provinces set up testing facilities in the early 1930s, that would continue their services in roughly the same way for almost forty years.[17]

## Minkema's Breeding Plan

Several developments induced the CBV to review the stations' testing procedure in 1967. The most important were the advent of artificial insemination and the loss of the breeding associations' near monopoly on pig breeding. While the testing stations had evaluated both sows and boars on the basis of their progeny, the introduction of AI in the early 1960s caused a shift of emphasis towards the boars, because the technique markedly increased their hereditary influence. At about the same time, private pig breeding companies were established by feed companies (such as Hendrix Feed Industries) and slaughterhouses. They took their lead from chicken breeding companies, which had demonstrated the commercial potential of hybrid breeding techniques. They also hoped to gain more direct control over the production of high-quality meat in this way. Over the course of the 1960s, these private companies started to represent serious competition to the cooperative breeding associations overseen by the CBV, to the extent that some cooperative breeders even worried that their days might be numbered.[18]

To review the stations' testing method, the CBV set up a working group of Wageningen agriculturalists, animal husbandry advisers, and CBV board members. Rommert Politiek was appointed chair and the agricultural scientist Durk Minkema secretary. Within a year, the group presented their report, which included a list of recommendations.[19] As expected, the report pointed out that it would be more effective to focus the stations' activities on the breeding boars, particularly the boars of the top breeders, as these were most influential in determining the genetic make-up of the next generation. Furthermore, because the three-year selection procedure to obtain a reliable assessment of a boar's genetic merit was deemed too slow, two alternative selection methods were suggested to speed up the process.

In the first, potential breeding boars might be judged solely on the basis of their own characteristics, particularly those that were known to have a relatively high heritability, such as feed conversion, growth rate, and backfat thickness. In the second, to gain a first impression of a boar's carcass and meat quality (which could be determined with precision only after slaughtering), the traditional method of testing four sibling piglets could be used, with the proviso that, in this case, the method was not intended as a progeny test of the piglets' parents, but to provide information about the two brothers in the quartet. After the testing procedure had been completed, only the two female piglets of the quartet were to be slaughtered; their performance then served as a proxy for that of their brothers.[20]

The provincial associations and the CBV endorsed the conclusions reached by Politiek's working group and saw to it that the testing stations implemented the report's recommendations.[21] Some years later, however, the CBV felt that the changes in the selection system did not suffice. By the mid-1970s, pork prices on the European Common Market had fallen sharply. Added to the rapidly rising labour costs, this caused serious problems for pig farmers.[22] In 1974, the situation had deteriorated to the point that pig farming journals characterized it as "catastrophic."[23] Two years earlier, the CBV had demonstrated its awareness of the impending crisis by appointing the Wageningen-educated breeding specialist Piet Reekers as its director. Reekers had previously been in charge of the pig breeding program of the Hendrix company Euribrid.[24] Under his direction, the CBV asked breeding expert Minkema to have another look at the selection system to find additional ways to increase efficiency.

Before long, Minkema came up with two suggestions to further intensify and speed up the selection of boars. The first was to reduce the time it took to test a potential breeding boar. Following the example of the dairy cattle breeders, the AI associations had set up a testing and waiting system for boars that had had shown promise on the basis of their external qualities and the sibling test. These boars first inseminated a small number of sows and then entered a waiting period until the test results from their progeny enabled a reliable verdict on their qualities as sires. The costly waiting period might be dispensed with, according to Minkema's calculations, provided a greater number of boars were tested to increase the chances of finding really good ones. Furthermore, he recommended that breeding boars be used for one year only. Shortening the generation interval between successive generations of boars would speed up genetic improvement and, at the same time, reduce the risks involved in this faster route.[25] "The associations are taking the highway," the pig farming magazine *Varkenshouderij* commented.[26]

Minkema's second suggestion was to focus the selection process more narrowly on meat quality. As in cattle breeding, indexes were calculated for the economically important hereditary characteristics of breeding stock such as growth, fertility, piglet mortality, litter size, feed conversion, and meat quality. The relative economic value of each of these properties was accounted for in the index calculations by multiplication factors.[27] Minkema's analysis showed that focusing the selection process exclusively on meat quality, which had a high heritability and monetary value, would yield the best overall results.[28]

Again, the CBV accepted Minkema's analysis and adjusted its breeding program accordingly.[29] Yet in this case, not all members of the breeding associations were happy with the change. The sector had changed beyond recognition since the war, and pig farmers' priorities as to which characteristics their pigs should be selected for had diverged. Between 1950 and 1970, the number of farmers keeping pigs in the Netherlands had decreased from 271,000 to fewer than 76,000, and it would drop even further, to 42,000, in 1980. Even more striking was the simultaneous increase in the number of pigs, which grew faster than anywhere else within the EEC, from roughly 1.8 million in 1950 to 10 million in 1980.[30] In the 1950s, pig husbandry had still been a branch of the mixed farms, but in the 1960s the sector began to specialize. A division of labour arose that resulted in what was called the pig pyramid. The breeders, who specialized in breed improvement, were at the top of the pyramid. They sold part of their stock to the multipliers, who bred these animals with the sole purpose of producing large numbers of piglets for the fatteners, who in turn grew and finished them for the slaughterhouses. By the 1980s, about 30 per cent of the pig farmers had specialized as breeders or multipliers; the rest had become fatteners.[31] As a result of this division of labour, farmers came to prefer a different type of pig, depending on their position in the pyramid.

The slaughterhouses at the base are often left out of visual representations of the pig pyramid, yet this disregards their pivotal role.[32] Sixty per cent of all Dutch pork was exported, and slaughterhouses faced fierce competition on the European market.[33] A European classification of pig carcasses, available since 1972, enabled quality comparisons between the products of the EEC countries; the better the meat, the higher the sales.[34] The slaughterhouses thus profited greatly from the new selection focus introduced by Minkema. Multipliers and fatteners, however, focused on other properties. Understandably, multipliers were most interested in fertility and litter size, while feed conversion and growth rate were crucial for fatteners. Representing the middle sections of the pig pyramid, both fatteners and multipliers had voiced their concern about the new focus on meat quality from the beginning and would continue to do so ever more loudly after 1975. Besides this, the pig fatteners complained that the slaughterhouses ignored their repeated request to be paid a better price for better-quality meat. It was a buyers' market, however, and the slaughterhouses saw no reason to give in.[35]

The CBV partly acknowledged these concerns, putting considerable effort into convincing the slaughterhouses to respond to the multipliers and fatteners' demands. Yet even threats that selection for quality would have to be relaxed if the slaughterhouses continued to refuse to pay more for better meat did not produce the desired effect.[36] At the same time, the CBV held its ground in the discussion with the multipliers and fatteners about the focus of selection, arguing that the decision to focus on meat quality was taken on "objective, scientifically corroborated" grounds. Considering the importance of the export market, there was simply no better way, as the experts had shown, to help the sector maintain its internationally competitive position.[37] Also, the CBV contended, it would be much more difficult to select for properties such as feed conversion and fertility, as these had a much lower heritability than meat quality. And it would be "extremely difficult" to devise an index for fertility that would satisfy all parties involved, as each defined fertility differently. Should the focus be on litter size and the number of litters a sow could produce, as the multipliers preferred? Or should it be on the production of strong, healthy pigs with a low mortality rate, as the fatteners required? Moreover, the biological antagonism between these different properties – pigs from large litters were less robust – made it impossible to combine them optimally in a single breed.[38]

By 1980, however, the opposition to the CBV's selection policy had grown so strong that it could no longer be disregarded. Once again, a committee was set up to find a solution. Whereas the earlier investigations had been conducted, at the CBV's request, by agricultural scientists from Wageningen Agricultural College and the closely affiliated public institute for animal breeding research IVO (*Instituut voor Veeteeltkundig Onderzoek*), the CBV now only appointed representatives of the provincial breeding associations and the AI associations to the committee. It should be added though that most of these were also Wageningen graduates.[39]

Finding a way out of the dilemma proved to be difficult, and the breeding journals started to complain after some time that the committee was slow and that its objectives lacked transparency.[40] Then an unexpected event broke the impasse. In 1977, the CBV had invited the private pig breeding companies that had entered the scene in the 1960s to have their various breeding lines "objectively compared" to the stock of the cooperative breeding associations. Unlike the associations, the private companies kept the details of their breeding programs to themselves, and a comparison of the end products, the CBV argued, would at least give pig farmers an idea of their respective merits. Several breeding companies agreed to participate in a comparative fattening test.[41]

The IVO executed the test and presented its report in October 1981. The results shocked the CBV. The pigs of the private companies did better than the associations' pigs on all counts, except meat quality.[42] In their reaction, the CBV tried to limit the damage by pointing out that the scale of the experiment had been too small to translate the results into economic terms.[43] But it was to no avail: as far as the private companies were concerned, it was beyond dispute that their pigs had won the contest, and the breeding journal *Varkensfokkerij* considered it likely that the companies' pigs were also the most profitable ones.[44] The general feeling was that the CBV's breeding strategy had failed. Finally, there was now clear evidence that Minkema's approach had had an adverse effect on the qualities that were important to the multipliers and the fatteners.

The CBV took several measures to remedy the situation. For instance, piglet growth rate, which had received no attention until then, was included in the program of the testing stations. Investigations to find ways to select for fertility were also started.[45] The report on the CBV's breeding program, commissioned a few years earlier, finally came out in December 1981, and it confirmed that fertility should become a focus of selection. Yet the report also argued that this adjustment would not suffice to bring the selection system of the associations up to date. What was urgently needed, the authors argued, was an experimental investigation of a new approach to breeding that cast aside a principle that had been sacrosanct in the cooperative pig breeding world for half a century: purity.[46]

The new approach, hybridization, would change Dutch pig breeding practices more than any other measure taken by the CBV. The method had been pioneered by the new private breeding companies, and the introduction of artificial insemination in the 1960s had constituted an important stimulus to explore it further.

## AI in Pigs

The first controlled AI experiments with pigs were conducted in 1956 by veterinarian Chris Willems, at the Faculty of Veterinary Science of Utrecht University in 1956.[47] In the 1960s, after a considerable number of technical and practical complications had been solved, the technique found its way to the pig farmers. AI associations were established that followed the model of the cattle breeders' associations and in many cases also shared technical equipment and facilities with them.[48] As the chapter on dairy cattle and other studies of the history of AI in livestock breeding have shown, the fact that AI would in due course bring about a rationalization of reproduction does not automatically explain why the technique was introduced in the first place.[49]

Farm pigs were not plagued by infectious genital diseases like the Dutch dairy cattle were. Yet there were other afflictions that were spread by close contact, such as foot-and-mouth disease and swine fever. According to both veterinarians and agricultural experts, replacing natural mating by AI would help to prevent these diseases. Additional bonuses were the promise of greater efficiency, as the animals themselves would no longer have to travel, and of faster genetic progress, since the best boars could inseminate about ten times as many sows via AI. According to the experts, the advantages of the technique were beyond dispute, so they started a vigorous, almost aggressive campaign to convince the pig farmers to adopt it. The pig farming journals published a stream of articles in which AI was presented as the rational alternative to natural fertilization that all serious breeders should adopt without hesitation.[50] Natural mating was depicted as verging on irresponsible and the epitome of sloppy farming practices.[51] Herd-book inspector Hendrik Bakker wrote, only half-jokingly, that there was surely no need for scientific experts to force the farmers to do the right thing.[52]

The top breeders did indeed adopt the new technique almost instantly. Most multipliers, however, were not interested. They kept deploying their own boars for natural mating and would ignore AI until the mid-1970s.[53] The percentage of sows inseminated by means of AI would rise to about 10 per cent in the 1960s, but seemed to hit a ceiling there, confirming that it was predominantly the breeders who used the technique.[54] The percentage rose to a maximum of 18 per cent during the outbreaks of foot-and-mouth disease in 1962 and 1967, when transporting pigs was prohibited in affected areas. Yet once the disease was contained, it would drop again, and in 1973 it was back to 10 per cent.[55] The main reason was that the multipliers, unlike the breeders, saw no advantages to the technique. Their objective was to produce as many piglets as possible at low cost. For the multipliers, "every piglet is a good piglet," as M. Veenstra, a board member of a large AI association put it somewhat derisively. Yet this remark should be offset against the fact that there was as yet no index for fertility, the characteristic that mattered most to the multipliers but for which the AI boars were not selected. In the multipliers' calculations, keeping their own boars was simply the most cost-efficient option for achieving their aims.[56] AI pioneer Willems had predicted in 1962 that all farmers would soon switch to AI, but there was little incentive for the multipliers to make this expectation come true.[57]

Ultimately, in the mid-1970s, the multipliers would also switch to AI boars. This was not, however, because they finally acknowledged the superior qualities of these sires. From 1974 onwards, the recommendations in Minkema's report resulted in a narrower focus on boar selection for meat quality and, as we saw, the multipliers and fatteners had had their reservations about this new course from the start. Rather, it was the increasing scale of their holdings that made the multipliers change their mind and, again, their decision was based on a calculation of costs and benefits. When the number of sows they kept surpassed 200, it was no longer possible to have all their animals inseminated more or less simultaneously, as an expected progeny of about 2,000 piglets was too much to handle all at the same time. They had to switch to a system of having their animals inseminated in batches of ten to twenty sows and having these give birth and suckle their piglets in rotating groups spread out over the year. Under this scheme, it was no longer efficient to leave the rather elaborate and unpredictable reproductive act to the whims of the boars and sows, as this resulted in sows giving birth over an indeterminate period of time. With AI, it was possible to fine-tune the reproductive cycle, and (in tandem) the work cycle, by assembling groups of sows in heat and inseminating them at the same time.[58] The changeover was facilitated by the introduction of "do-it-yourself AI" in 1972, which lifted the proscription under which only veterinarians were authorized to carry out the procedure.[59] After the multipliers had switched to AI, natural mating rapidly receded into the background. The percentage of pigs inseminated artificially would continue to rise until it reached about 98 per cent, higher than in any other livestock species.[60]

Apart from enabling breeders to use their best breeding boars on a wider scale and multipliers to rationalize their practices, AI fulfilled yet another important role in the transformation that pig breeding underwent from the late 1960s onwards.[61] The very fact that it made the distribution of hereditary material much easier raised the issue of ownership. Whereas the traditional breeding associations had held a virtual monopoly over breeding until then and had stimulated the free exchange of breeding stock among their members, the rise of private companies induced the associations to restrict the dispersal of their genetic capital. To protect their investments, the new companies maintained strict control over their animals by offering them exclusively, on a contract basis, to their buyers. The cooperative breeding associations had never looked at the breeds kept by their members as their property in this sense. Initially, the private companies could freely use the associations' AI boars if they so wished, whereas the companies' boars were made available only under contract. When the private breeding companies started to become serious competitors, however, the CBV gave up its principle of free exchange. In 1974, it decided that permission from the associations was required for all sales of breeding stock.[62] Five years later, regulations were drawn up to prevent farmers who performed inseminations themselves from reselling the sperm of AI boars to other parties.[63]

Like the breeders' associations, the AI associations were independent organizations, yet since the latter owned the pedigree AI boars – there were about 320 of them in 1972 – the AI and breeders' associations entertained an ever closer relationship. In 1976, for instance, they combined their administrations into a single computer system.[64] At the same time, however, the collaboration generated a conflict of interest, as the AI associations also kept the boars of the private companies at their stations, and these boars provided increasing competition to those of the cooperative associations.[65] An initially successful collaborative attempt to create new breeding lines undertaken by the CBV and the private company Coveco ultimately failed, due to what CBV director Reekers called "the problem of exclusivity": in the end, Coveco was unwilling to freely share the results of the collaborative project.[66]

In due course, however, the internationalization of the breeding market and the growing investments required to produce competitive new breeding stock virtually condemned the parties to each other, particularly when the European monetary union dawned on the horizon. Referring to "the magical year 1992" (when the Treaty of Maastricht would be signed), Wageningen researcher Hein van der Steen wrote: "The Dutch pig breeding organizations must not miss the boat."[67] Following the example of cattle breeding, the AI associations, originally twenty-four in number, had already merged into five large associations, for reasons of efficiency, in the early 1970s.[68] The provincial breeding associations also joined together to form four regional associations in the same period, and in 1989 three of these joined forces in a single herd-book association, the NVS (*Noord-Nederlands Varkens Stamboek*). Finally, over the course of the early 2000s, all breeding associations and most of the private companies and AI associations merged into a single cooperative, the Pigture Group, later called Topigs. The company developed a strongly centralized breeding program and obtained a market share of 85 per cent in the Netherlands. After a merger with the Norwegian company Norsvin in 2014, Topigs Norsvin became one of the leading suppliers of pig genetics worldwide.[69] The global market is now dominated by a mere handful of such firms, of which the Pig Improvement Company (PIC) is the largest. PIC originated in the early 1960s, when a group of Oxford pig farmers who were dissatisfied with the results of purebred breeding decided to explore hybrid breeding techniques.[70] Some of their Dutch colleagues followed the same path in those years.

## Hybrid Pig Breeding

Purebred breeding was the norm in pig husbandry in the early decades of the twentieth century. Attempts to copy the Danish system of crossbreeding to obtain a vigorous $F_1$ generation had failed, and both the breeders and their scientific advisers considered purebred breeding a rational alternative for producing progeny of predictable quality. During the economic crisis of the 1930s, when the export market tumbled into free fall, the government aimed its protective measures at the organized farmers, which provided an additional incentive for the pig breeders to become members of the provincial breeding associations and to stock their farms with purebreds.[71]

After the sector had recovered from the Second World War – when pig numbers dropped from 1.5 million in 1940 to 77,000 in 1945 – the emphasis on purebred breeding was maintained and even reinforced by government regulations. For instance, even while the provincial associations registered pigs of various breeds in their herd books, the government prohibited keeping more than a single breed on any one farm.[72] The Dutch breeders saw their efforts at breed improvement rewarded by an increasing foreign interest in their purebreds. The two most widespread breeds in those years were the time-honoured Dutch Yorkshire and the Dutch Landrace, a new breed created in the 1930s by adding some Danish blood to the Improved German Landrace.[73]

The private breeding companies that were established in the early 1960s chose a different approach. They aimed for hybrid vigour, following the hybrid-corn breeding model, which, as explained in the previous chapter, was based on the hybridization of unrelated pure lines. The private companies' interest in the model was also due to the biological lock it created: the crossed offspring could not be bred from profitably, so farmers became dependent on the companies to renew their stock. Euribrid, the Hendrix Feed Industries subsidiary that pioneered hybrid-chicken breeding in the Netherlands, was among the first to enter pig breeding in the early 1960s and developed a hybrid that was advertised under the brand name Hypor. Other feed factories, the slaughtering industry, and a few private breeders also established breeding companies. As in chicken breeding, the government was by then prepared to relax its control over the sector: on request, breeders could be exempted from the regulation that prohibited them from keeping more than a single breed.[74]

Piet Reekers, then working at Euribrid, explained the advantages of hybrid breeding in a pig farming journal in 1967.[75] The original method used in hybrid-corn breeding involved heavy inbreeding to make sure the parental lines were as pure – homozygous – as possible. Combining them then resulted in a uniform, heterozygous hybrid. In applying the method to pigs, however, geneticists found that they suffered even more from the adverse effects of inbreeding than corn and chickens did. Euribrid therefore chose to work with synthetic lines, as they were called, which had been "purified" by selection only, without inbreeding. As the level of homozygosity in such lines was lower than in inbred lines, the heterosis effect in their crossbreds was weaker, yet this was amply compensated for by another advantage of hybridizing: the opportunity to combine different characteristics in a single line.

Reekers was referring to a problem here that constituted a fundamental obstacle to the improvement of pig breeding, particularly after the sector had developed into the pyramid of breeders, multipliers, fatteners, and slaughterers. Pigs were selected for a host of different characteristics, yet as mentioned earlier, it was impossible to combine all these traits in a single breed, because some of them, particularly growth rate and fertility, were antagonistic. "Miracle pigs" that performed optimally on all counts were unobtainable, Reekers asserted. Yet the ideal might be approached as closely as possible by selecting parental lines for only a limited number of desirable properties and then combining these lines in such a way that their crossed offspring would be endowed with the best possible combination of traits. Perhaps most significantly, this breeding system enabled the production of pigs that combined exactly those characteristics that the farmers in the several layers of the pig pyramid deemed important. For the multipliers, for instance, sows might be produced from mothers that excelled in litter size and fathers that produced robust piglets. The fatteners' wishes could be accommodated by mating prolific sows with a boar in which a high growth rate and high meat quality had been combined. Three or even four different lines might thus be used in consecutive crosses to obtain the desired combination of characteristics. Reekers conceded that it was obviously a costly and time-consuming system, requiring a high level of expertise. Discipline and strict procedures were essential to prevent the system from deteriorating into a "Wild West" chaos of uncontrolled crossing.[76]

At first, the risk that chaos would set in if the associations decided to switch to hybrid breeding was sufficient reason for the CBV to look upon the new system with suspicion. In the 1960s, several multipliers had set up experiments using the older technique of crossing pure breeds, to find out whether the heterosis effect would help to increase litter size.[77] The results of crossbreeding the Yorkshire and the Dutch Landrace were promising, and more and more multipliers tried their hand at this single cross over the course of the 1960s.[78] The CBV could not but condone the technique after some time, yet saw to it that crossing would not get out of control and that the hard-won purity of the parental breeds would not be ruined by unregulated experimenting. There were about 300 breeding boars at the AI stations at the time, and the CBV feared that even a single AI boar of dubious descent might do untold damage to the sector. The IVO was asked to check if the positive results that the multipliers had obtained could be reproduced in a controlled setting, and a blood test was devised to verify the parentage of pigs of crossed descent. Finally, the herd-book inspectors were instructed to assist the multipliers in picking their stock for crossing purposes.[79]

Until the end of the 1960s, the CBV continued to consider the breeding companies' new approach involving synthetic lines and multiple crosses as a bridge too far for the cooperative breeding associations. Yet when it appointed Piet Reekers as its new director in 1972, it appeared to be adopting a more positive stance. Reekers immediately set out to explore if and how the new technique might benefit the breeding associations. Building on the results the multipliers had obtained by crossing purebred Yorkshire and Dutch Landrace pigs, he had the populations of both breeds scrutinized for family lines that appeared most suitable for hybridizing purposes. A cross between two such lines was called the E line, and a double-cross involving four lines, the D line. The ultimate objective was to create a hybrid pig in which various traits were optimally combined.[80]

Reekers proceeded carefully and devised an elaborate monitoring system to prevent the procedure from getting out of hand. Keeping records of all the animals involved in the hybridizing program was facilitated by the introduction of the computer. With their membership spread throughout the country, it was more difficult for the CBV to control the breeders and the multipliers, and therefore the hybridizing experiments were executed on a small scale.[81] Nevertheless, after several years of experimenting, Reekers had to conclude that the results were disappointing. Part of the problem was that the multipliers lacked experience in detailed record-keeping and in selecting animals individually for crossing purposes. As a consequence, progress was slow – too slow, pig farmers complained, considering the pressing problems they were facing in the mid-1970s. To speed up the process, particularly with respect to increasing piglet robustness and litter size, the CBV decided that a third breed, besides the Yorkshire and the Dutch Landrace, should be added to the mix.[82]

The Duroc, a fertile and strong pig breed originally from North America, was found to be the most promising candidate for this role.[83] The CBV continued to heed the adage that caution was the mother of wisdom and asked the IVO to set up an elaborate testing program to check whether combining the three breeds would indeed deliver the hoped for results.[84] The pig farmers, however, wanted to move more quickly. They were still suffering the ill effects of the crisis that had set in in 1974 and their protests against the one-sided focus on selection for meat quality were growing louder and louder. The farming magazine *De Boerderij* reported in 1977 that more and more multipliers were turning to the private breeding companies for their boars.[85] Early in 1981, while the experiments were still running, the CBV reacted to the spreading unrest by allowing its members to use the Duroc in their crossing schemes.[86]

There is an obvious parallel here with the situation ten years earlier in cattle breeding. The dire circumstances in dairying at the time induced farmers to put their faith in the American Holsteins to increase milk production even before the experiments undertaken by Politiek and his colleagues had proven that the American cows would indeed perform better under Dutch conditions. Yet while the dairy farmers' gamble to switch to the Holsteins had paid off, the pig farmers had to backtrack when the results of the scientific test finally came in. As expected, Duroc hybrids produced more piglets, which were also more robust. Yet first-generation sows turned out to be nastily aggressive, and they had inferior udders. Also, overall carcass quality declined in combinations that included the Duroc. In sum, the Duroc was not going to solve the problems of the fatteners and multipliers.[87]

The solution was ultimately found, not by introducing an alternative third breed, but by splitting the Yorkshire into two separate breeds, an option that had been explored by one of the regional associations since 1979 and delivered its first, positive results three years later. One of these new Yorkshire breeds, the GY-S, was selected for meat quality, while the other, the GY-Z, was selected for litter size and udder quality. Judicious crossing of these new breeds with the Dutch Landrace pig then successfully resulted in the different types of pigs required by the multipliers and the fatteners. Remarkably, the splitting up of the Yorkshire was not based on the line-breeding approach of the breeding companies, in which individual pigs and their close relatives were isolated from the rest of the breed to form a separate line, but on conventional mass selection, involving the Yorkshire population as a whole. The program thus deployed traditional selection methods, yet in a new way.[88] Evidently, breeding methods were flexible, and old and new approaches could be amalgamated in varying combinations, depending on what circumstances required.

Hybrid breeding, involving both purebred breeds and synthetic lines, quickly became the standard pig breeding method in the 1980s. In this process, some multipliers specialized in crossing, thus adding a new tier to the pig pyramid: they performed the crosses of synthetic lines preceding the terminal cross that produced the piglets for the fatteners.[89] BLUP was introduced in the 1980s to rationalize the selection process. In recent years, genomic selection has played an increasingly important role.[90]

## The Breeder's Eye

Until late in the twentieth century, dairy cattle breeders gauged a sire or dam's hereditary qualities on the basis of its external characteristics, and the yearly dairy cattle shows were the apogee of the breeders' promotional activities to market their stock. Conformation and shows have hardly been mentioned in this chapter so far, yet that should not be taken to imply that their role was insignificant in pig breeding. On the contrary: the paramount importance of external qualities in pigs was uncontested. Whereas the link between the visible characteristics of dairy cattle, particularly the bulls, and their hereditary capacity for milk production was tenuous at best, conformation in pigs was directly related to their economically important characteristics. The controversy over whether a correctly built cow was a good milking cow had no equivalent in pig breeding, because visible external characteristics such as size, back length, hams, and the number of teats in sows were the very criteria that distinguished good pigs from bad ones. From the beginning, young pigs were entered into the herd-book registers only after a thorough assessment of their external traits, a procedure that would not change throughout the century.

Like the breeders of other livestock, the pig breeders held regional and provincial shows to present their best animals to potential buyers. Geneticist Arend Hagedoorn – predictably, we might say by now – voiced his concern that pig shows, like cattle shows, might stimulate hobby breeding and lapse into beauty contests.[91] However, leaving aside that pigs in "show condition" tended to be overly fat, most breeders were scarcely inclined to value their animals on the basis of conformation points unrelated to productive qualities. The top breeder Van Vloten chided his colleagues for talking hypotheticals when they brought up the question of whether a black-spotted skin should be seen as disqualifying a pig for pedigree breeding – an issue that also vexed the cattle breeders. Van Vloten urged them to focus on more important characteristics, such as meat quality.[92] When he suggested that progeny testing should replace exterior evaluation completely, however, animal husbandry adviser Theo Kees Rijssenbeek stepped in and criticized him for overstating his case.[93] So the prolonged debate in mid-twentieth-century dairy cattle breeding over whether animals should be bred for show or for production had no parallel in pig breeding. Conformation was considered of central importance in pigs, for directly economic reasons.

In 1920, animal husbandry adviser Egbert Dommerhold devised a points system for the two most important breeds, the Dutch Yorkshire and the Improved German Landrace, to evaluate the important parts of the body and thus to enable judges to compare their results and make them less dependent on personal preferences.[94] In 1927, the CBV prescribed this points system as mandatory for all associations to ensure that pigs throughout the Netherlands would be judged according to the same standard.[95] This quantification of the evaluation of conformation was not intended to do away with the breeder's eye, however. The decisive criterion for admitting a pig to the herd-book registers was not the total number of points attained for the individual characteristics, but the quality of its "general appearance" (*algemeen voorkomen*), which was to be assessed by the judges on the basis of their training, experience, and their natural talent for the job. Dommerhold acknowledged that it was difficult to put into words what exactly was meant by general appearance. Leaving no doubt as to its subjective nature, he ventured that terms such as "fineness," "type," and "nobility" might feature in a description.[96]

In the postwar period, when AI and new breeding methods entered the scene, external characteristics continued to be as important as before. The first screening a potential AI boar had to undergo as a piglet consisted of an evaluation of his conformation. Shows also remained important until the 1970s, gradually evolving into events with a much broader scope. Besides the competitive showing and trading of breeding stock, the shows were also the occasion for all kinds of educational activities for the farmers. For instance, some pigs were slaughtered to explain the details of good carcass quality to the farmers, experts gave lectures on the latest developments in pig husbandry, new feeding regimes were presented, and demonstrations were given of how to house pigs hygienically and efficiently, and how to get them into show condition. At a show in 1968, a new instrument was introduced that measured backfat thickness ultrasonically (Figure 3.2). This was an important innovation because it meant that slaughtering was no longer required to assess this property. Finally the shows were social gatherings that for many pig farmers and their families were the high point of the year (Figure 3.3).[97]

The shows also provided an occasion for the AI associations to present and advertise their boars. Initially these boars were entered into the show competitions, which made their external appearance even more important.[98] The associations put in extra effort to make sure their boars would stand out, as evidenced by the fact that, after the show tradition had come to an end in the early 1970s, they immediately relaxed the conformation requirements an AI boar had to meet.[99]

Remarkably, the rhetoric of an opposition between exterior evaluation and shows on the one hand, and scientific breeding on the other, did enter discussions on breeding methodology in the pig farming magazines after all. After the shows had been discontinued, agricultural scientists began to look back on them as the last relics of an outdated approach to breeding that had put more emphasis on traditional notions such as the breeder's eye than on the insights provided by science and technology.[100] Yet the ending of the show tradition had little to do with changing perceptions of the role of conformation and the

Figure 3.2. Measuring backfat thickness. From *Maandblad voor de Varkensfokkerij* 33, no. 3 (1970): 51.

breeder's eye in the selection of breeding stock. Several developments of a quite different nature were responsible for this.

To begin with, the educational activities that were organized at the shows were gradually taken over by various regional improvement organizations set up with government support in the 1950s and 1960s, which had a special section for pig farmers, called the *varkenshouderijkernen* (pig farmers' centres).[101] Second, once the AI associations had

Figure 3.3. A provincial pig show in the 1960s. From the archives of the Nationaal Veeteelt Museum, Beers.

merged into larger units beyond the provincial level, there was no longer any reason to enter their boars into provincial show competitions.

Before long, they only brought their boars to the shows for demonstration purposes, and by the end of the 1960s they stopped bringing them altogether and organized open days for the farmers at their AI stations instead (Figure 3.4).[102] They thus avoided the risk of infection, which had always posed a serious threat at the shows. Finally, the vertical integration of the sector that began to take shape in the 1960s changed the relations between the farmers in the pig pyramid in such a way that the shows lost their role as a sales market for breeding stock. Feed companies, breeders, multipliers, fatteners, slaughterhouses, and supermarkets entered into contracts that left the different groups of farmers with few choices. Which animals the multipliers and fatteners had to work with was decided on at a different level, and in this respect shows lost their function.

Thus, by the early 1970s, the social aspect of the shows was about all that was left of the ingredients that had been important for their popularity, and apparently this was not enough to prevent their decline. Farmers had better things to do than to prepare for and visit shows, an inspector of a provincial association wrote matter-of-factly in 1972.[103]

Figure 3.4. Demonstration of Hein, a Dutch Landrace boar, at an AI station in the province of Utrecht. From *Maandblad voor de Varkensfokkerij* no. 8 (1975): 10–11.

In any case, the shows were discontinued with few signs of regret. When a group of breeders in North Holland deplored the dwindling importance of the shows and the concomitant marginalization of their own role,[104] their animal husbandry advisers riposted with the rhetoric of modernization and scientific progress. Breeders should "set their eyes on the future" and realize that this development was "the *only* way to achieve rapid improvement,"[105] an inevitable result of "modern systems of selection" having pushed the role of exterior evaluation to the background.[106] Yet whereas the introduction of AI and index breeding unquestionably diminished the once overriding importance of shows in cattle breeding, a different story arises from the developments in pig breeding in these years. Inspector H. Reintjes gave a more balanced assessment of what had happened when he wrote in 1972: "The argument that exterior evaluation is no longer important is one-sided ...

Rather, the means available for adequate judging have been expanded considerably over the course of time."[107]

## Pigs Are Not Chickens

Like chicken farming, pig farming had become highly industrialized by the end of the twentieth century. In both sectors, the breeders had been receptive to the advice of their scientific advisers throughout the century, and on various occasions the pig breeders called upon Wageningen agriculturalists to help them solve imminent problems. As a consequence, pig breeding clearly became more scientific: in the end, breeding decisions were taken by geneticists working at a small number of specialized commercial companies.

At the same time, this chapter shows that what was rational from the scientists' point of view was not necessarily the best option for the breeders. Some of the scientific solutions proffered were too simplistic, or else practical realities stood in the way of their implementation. The pigs themselves also played a key role, because their biological traits effectively precluded certain options preferred by the scientists or the breeders. Thus the choice for a particular breeding method was not determined by scientific considerations alone, but also by other, partly contingent factors. For instance, when Wageningen experts advised the breeders to focus on purebreds in the 1920s, it was not because they believed this to be the best alternative; the Danish breeders had already demonstrated that crossbred pigs performed better than purebreds. Pig breeding in Denmark was under government control, however, and the Dutch scientists knew from experience that unregulated crossbreeding would result in chaos. Then again, there were no practical obstacles to progeny testing, and the breeders readily accepted the scientists' proposal to copy the Danish system on this point.

In the 1960s and 1970s, the CBV invited scientists to overhaul the selection system on several occasions, and followed the suggestions the scientists came up with. The results were mixed, however. Minkema's advice to focus on meat quality did not turn out well for the multipliers and the fatteners, who were more interested in other traits. Selection for meat quality, Minkema had reasoned, was best for the national sector as a whole, yet this ignored the diverging interests of the farmers in the different layers of the pig pyramid. We encountered a similar situation in cattle breeding, when Rommert Politiek urged the dairy farmers not to give up on the dual-purpose red-and-white dairy cow, as this might jeopardize the national beef supply – a plea that fell on deaf ears as the farmers in question were well aware that milk brought in more money than meat. Likewise, the multipliers initially rejected AI, despite a vigorous campaign by the scientists, because they had priorities other than breed improvement; for them, natural mating was more practical in management terms. They changed their minds, however, when the rising numbers of sows on their farms made natural mating impractical.

The private breeding companies that entered the field in the 1960s hoped to achieve better results by scientifically controlled crossbreeding and hybridizing, following the examples of the Danish breeders and of corn and chicken breeding. While the hybrid-corn method worked reasonably well with chickens, it can at best be said to have inspired new approaches in pig breeding. After all, the crux of the hybrid-corn method – heavy inbreeding followed by crossing – was not an option in the case of pigs, because they took badly to inbreeding, even more than chickens did. Thus, all that remained was hybridizing non-inbred lines within breeds. Besides the benefits of hybrid vigour and of creating a biological lock, the major advantage of the hybrid-corn method in pig breeding was that it enabled the breeders to overcome the natural antagonism between several of the commercially important traits in pigs, particularly growth and fertility. In essence, there was nothing new about this method, as combining different parent lines to obtain a crossbred that combined the best qualities of both had been practised for centuries, for instance by breeders of mules and hinnies. The only difference was the systematic approach, aided by the instruments of quantitative genetics, that the scientists brought to the field. By rationalizing the hybridizing technique, they took it to an unprecedented level.

The organized pig breeders' eagerness to avail themselves of Durocs without awaiting the results of the scientific tests resembles that of the cattle breeders who began to import Holsteins long before the scientific experiments investigating their merits were completed. Once again, the breeders demonstrated their faith in the scientific approach and their readiness to take chances.

Finally, the history of pig breeding provides another illustration of the inadequacy of the "art-to-science" scenario as an explanation of how breeding became scientific. Contrary to what was suggested by the scientific experts' rhetoric, the much-disputed breeder's eye never lost its importance in pig breeding practices. Scientists – and some breeders as well – deployed the metaphor of the breeder's eye to juxtapose the objective, rational approach to breeding with the traditional notion of breeding as an art. Yet the subjective evaluation of conformation remained an indispensable element in the selection of breeding stock, for commercial breeders as well as scientific experts.

# 4 Just Not Like Any Other Sheep Breed: The Texel

In the nineteenth century, Texel sheep were mainly found in a clearly defined geographical area, the Isle of Texel, which lies just north of the Dutch province of North Holland. Hence they were known as *Texelaars* (Texels). The island's soil is sandy and poor, and the Texels resembled the sheep found in other taxing environments, such as moorlands and high hills. Of medium stature and wiry, Texels were kept by the islanders for their wool, manure, and milk (Figure 4.1). Meat was also an important product; to be fattened, the lambs were sold to sheep farmers on the richer pastures of mainland North Holland. Cattle did not thrive on the island, and sheep were the farmers' mainstay. In the Netherlands, this was fairly exceptional: in most regions (mixed) dairy farming was more profitable, and there were few specialized sheep farms outside North Holland. In the nineteenth century, many mixed farmers on the Dutch mainland did keep sheep, but only in small numbers, and mainly for the production of manure. The Isle of Texel, on the other hand, with its area of 161 square kilometres, was home to some 35,000 sheep that were kept by about 300 farmers. Their wool and meat were of excellent quality, and Texel sheep were a widely known type.[1]

Their relative isolation on the Isle of Texel did not prevent the sheep farmers from experimenting with different breeds. The European Merino craze of the early nineteenth century did not leave them unaffected, but, as in many other places, these highly demanding sheep did not prosper on the island.[2] From the mid-nineteenth-century onwards, several English breeds were tried, rather haphazardly, yet besides adding to the mix of a type that was already ill-defined they left no permanent trace. More systematic attempts at improvement were taken in the closing decades of the century. By then, the rise of the sheep industry in Australia, New Zealand, and Argentina had

Figure 4.1. The Texel in the early nineteenth century. From Numan, *Handleiding*, vol. 1, figure V.

resulted in falling wool prices, and sheep manure was becoming less valuable due to the introduction of artificial fertilizers.[3] Sheep that had been kept especially for these purposes, such as moorland sheep, would rapidly decline in numbers after 1900.[4] The Texel farmers were affected less, because their sheep also produced meat of good quality. To compensate for the dwindling value of wool and manure they had begun to transform their sheep into specialized producers of lambs for the English market. For unclear reasons, Dutch consumption of mutton and lamb was negligible – and still is.[5] In England, however, demand was high and provided an opportunity for the sheep farmers to join the thriving export market that provided an incentive to Dutch livestock farmers as a whole.[6] In 1864, for example, over 261,000 live sheep crossed the Channel, a number that remained fairly stable for the rest of the century.[7]

In their attempts to improve the Texel as a meat-producing sheep, farmers on the island and on the North Holland mainland experimented with various breeding methods. By the early 1900s their methods had diverged, with the islanders focusing more and more on purity, while the mainland farmers tried their hand at a variety of crossing schemes. As a result of all these efforts, the Texel would emerge as a standardized breed in the 1920s. Within a few decades, it would also become the dominant Dutch breed. The history of sheep breeding in the Netherlands is thus, for the most part, the history of the Texel and its derivatives, such as the Swifter.

The story of the Texel's origin once again illustrates the motives that may induce farmers to focus on a single, uniform breed, and it highlights in particular the significance of the breed concept as the embodiment of a commercial brand. After the Second World War, Wageningen scientists attempted to improve the Texel in various ways by introducing crossbreeding, artificial insemination, and index breeding. The results were nowhere near what they had hoped for, however. The crossbreeding experiments were redirected by the breeders and resulted in the creation of a new breed – the Swifter – and AI and index breeding never really got off the ground. This failure was mainly due to the scientists' disregard for the overriding commercial importance breeders attached to the distinctive characteristics of their sheep. Nevertheless, by the end of the twentieth century the Texel had been successfully "modernized" – not by Wageningen scientists but by the breeders themselves, using their most traditional tool, the breeder's eye.

## Creating the Texel

Around 1890, the number of sheep in the Netherlands as a whole was declining, yet the Texel flocks together still comprised about 30,000 head of sheep, and farmers continued to depend on them for their income. A typical Texel farmer kept between 100 and 500 sheep, partly for their wool, but mainly for their meat. All farmers had their own rams and bred their own sheep. Some were more interested in breed improvement than others, but few were specialists and they all depended on selling lambs for their living. The lambs, after being sold to mainland farmers for fattening, were taken to livestock markets in places like Leiden, Purmerend, and Schagen, to be exported to England. Their popularity is demonstrated by the fact that the Texel farmers often sold their lambs even before they were born. The English customers particularly liked the Texel lambs for their lean meat, a characteristic that set them apart from many British breeds that produced more fatty types of meat. By 1900, the Texels were less sturdy than they had been half a century earlier, but more suitable for fattening.[8] The Dutch agronomist Winand Staring noted as early as 1870 that the Texel sheep had been "completely changed and improved."[9] Documentation of this transformation is scarce, as the breeders did not write down how they proceeded. However, the transition to a predominantly meat-producing type can be reconstructed in broad outline from scattered pieces of information.

In the second half of the nineteenth century, the Texel breeders regularly imported English rams of various breeds that were known to produce meat in ample quantities: the Lincoln, the Cotswold, the Wensleydale, and the Leicester are the most frequently mentioned.[10] In 1888, Cornelis Dijt, whose father Hendrik owned the largest Texel farm at the time, with about a thousand sheep, made a trip to England to purchase suitable rams. The diary of his sojourn gives a glimpse of his appreciation of English breeding practices and of his criteria for good breeding stock.[11] Dijt was particularly interested in the Leicester and the Lincoln and he visited several farms and markets. Some of the sheep he scrutinized with his breeder's eye met with his approval, but the verdict "ragged sheep" appears more often in his notes.[12] He particularly disliked "small and coarse" lambs, sheep that were "weak in the hindquarters," rams with too much wool or a "sloping croup," and rams that were as "small as cats." What he was looking for were rams that were not just "fine" (*puik*) but "extra-fine" (*puik-puik*).[13]

Dijt knew a good ram when he saw one, yet he also paid attention to other aspects. For example, he preferred rams born as twins, or at least from a herd in which twins were abundant.[14] He was particularly appreciative of sheep that prospered in a poor environment.[15] And he preferred to buy his animals from good breeders. His notes reveal an important criterion for evaluating the skills of a breeder. After a visit to a breeder of Leicester sheep he jotted down: "He has a good farm and he has clearly paid care and attention to getting them [his sheep] as alike as they are."[16] Another flock was similarly praised as "really good, and being really similar to each other."[17] So for Deijt, a good breeder had a uniform flock, and presumably this was also what he himself was aiming for in his breeding work.

Considering the many different breeds that farmers on Texel experimented with over the course of the nineteenth century, uniformity was probably not the most conspicuous characteristic of the island's flocks. In the closing years of the century however, more and more breeders, the Dijts definitely among them, decided to aim for uniformity, implying that their breeding method shifted from haphazard crossbreeding to consistently selecting a more clearly delineated type. A few decades later they had achieved this goal, and various sources indicate that they had also developed a sophisticated breeding method along the way.

For example, in early November, the beginning of the breeding season, Texel breeders did not simply introduce the rams into their flocks. Holding them on a leash, they guided each ram along the ewes he was designated to mate with at regular intervals. Thus the rams and ewes were matched according to plan. A further measure taken by the islanders to make sure the lambs' fathers were known was the regulation that all rams had to be housed or at least constrained in their movements between 1 October and 1 December. Finally, the breeders kept track of the lineage and age of their sheep using an elaborate system of earmarks.[18]

The quality of the rams was judged annually at ram shows, which were an important social event on the island. The breeding ewes were also selected carefully. As with the rams, breeders preferred their ewes to be born as twins and selected them for this trait. After the turn of the century, over two-thirds of their flocks produced twins.[19] Every year, 25 per cent of the ewes were replaced. These animals, mostly three or four years old, were sold to mainland North Holland, where they were used as breeding ewes for several more years. Breeders made sure they had the first pick of the new lambs, and special care was taken of future breeding stock.[20]

The breeders' efforts paid off. In 1908, the annual agricultural exhibition of the Holland Agricultural Society was organized on Texel, and the breeders collaborated to turn the show site into "a huge white field" of sheep.[21] Farmers from all over the country visiting the event were impressed and the Texel sheep and their breeders were highly praised in almost every review of the exhibition.[22] The *Nederlandsch Landbouw-Weekblad*, an agricultural weekly, reported that "Farmers who were not yet aware of the high quality of the sheep bred on Texel, most certainly are now."[23] The selection system and the tracking of lineages was singled out for special commendation in an article in *De Schager Courant*, and its author went so far as to state that the Texel breeders had demonstrated "a practical application of the laws of heredity."[24] It was probably on this occasion that the name "Improved Texel" was used for the first time, by F.B. Löhnis, an influential agricultural inspector: "The old Texel type is as good as gone; [the Texel breeders] have succeeded in breeding an Improved Texel breed, which today is only bred purely and is much sought after."[25] The name would stick and was widely used in the following decades (Figure 4.2).

Figure 4.2. The Improved Texel. From Kroon, *De tegenwoordige richtingen*, 142.

An indication that the Texel breeders had not only successfully turned their sheep into a pure breed, but were also striving to turn it into a recognizable brand, is provided by an experiment conducted on the island by Hagedoorn, the geneticist. In 1910, the Holland Agricultural Society invited him to assist the Texel breeders in their endeavour to consolidate their breed. Hagedoorn, freshly graduated from the University of Amsterdam, wrote an outline of the experiments he intended to undertake, stating that reducing the variability of the type was his prime objective, because it had a negative influence on the marketability of the lambs. The characteristics he had in mind in particular were nose and fleece colours: some sheep had piebald noses, whereas they should have been black, and some ewes produced lambs with black instead of white wool. Such traits did not affect the animals' productive quality as meat sheep, which indicates that Hagedoorn's assistance was primarily sought to improve the Texel as a well-marked commercial brand. Conveniently, the unwanted traits were qualitative, and therefore amenable to a Mendelian approach, according to Hagedoorn. Assuming they were determined by one or only a few recessive Mendelian alleles, he explained how simple Mendelian factor analysis could be used to assess whether animals were homozygous or heterozygous for the desirable traits.[26]

Not all sheep breeders liked this approach, as it included inbreeding – backcrossing progeny with their parents – yet Hagedoorn found an enthusiastic supporter of his plan in one of the major breeders on Texel, Jacob Sijbrand Dijt, the older brother of Cornelis. He performed the crossing experiments Hagedoorn had proposed and after some time reported that "what we have thus far found on our farm leads us to expect successful results."[27] These results would never be forthcoming, however. Meanwhile, as would happen many times during his later career, Hagedoorn was criticized by the farmers' scientific advisers, such as the agriculture adviser Cornelis Nobel and veterinarian Aryen van Leeuwen, who rejected his approach as unrealistic. While the Mendelian reasoning behind Hagedoorn's crossing experiments might be theoretically sound, such experiments "should stay within the walls of testing stations, laboratories and zoos," remarked Van Leeuwen. Even if only a few Mendelian factors were involved, the number of test crossings required to find a reasonable number of homozygous animals would quickly get out of hand. Moreover, a great many animals, including numerous heterozygotes with no visible faults, would have to be discarded for reasons that had nothing to do with their productive qualities. No breeder could afford such experiments; they had to make money from their sheep, Van Leeuwen argued.[28] Nobel agreed: Hagedoorn was obviously a stranger to the world of practical sheep breeding, otherwise he would have known that results were only to be expected from the breeders' conventional methods: pedigree analysis and patient selection. Furthermore, Nobel questioned Hagedoorn's assumption that single genes were responsible for the Texel's undesirable traits; it was as yet unproven.[29] It seems not unlikely that Dijt ran into exactly the kind of practical difficulties that Nobel and Van Leeuwen had foreseen and that this explains why he never reported the results of any of his experiments. Dijt's objective, however, was clear: he aimed to purify the Texel as a breed and thus improve it as a brand.

The mainland breeders chose a completely different approach. Besides the Texel lambs they bought from the islanders for fattening, they also kept their own Texel ewes to produce lambs, and they aspired to make the latter even better than the imported lambs by continuing a practice the island breeders had abandoned: crossing the Texel ewes with sires from English meat breeds such as the Lincoln, Wensleydale, and Leicester. Their richer pastures, the farmers reasoned, enabled them to raise more demanding sheep that, if taken proper care of, would grow faster and produce even more meat than the Texel lambs. Yet it turned out to be no easy task to outdo the island breeders and improve upon the quality of their lambs. In a 1909 article in *De Veldbode*, Nobel pointed out what he saw as the core of the problem: the farms and flocks on Texel were considerably larger than those on the mainland, which gave the famers ample opportunity for selection within their breed. The mainland farmers would have to collaborate to obtain comparable results. He therefore proposed that a sheep breeders' society be established to stimulate the farmers to work together and devise a controlled system of breeding.[30] His call was received enthusiastically by the mainland breeders, and on 10 September 1909 the Society for the Improvement of Sheep Breeding in North Holland (*Vereeniging tot Verbetering van de Schapenfokkerij in Noord-Holland*) was founded. Nobel became a member and developed an elaborate breeding system.[31]

The system entailed systematically crossing the various breeds or types available on the mainland, to find out which combination worked best. Nobel probably wanted to include as many mainland farmers in his program as possible, because he initially came up with fifteen different breeding combinations – a clear illustration of the multiple approaches that the mainland breeders were trying out to improve their sheep. The list included purebred mating (e.g., for the Texel and Wensleydale), several schemes in which different breeds were crossed (e.g., Texel x Lincoln, Texel x Wensleydale), and a miscellany of combinations with crossbreds (e.g., Texel x Crossbred Lincoln, or Crossbred Texel x Crossbred Wensleydale). Farmers were supposed to help each other in procuring the stock for their preferred combinations.[32]

The necessity of collaboration was evident from the situation the society's inspectors encountered on the farms in 1909, at the start of the breeding experiments. A total number of 30 rams and 413 ewes were deemed good enough to participate, yet after these animals had been divided into the 15 different mating combinations, mostly very small groups remained, the largest comprising 8 breeders with 8 rams and 116 ewes.[33]

A complication that aggravated the situation was that there were very few English rams available for the crossing schemes, and they were of uneven quality. This problem had a long history. With support from the regional agricultural society, many different rams had been bought in the last quarter of the nineteenth century – Lincolns, Leicesters, Cotswolds, Border Leicesters, Hampshire Downs, Southdowns, and Wensleydales – but the results were generally found to be unrewarding.[34] A breeder even complained about the "noticeable deterioration of our sheep" in 1895.[35] And it was not only the breeders who were dissatisfied with the quality of their lambs. The

Dutch consul in London warned the breeders in 1889 that he "had repeatedly heard complaints about the low weight" of the Dutch sheep offered to the London market.[36] Also, English buyers were said to find the lambs' meat too fat.[37]

The reasons for this lack of progress were manifold. Besides misfortunes such as dying rams and lambs, there were significant differences between the testing farms, such as in the way the sheep were kept and in the types of soil on which the lambs were raised. Some rams were excellent; others were inferior, regardless of the breed they belonged to. The ewes also varied in quality from one farm to the next. All that could be said after several years of experimenting was that Wensleydale rams seemed to perform more consistently than rams of other breeds.[38]

At this point, one might begin to suspect that Nobel's real motive for setting up his system in 1909 was to prove once and for all that crossing was unproductive. Whatever his original motive, this was the conclusion he would arrive at after a decade of experimenting. Nobel proceeded step by step, however. After a few years, he became more restrictive about the animals that were allowed to enter the system. A list of disqualifying traits, such as an overbite, a hairy coat, bad posture, or insufficient development was introduced in 1911, and it grew longer every year. Known descent became a prerequisite in 1913, and from 1917 onwards, extra evaluation points were awarded for every known ancestral generation of a sheep.[39]

Most important, Nobel discarded more and more mating combinations over the years. In 1911, he dropped eight of the fifteen options in the absence of a clear rationale for identifying and distinguishing between the different types they involved. This left only the combinations that involved purebred Texels, Lincolns, or Wensleydales, either for purebred breeding or for crossing, and an odd category called "mixed." In 1917, the crossbreeding combinations were terminated because of inconsistent results, so that only purebred breeding with Lincolns, Wensleydales, or Texels remained. Tellingly, a new category established to accommodate breeders who wanted to continue experiments with crossbreeding was abolished a year later due to lack of interest among the breeders. Intentionally or unintentionally, Nobel's program had apparently put paid to the breeders' belief in the effectiveness of crossbreeding.[40]

Agricultural adviser D.L. Bakker hailed the breeders' change of mind as a rational decision backed up by Mendelian theory. Purebreds, he asserted, might be regarded as homozygotes for all practical purposes, and crossbreds were heterozygotes, which explained why the former produced consistent results when bred among themselves, whereas the latter did not. The Texel, as it had recently been developed on the island, could now be considered a pure breed, on a par with the Wensleydale and the Lincoln, so it was a wise decision to focus on these three breeds, according to Bakker.[41] In the *Texelsche Courant*, the island newspaper, he urged all breeders to cooperate with the mainland breeders to bring the Texel to "the highest stage of perfection."[42] Most Texel breeders had kept their distance from the mainland breeders' society until then, but in 1917 several dozen of them joined the society.[43]

In the same year, the society advised its members to define a detailed standard for the perfect Texel. On the mainland, too, the breed was on its way to becoming a commercial brand, as evidenced by the insistence of the members on details of conformation that had no relation to productivity, such as a fairly short tail (which is still a prominent defining characteristic of the Texel), a wide head with a black nose, and a white fleece without patches of black wool.[44] Animals that did not meet this standard were refused registration in the society's flock book. Standardization was a recurrent issue for several years, and a detailed description of the Texel was agreed upon in 1925.[45]

The Texel's rise to prominence as a breed was further signalled by the gradual demise of the Wensleydale and the Lincoln. The Texel did best at the yearly shows, and more and more sheep farmers on the mainland gave up the English breeds. Other Dutch provinces also became interested in the Texel; they established their own flock books between the 1920s and 1940s. By 1925, the North Holland society counted 141 members who exclusively bred Texel sheep. Only four breeders had Lincolns, and only a single member still had Wensleydales. In 1926 the society officially changed its name to *Texels Schapenstamboek in Noord-Holland* (Texel Flock Book Society in North Holland).[46]

By 1940, the Texel had become "the most popular breed" in the Netherlands as a whole, according to agricultural adviser Jacques Timmermans (Figure 4.3).[47] In the words of his colleague E.J. Bats: "[T]he Texel can be considered the ideal breed for our country and there is no need for other breeds."[48] Foreign interest underlined the Texel's reputation as a meat breed. The English market collapsed after the crash of the stock market in 1929, but France and Belgium, among a growing number of other countries, soon took its place. Besides slaughter lambs, Texel breeding stock also found its way to various countries, which established their own Texel breeders' societies. In the second half of the twentieth century, the Texel would grow into one of the principal meat breeds worldwide.[49]

Figure 4.3. Lamb sale at Den Burg, Texel, around 1950. Private collection.

## The Swifter

The dominance of the Texel went unquestioned until the 1970s.[50] In 1974, however, Marten Bekedam, a scientist at Wageningen Agricultural College, published the first results of an experiment in which he had crossed the Texel with Flemish sheep.[51] Bekedam had studied sheep fertility and reproduction since the late 1950s, but he had not worked on breeding before.[52] There was a natural connection with his earlier work, however, as crossbreeding can be used to increase fertility. There were many examples of such experiments in the literature, and crossing was routinely used by English breeders, who deployed "terminal sires" of a meat breed to obtain fast-growing lambs from mothers of a different breed that excelled in fertility or maternal traits.[53] Producing meat lambs in this manner was also what the mainland breeders in North Holland had unsuccessfully attempted in the early twentieth century. Whether Bekedam was aware of this history or not, he realized that a strictly regulated and monitored breeding program would be needed to turn such an approach into a success. Ironically, as we will see, Bekedam in the end turned his back on the experiment, as the farmers whom he had engaged in his endeavour insisted on such a strict adherence to the program's regulations that his own work was impeded by it.

Bekedam's choice of the Texel as a terminal sire for his experiment was unsurprising. Over 90 per cent of all Dutch sheep were Texels, and it was the pre-eminent Dutch meat breed. Moreover, breeding Texels was not without its problems, and crossing seemed the ideal method to compensate for their shortcomings. Bekedam published an analysis of fertility and lamb mortality among Texel ewes in 1971, concluding that too many lambs died during or right after birth. The best way to remedy this, he argued, was to reduce the number of singleton lambs. Texel lambs were rather big to begin with, but the single lambs especially were often so large they could barely pass through the ewe's birth canal. By increasing the percentage of twin lambs, Bekedam reasoned, more lambs would survive, and the Texel's fertility in terms of the number of healthy lambs produced would go up at the same time. Crossbreeding a Texel ram with ewes of a suitable breed would be the fastest way to achieve this.[54]

A breed used regularly for this purpose was the Finnish Landrace or Finnsheep, well known for its ability to produce triplets and even quadruplets. Yet Bekedam rejected this option. Finnsheep had no specific breeding season and produced their lambs year round. The Texel was strictly seasonal and had its lambs in winter or early spring. Changing this cycle would be too drastic a change for the Dutch farmers, Bekedam believed, and he went on the lookout for a more fitting breed.[55] He eventually found it at a farm in Achtmaal, a small Dutch village close to the Belgian border.[56] That is, he found a group of unregistered ewes of an unspecified breed that seemed to be related to the Belgian Milk Sheep. Bekedam considered them perfect for his purpose because of their high prolificacy and milk production, and their wedge-shaped conformation, which made for easy lambing. Between 1967 and 1969, Wageningen Agricultural College acquired 20 ewes and 7 rams of this type, and by November 1973 the flock had grown to 138 ewes. Over the years they were transformed into a proper breed by inbreeding and selection, and with some creative use of history Bekedam christened them Flemish sheep.[57]

From the moment he bought the first ones, Bekedam selected the Flemish ewes for ease of lambing and for producing at least two lambs. Another benefit of the type was that the ewes could already be bred in their first year, as opposed to the Texel, which only reached reproductive maturity in its second year. Within five years, Bekedam had succeeded in raising the birthrate in his ewes by 0.4 lambs. The crossbreeding experiment was started in 1970, on an experimental farm in the village of Swifterbant. The best ewes were mated with Texel rams to produce the $F_1$ lambs (first filial generation). The first-generation ewes were meant to produce larger litters, with smaller lambs and lower mortality. Like their mothers, they were crossed with a Texel ram to produce the $F_2$ lambs, which were three-quarters Texel and one-quarter Flemish, and the intended end product of the crossing scheme. A quantitative comparison of Bekedam's $F_1$ and $F_2$ sheep with the Texel showed that there was great promise in the procedure. Besides lower mortality and larger birthrate, the ewes needed less assistance during lambing due to the smaller lambs. Also, the crossbred ewes were milkier than Texel ewes, resulting in excellent growth rates for the $F_2$ slaughter lambs. The only setback was that the lambs' carcass quality was not quite as good as that of purebred Texel lambs, but Bekedam believed that even this might be improved by using better Texel rams. In conclusion, he stated that the procedure would increase the farmers' revenue by 20 to 30 per cent, compared to breeding with the Texel ewes. In a later calculation, he estimated that this might result in extra income of between 8,700 and 15,600 guilders per farmer.[58]

The initial reactions of the Texel breeders to Bekedam's results were, with a few exceptions, cautious or downright dismissive.[59] Many of them rallied to their breed's defence. The better meat quality of the Texel was of course brought up: farmers feared that the excellent reputation of Dutch lamb meat might be ruined. Most of their reactions emanated from a heartfelt disappointment that their favourite breed's superiority was being challenged. In the words of a particularly impassioned breeder who was interviewed in the sheep breeding journal *Het Schaap*: "Dear lovers of sheep, please do try the Texel."[60]

The breeders did not close their eyes to the Texel's shortcomings though. They acknowledged their problems in giving birth, which made it a very labour-intensive breed. They also agreed that fertility in terms of birthrate – although it had not been considered a problem until then – might benefit from selection.[61] A further blow was dealt to the Texel enthusiasts by the outcome of a French carcass competition in 1980, in which the Texel was awarded a dismal seventh place. The breeders' incredulity over this result was poignantly expressed in the title of a report on the event published in *Het Schaap*: "The best, but still only seventh place." There was no doubt among the farmers that their Texels were indeed the best in terms of general conformation. In particular, they found the heads of the winning sheep much too feminine. Quality, they felt, should not be judged on the basis of a sheep's carcass alone but on its conformation as a whole.[62]

Nevertheless, the call for a more structured, comparative, and quantitative approach to breeding Texels grew stronger, especially among the farmers associated with the NTS *(Nederlands Texels Schapenstamboek)*, the National Texel Flock Book Society, that was established in 1979.[63] Yet the members of the oldest society, the Texel Flock Book Society in North Holland, continued to reject such an approach. For them the breeder's eye remained essential in judging the quality of a sheep. The issue was important enough for them to decide they would not join the NTS.[64]

What possibly tipped the scales for many breeders to try their luck with Bekedam's new crossbreds was the 1979 decision by the European Court of Justice that the French restrictions on the import of British lamb meat and mutton were illegal, meaning that the Dutch lost their privileged position on the French market – their most important market at the time.[65] This decision came on top of a steady decline in the revenues from sheep breeding that had been going on for years. Whereas an average ewe had brought in 104 guilders in 1972, its price had dropped to a dispiriting 22 guilders by 1980.[66]

While Bekedam had set up his project at the end of the 1960s to investigate the options for further growth of the sector, farmers now began to see it as an escape route in their struggle to stay in the sheep business. In July 1981, eight breeders decided to work together "based on the conviction," as stated in the minutes of their meeting, "that the system of breeding created by Wageningen based on a Flemish/Texel sheep, the so-called $F_1$-F/T product, has a future." They decided to establish a breeders' society for Bekedam's new type of sheep to foster its improvement.[67] Wageningen Agricultural College, the supplier of Flemish sheep, was an indispensable partner, and Bekedam was invited to become a member of the advisory board.

In accordance with Bekedam's scheme, the society's $F_1$ ewes were to be mated to an excellent Texel ram to produce lambs for slaughter. In their definition of an $F_1$ ewe, however, the breeders added a clause that would give Bekedam's project a fundamentally different direction. Not only Texel-Flemish crossbreds would count as $F_1$ sheep, the description stipulated, but also the offspring of $F_1$ animals that were bred among themselves. In Mendelian parlance, such second-generation offspring should have been designated as $F_2$, yet the breeders reasoned that all animals that were 50 per cent Texel and 50 per cent Flemish would count as $F_1$. The offspring of two first-generation animals obviously met this requirement. The breeders considered this ratio important; deviations were not permitted.[68] They also intended to keep strict control over their animals' lineages, as is evident from the regulation that all sheep, regardless of whether they were used for breeding purposes or not, should be entered into the flock-book registers. This was all the more necessary because it was hard to tell the various crossbreds of the first and second generation apart on the basis of their conformation. As expected, the second-generation animals in particular showed a lot of variation due to recombination.[69]

The breeders did not leave it at this. By breeding the $F_1$ sheep among themselves and carefully selecting the offspring, they aimed to create a new breed, with its own breed name and a proper standard. Their motives for these adjustments to Bekedam's breeding scheme are not difficult to fathom. If they had followed Bekedam to the letter, they would have had to maintain two different flocks on their farms: Flemish sheep to produce the $F_1$ generation, and the latter to produce the slaughter lambs. This was impracticable, especially considering that most farmers kept only a small number of sheep as a sideline. Turning the $F_1$ sheep into a new breed and mating the ewes to a Texel ram to produce the slaughter lambs was a much more expedient option.

The location of Bekedam's experimental farm, Swifterbant, provided the name for the new breed: the Swifter (Figure 4.4).[70] It was advertised as more prolific than the Texel and produced healthy lambs in its first year. After several years of continued selection, the Swifter lambs were said to be worth 98.5 per cent of the price of purebred Texel lambs, a figure that clearly appealed to farmers who were struggling to keep up sheep farming and were looking for alternatives to the Texel to increase productivity.[71] Membership of the society rose to 55 breeders in 1983, 105 in 1984, and 163 by the end of 1986.[72]

The rapid growth of the association had a drawback, however. Within a few years, there was a shortage of Flemish ewes. Wageningen Agricultural College still had the only flock, and the flock-book regulations of the Swifter stipulated that these Wageningen animals, or animals directly descended from them, were the only ones that would be officially admitted as parents of $F_1$ Swifters.[73] To overcome this problem, most Texel breeders interested in producing Swifters reversed the sexes of the parents in Bekedam's original scheme to produce the $F_1$: they used Flemish rams, of which they only needed one or a few, as sires for their Texel ewes. This was more economical for them than performing Bekedam's cross with Flemish ewes anyway, since they already owned the Texel ewes.

Some of the flock-book regulations evoked criticism from the breeders. The requirement to register each and every animal was felt as a burden. Even more difficult to obey was the regulation that required the mother of a breeding ram to have given birth to at least two lambs as a one-year-old, and at least three in both her second and third year.[74] Texel breeders in particular found this requirement unreasonable for their ewes.[75] Yet a majority of the breeders supported the measure, as

Figure 4.4. The Swifter. From the archives of the Nationaal Veeteeltmuseum, Beers.

it concerned one of the principal objectives of the new approach: to produce more lambs.[76] Furthermore, an increasing number of breeders called for a standard of conformation for the Swifter. In Bekedam's experiment, conformation had played no role, yet since the farmers saw the Swifter as a new breed, the question of a standard became as relevant to them as it had always been to Texel breeders.

"I think [the Swifter] should be a recognizable breed," a Swifter breeder said in a letter to the society's board. "We would end up with a host of different Swifter types if everybody just bred according to their own whims."[77] Another breeder reproached the board for ignoring the issue and requested a detailed description.[78] Yet the society, no doubt with Bekedam's full support, was determined to keep its focus on functionality. By the end of 1985, the society's committee on breeding came up with a rather non-specific description of a "well-developed," "correct," and "proportional" type of sheep, that was mainly defined by its productive characteristics.[79] Unsurprisingly, this did not satisfy the discontented breeders. They agreed that the Swifter society should not take the Texel's breed description as an example, because it had led to animals that were too compact, resulting in the ewes' well-known problems in giving birth.[80] For most breeders, however, even though the incentive to breed Swifters was to create a more functional animal, clearly defined breed characteristics also added to the breed's economic value.

An additional reason for their insistence was the remarkable fact that, in the 1980s, selling Swifter breeding stock was more lucrative than selling $F_2$ slaughter lambs. By the end of the 1980s, 420 breeders had officially registered Swifters.[81] Of the 18,937 lambs born in 1991, only 2,379 were $F_2$ animals. This discrepancy can be found in all preceding years of the flock book's existence. A 1985 survey stated that "experiences with $F_2$ lambs are rare."[82] Inspectors even had difficulty finding outstanding $F_2$ sheep to be shown at the biannual Day of the Sheep (*Dag van het Schaap*) show of 1988.[83] Apparently, it was not the $F_2$ slaughter lambs that were bringing in the money, but the $F_1$ sheep, showing that the Swifter was rapidly becoming popular among farmers as a new breed. The Swifter Flock Book Society acknowledged this in 1989 when it stated that the $F_2$ lambs would "become important in the future," after the new Swifter breeders had built up their flocks.[84] So it was the great interest in the new breed that enabled its early adopters to take a shortcut – selling Swifters – that brought in money faster than Bekedam's long path ending with $F_2$ slaughter lambs. In this light, the breeders' calls for a standard are all the more understandable: it would strengthen the Swifters' marketability.

The society held its ground, however. It even stepped up the prolificacy requirements for the Flemish mother of a Swifter breeding ram from eight to nine lambs in her first three years.[85] The board justified this decision by noting that the improvement in birthrate that Bekedam had accomplished on his experimental farm appeared to be only partially realized on the farms of the Swifter owners, due to insufficient selection for fertility among the popular ewes of the new breed.[86] The loss of the heterosis effect was also mentioned: Texel-Flemish crossbreds profited much more from it than $F_1$ sheep that were bred among themselves.[87] Strict adherence to the society's breeding goals was therefore essential, according to the board.[88]

The board's strictness even created a conflict with Bekedam. In 1983, Bekedam's experimental farm at Swifterbant, by then called the A.P. Minderhoudhoeve, became a member of the Swifter Flock Book Society, yet it retained its own computerized registration system. Bekedam insisted on registering and using breeding rams that he considered promising from a scientific viewpoint, even when they did not meet the society's entrance requirements.[89] This caused problems when the descendants of these Minderhoudhoeve rams were sold to farmers:

buyers might find that they were not accepted by the Swifter society for registration.[90] It did not help matters when the society decided to "close" its flock book in 1987, meaning that only sheep with officially registered parents could be entered.[91] This effectively shut out part of the progeny of the Minderhoud sheep. Bekedam's growing frustration with the society's course of action induced him to resign as a member of the advisory board. He accused the society of promoting "hobby-ism" and of putting its own interests above those of the sector. At some point, he even advised the buyers of Minderhoud sheep to have their animals registered in the flock book of the Texel society (the NTS).[92] Although the interests of breeders and scientists clearly diverged here, it should be kept in mind that it was the society's adherence to the core of Bekedam's own program – the improvement of fertility – that had caused the conflict in the first place. Attempts to settle the disagreement failed, yet Bekedam's influence had been waning since his retirement in 1986.[93] In 1988, the Minderhoudhoeve gave in to the society's principles, and the two registration systems were merged.[94] Increasingly, however, the society went its own way.

When the society started organizing regional meetings towards the end of the 1980s, the issue of conformation – which Bekedam considered irrelevant – resurfaced at every single meeting.[95] "Demonstrations" of different types of Swifter sheep were organized, the term having been deliberately chosen to avoid any association with traditional shows at which animals were ranked on the basis of exterior evaluation.[96] By the early 1990s, the board was prepared to try and capture the Swifter's conformation in more exact terms.

A suitable tool for realizing this appeared to be the so-called EUROP classification system, a method for evaluating muscle development in live animals, based on external evaluation. EUROP was an acronym whose letters represented categories of muscle development.[97] The society's breeding committee adopted the system, arguing that they "should not judge on the basis of what is beautiful or what is not" but of what was functional.[98] It was also deemed important to get all the Swifter breeding rams together at an annual event, as was customary among other breeders' societies. From 1991 onwards, young rams were evaluated at such events on the basis of their EUROP classification, as well as on their growth after 100 days, the quality of their testicles, and hereditary defects.[99] The evaluation was not mandatory; its only aim was to edify the breeders.[100] Nevertheless, the way it was set up opened the door to a more traditional type of exterior evaluation. Rather surprisingly, in 1992 the Swifter board turned to the experienced judges of the NTS to judge their rams' conformation and to help them get a better idea of what a Swifter ram should look like.[101] Moreover, even though the verdict of NTS judges did not always match the EUROP classification,[102] it was the NTS evaluation that was made mandatory in 1993, not the EUROP scheme, and the members supported this decision.[103] Thus, during the first twelve years of its existence, the Swifter society moved from completely rejecting the traditional focus on external traits to accepting the evaluation of conformation as a cornerstone of selective breeding.

The breeders still took pride in the "scientific" origin of their breed at Wageningen Agricultural College, and they continued to see their Swifters as a utility breed, placing high demands on its functional characteristics. It was their practical and pragmatic decision to turn the Swifter into a breed and, when its popularity rose, a recognizable brand, that induced them to also set great store by the Swifter's exterior characteristics. Thus, it would seem that the breeders did not regard turning to the NTS for assistance as illogical. After all, the Texel was the quintessential meat breed, and the NTS judges knew exactly what to look for in a good ram. What worked well for the Texel as a typical meat breed, the society appears to have reasoned, should work well for the Swifter, too.

Thus, the Swifter was as much a product of Bekedam's initiative to develop a new type of sheep according to scientific principles, as of the breeders' practical and economic considerations to make the plan feasible. While Bekedam's scientific crossbreeding scheme may have appeared the most productive approach on paper, from the farmers' perspective the creation of a well-marked breed was indispensable to turn theory into practice.

## Breeding By Numbers or By Eye

By the end of the 1960s, there were twelve Texel flock-book societies, spread across the country. They were overseen by an umbrella organization, the *Centraal Bureau voor de Schapenfokkerij* (CBS) but had considerable autonomy and a regional focus. They each had their own board, flock-book registers, and inspectors; they organized their own exhibitions and activities; and many had slightly different preferences regarding the ideal type of the Texel.[104] The government supported the societies but, after reorganizing the Ministry of Agriculture in 1969, announced it would end its sponsorship in 1972. The CBS responded by making plans to merge the regional societies into a single national one for reasons of efficiency, and at the same time advised the breeders to take a good look at the differences between the various types and to think about ways to improve the Texel.[105] After almost a decade of deliberations the NTS was established in 1979, replacing the CBS and uniting all but one of the regional organizations.[106]

As we saw earlier, the Texel Flock Book Society in North Holland, the oldest and largest in the country, decided not to join the NTS. It was acclaimed as producing the best breeding stock and the top breeders' sheep were in high demand in the Netherlands and beyond. Having created the breed in the early twentieth century, it was also the most dedicated society when it came to preserving what they considered the proper type of the Texel. The society did not need the national merger to survive; unlike most of the others it was able to support itself as an independent organization and cherished its autonomy.[107] This decision would have far-reaching consequences for the newly formed NTS.

The NTS wasted no time in devising plans for improving the Texel. In a 1974 report, Bekedam and his colleagues Albert Visscher and J.A. Beukeboom of the government institute for animal husbandry research IVO had suggested how to proceed. Based on earlier, small-scale experiments in which lambs had been weighed to calculate growth indexes, they had recommended a quantitative approach to rationalize breeding practices.[108] The NTS agreed: the structural reorganization of the flock books was an excellent opportunity to develop a national breeding policy, based on quantification and with a special place for the calculating power of the computer.[109] According to Jan Geluk, the newly appointed president of the NTS, the aim should be to put sheep breeding in the Netherlands on a firmer professional footing.[110]

At the request of the NTS, Albert Visscher set up a program to determine breeding indexes for growth. The breeders' cooperation was crucial to the program, because large quantities of data were required for the index calculations, not only on lamb growth over time, but also on environmental factors such as the farm and the soil they were raised on, and on the farmers' feeding and management regime.[111] To get the breeders on board, Visscher and his colleagues gave lectures and published articles in the sheep breeding journal *Het Schaap*.[112] This was definitely needed, as many breeders were apprehensive about what the program might do to their animals' conformation, which they continued to see as an indispensable element of the breed's quality and marketability. Visscher acknowledged this concern and promised he would keep it in mind, adding, however, that the Netherlands was ten to twenty years behind other sheep breeding countries in implementing quantitative methods.[113]

In 1983, lambs began to be weighed to assess their growth rate. Complications arose from the beginning. To obtain optimal results, a lamb would have to be weighed several times during the first months after its birth. For reasons of accuracy, the investigators did not want this task to be delegated to the farmers, implying that farms would have to be visited several times. This was deemed too costly and time-consuming, however, and on the basis of growth data available from the earlier experiments it was decided that the lambs would be weighed only once, at 135 days, when they were about ready to be sold (Figure 4.5). Obviously, this came at the cost of precision in calculating the growth indexes.[114]

Correction factors needed to be calculated to compensate for seasonal, local, and management influences. Yet collecting sufficient data for these calculations proved to be a challenge. Useful data on 6,566 lambs were gathered from the 142 farms that had signed up for the weighing program. Initially, the inspectors intended to determine correction factors for a host of external influences, such as the region in which the farm was located, the type of farm, the date of birth and sex of the lambs, litter size, the mother's age, and the state of the fleece at the time of weighing (wet or dry). Yet as it turned out, insufficient data were available for calculating correction factors at the level of the individual farm; the number of lambs per farm was too small for this. The farms therefore needed to be grouped. Several other factors had to be dropped from the calculations as well. Finally, due to the participation of many small farms, yet another compromise had to be made for the 135 days point for weighing. In practice, lambs were weighed between 90 and 150 days and then had their weight corrected to correspond to the 135 days standard.[115]

All these limitations of the weighing program were minor imperfections in comparison to the shortcoming inherent in the final results of the index calculations. After correction, the average weight at 135 days of all the lambs on a farm provided an indication of the hereditary predisposition of each lamb on that farm: if its weight was higher or lower than the farm's average, this might be ascribed to hereditary factors. The problem was, however, that the calculations did not allow for comparisons across farms; what was found to be an excellent lamb on one farm might count as a below-average one on the next. Thus, the usefulness of the growth index was restricted to the farm for which it was calculated.

The rams that had sired the lambs could not be compared across farms either. To make such a comparison possible, they would have had to be mated with a random sample of ewes from a random sample of environments. The use of AI in dairy cattle breeding enabled a bull to service cows on many different farms, yet Texel rams were typically used for natural mating on a single farm, implying that the influence of the ram could not be separated from the influence of the farm.[116] This

Figure 4.5. Weighing at 135 days. From *Het Schaap* no. 3 (1986): 9.

also entailed that the best statistical tool for calculating indexes, the BLUP method, could not be used. There were ways to overcome this limitation, however. The investigators proposed using the indexes of the grandparents of the lambs as extra input in the calculations. These indexes were based on data from different farms, and might therefore be used to filter out at least some of the environmental effects. To obtain these data, the weighing program would of course have to be continued over several generations, but the investigators had planned to do this anyway, and if a sufficient number of farmers participated in the program, such data would automatically be forthcoming in due course.

In a 1986 report, the investigators gave a first estimate of the results to be expected from the weighing program: if a ram lamb was x kilograms heavier than average on day 135, he would pass on 21 per cent of these extra kilograms to his descendants. Even though the report considered the limitations of the program in detail, it ended on a positive note: "All in all, these results are encouraging and, despite the costs, they should be an incentive to continue the weighing program, and, above all, to use the results of the weighing program, the indexes, for selectively breeding Texel sheep."[117]

The breeders were less convinced. Their criticism of the program focused in particular on its possibly detrimental effect on the Texel type. In 1982, a Texel breeder wrote: "It is a shame to see that the breeding business leaves no room for breeders to focus on beauty. Both the nobility and the meat quality of an animal are of the utmost importance, and it is both these aspects that lend the Texel its desirability [...] One might question the appropriateness of sheep farmers (and sometimes even breeders) being induced by 'paper people' to try 'something new' on their farm based on a (theoretical) expectation of higher profit."[118] Other breeders argued in favour of renewed respect for the abilities of the experienced breeder, whose eye for detail and type guaranteed the Texel's quality. The quantitative approach only included aspects that could be expressed in numbers, yet the true breeder did not need such numbers; "keeping his eyes open when buying his ram," was all he had to do to select animals for any desirable property, including quantitative ones.[119] Nevertheless, the NTS kept defending the program and openly expressed its annoyance about the opposition to it, saying it was "a shame that some breeders fail to properly understand the report by Visscher."[120] The board took heart, however, from a grant awarded by the Ministry of Agriculture and Fisheries, which kept the costs of the program down to a guilder and a half per lamb.[121]

Participation in the weighing program would increase to a maximum of 345 farms in 1990, i.e., about 20 per cent of all active NTS members. Thereafter, however, their interest waned. In 1994, only 111 farms signed up and two years later – the last year the program was mentioned in the NTS annual report – only 76 remained. After 1996, the weighing program silently sank into oblivion.[122] Why did the breeders lose interest? As expected, an important drawback was that the growth index was only of use on a single farm, which implied it was not really helpful in marketing breeding stock or in choosing a breeding ram. Breeders frequently complained about this.[123] Moreover, the IVO could never live up to its promise of making it possible to compare growth indexes across farms by providing grandparent data. Such data simply did not become available in sufficient quantities, and the grandparent solution died a quiet death without ever being mentioned again.

The problem with the collection of sufficient data was twofold. First, after several years of weighing, most breeding rams had still not been weighed and therefore did not have a growth index. Even breeders who had embraced the quantitative approach continued to buy rams on the basis of their excellent conformation, not on the basis of their growth index. "I have been participating in the weighing program for four years now," a breeder of Texels stated, "and buyers rarely ask for this information."[124] Second, the reputation for excellence of the North Holland Texels, particularly those from the island, proved to be an obstacle. North Holland breeders had shown little interest in the weighing program from the start; they continued to select their breeding animals on the basis of conformation. And they had every reason for doing so, because it was these North Holland breeders who dominated the shows and won the majority of the prizes. Some of the most successful breeders came from families that had been breeding Texels for generations and had their names attached to distinct bloodlines – breeders recognized "Commandeur sheep" or described their flock as being "of Kikkert-blood." Annual outings of regional departments of the NTS would often have one of the renowned farms on Texel as their destination. Breeders looking for an outstanding breeding ram sought out the same farms, and many regional champion rams traced their lineage directly to a North Holland flock.[125] Thus, the breeders from Texel and North Holland had a disproportionate influence on Dutch Texel breeding as a whole and, as indicated, most of their rams came without breeding indexes. In the words of a board member of the Texel Flock Book Society in North Holland: "They [the top breeders] probably fail to see what financial benefits the indexes might bring them."[126] This effectively thwarted the implementation of the grandparent solution.

The second reason for its failure was that breeders elsewhere in the country also lost faith in the growth index. When it implemented the weighing program, the NTS advised its members to make a major adjustment to the Texel's conformation. The characteristics of the breed had verged more and more towards the extreme over the 1960s and 1970s. The Texel's body had become smaller and shorter, with a wide head featuring a pronounced "stop" between forehead and nose bridge, a short neck, and an almost arched backline (Figures 4.6–4.7). This "luxury type," as it was called, had contributed in no small measure to the branding of the breed, yet also to the Texel's problems in giving birth and its high lamb mortality; the short neck, moreover, was said to make grazing difficult. This trend had to be reversed, according to the NTS. The Texel should become larger and wider to make it functional again and less labour-intensive. The focus of the quantitative program on growth fit in with this objective, because it was known to result in larger animals.

In the 1980s, the NTS instructed its inspectors to give more weight to size and a longer back in their evaluations, and although some supporters of the luxury type clung to their preferences, by the end of the decade the majority of the NTS breeders had accepted that breeding a larger type of Texel was advisable. The titles of articles on breeding

Figure 4.6. Texels of the luxury type. From *Het Schaap* no. 4 (1985): 25.

and shows in *Het Schaap* clearly reflected this new course, examples being: "Trend toward larger sheep sets in," "Functionality wins," and "Excellent young sheep, both broad and typical."[127] Mart Nijssen, chief inspector of the NTS, noticed in 1989 that ram lambs at the shows had become some 10 kg heavier in just five years. More and more sheep were "well-developed," having the desired length and width, with a muscularity that was "less extreme," but still excellent.[128] Most important, even the breeders in North Holland and on Texel agreed that the luxury type, for whose creation they had mainly been responsible, would no longer do. Some breeders, for whom breeding Texels was as much a hobby as a source of income, continued to defend the extreme type, and in 2003 a group of seven aficionados even established their own society, *Texelaar Elite Schapen* (TES), to preserve it.[129] However, by the mid-1990s, most members of the Texel Flock Book Society in North Holland were breeding larger sheep. Top breeder Kees Kikkert said in 1994 that "the smaller animals should be kept away from the shows," as they no longer represented "proper breeding."[130] Inspectors even began to warn the breeders that the Texels were now so large and fast-growing that they threatened to become too fat. This induced the NTS to introduce the EUROP classification for carcass quality mentioned earlier.[131]

Figure 4.7. The Texel's characteristic head. From *Het Schaap* no. 4 (1985): 27.

By this time, the interest in the scientific weighing program was rapidly declining, and the reason should be clear now. The scientific approach to selective breeding, based on breeding by numbers, had been overtaken by the breeders' practical method, based on the evaluation of conformation. The aim the NTS had set itself when it was established in 1979 was reached within some fifteen years, but it was the breeder's eye that had been instrumental in accomplishing this, rather than measuring body weights and calculating indexes.

To a large extent, it was the small scale and structure of the sector that prevented the scientific program from realizing its potential. Sheep farming was at best a sideline for mainland farmers. As a rule, dairying was more profitable in the Dutch flatlands, and farmers tended to run a small flock of sheep behind the cows to graze the pasture down. The number of specialized sheep farms was small, reaching a maximum of 8 per cent of all farms with sheep in 1990. Although the average number of sheep per farm had grown from twelve in 1950 to seventy-seven in 1995, the majority of farmers still had fewer than fifty ewes and one or two rams to mate with them.[132] The data the inspectors were able to collect on these sheep and the farms they were kept on proved to be insufficient to perform the intricate index calculations successfully. There were simply too few weighing data and too many environmental factors to be reckoned with. Moreover, the non-random sample of ewes the rams were mated with prohibited across-farm comparison and also compelled the scientists to deploy less than optimal calculation methods. Finally, the data needed for the grandparent solution were not forthcoming. Despite Albert Visscher's reassurances, his program largely ignored the breeders' concern with the Texel's type characteristics. Too many breeders continued to choose a breeding ram on the basis of his looks rather than his growth index, and since the best rams often did not even have an index, too little father-grandfather data became available, meaning that a major benefit of the weighing program, across-farm comparison, never materialized.

It would be too simplistic to conclude that the breeders' traditional selection method worked better than the scientific approach. If the scientists had had the breeders' full cooperation, their program might arguably have worked as well, and possibly even better. What differentiated the two approaches was that the NTS campaign to improve the Texel's type was supported by the vast majority of the breeders – even by the top breeders in North Holland. Unlike the scientists, the NTS did take the breeders' concern with the Texel's external characteristics into account: quality of type continued to be valued at the shows, and the North Holland breeders' approval of the new course instilled trust in their NTS colleagues that the Texel's defining traits would be preserved.

With hindsight, one might say that the deck was stacked against the scientific weighing program from the start; the scientists had defined their breeding goal too narrowly to get the majority of the breeders on their side.

## AI in Texel Sheep

Like the growth indexes and the crossbreeding program, artificial insemination in sheep originated with Wageningen agriculturalists. Following the dairy cattle breeders, pig and chicken breeders had adopted AI in the 1960s to prevent diseases or improve their breeds. It seemed only natural to assume that the sheep sector might also benefit from AI. In principle, the technique should be applicable to any breed. The Texel, however, was just not like any other breed.[133]

The first problem that had to be overcome to make AI work in sheep, the scientists realized, was to find a practicable way of determining when a ewe was fertile. The Texel was a seasonal breed, the ewes having their oestrus periods between late summer and late fall. They went through consecutive cycles of about seventeen days, during which a fertile period of between twenty-four and thirty-six hours occurred. The cycles continued until the ewe was pregnant or the season was over. Experienced breeders could tell from a ewe's behaviour when she was fertile. Also, a ram with an anti-mating apron girded around his lower chest might be used to seek out the ewes in heat. These options, however, were considered too cumbersome and time-consuming for trained inseminators to implement AI efficiently. The best solution, according to the scientists, would be to apply hormones to induce all the ewes in a flock to ovulate at the same time. As an additional advantage, the lambs would then be born within a short time span. A small-scale experiment conducted in the early 1960s showed promising results, although the procedure was expensive and the percentage of non-viable lambs quite high.[134]

More extensive experiments with Texel ewes were started in 1966, in the veterinary obstetrics and gynaecology clinic at Utrecht University. With a success rate of 93 per cent, using progesterone to induce ovulation proved to be perfectly feasible. After natural insemination by a ram, 88 per cent of the treated ewes became pregnant, which was also quite satisfactory, when compared with the natural pregnancy rate of 95 per cent. Moreover, an extra hormonal injection of PMSG (pregnant mare serum gonadotropin) resulted in a significant increase in the birthrate, from 1.35 to 1.89 lambs. To the investigators' disappointment, however, artificial insemination of the treated ewes resulted in a pregnancy rate of only 47 per cent.[135] The Utrecht researchers decided to collaborate with Wageningen animal scientists to find a way to obtain better results. Foreign research clearly indicated this should be possible. In Russia, for example, AI had been routinely used by sheep farmers since 1928; in 1967, some 39 million sheep were artificially inseminated, about 60 per cent of all Russian sheep. France and Australia also used sheep AI on a large scale.[136]

It was soon found that some anatomical details of Texel ewes' reproductive organs were atypical. Tailor-made equipment had to be designed to accommodate these peculiarities, and the ewes had to be held in a special position to be successfully inseminated. Working out the most effective procedure took several years. Other research questions were whether it was best to inseminate ewes in their first or second oestrus cycle, and whether multiple inseminations enhanced the chances of success. The investigators noticed that success rates depended significantly on their experience in collecting and administering sperm. As the experiments progressed, pregnancy rates went up nicely, yet a worrying result was that the best results were obtained by doubling or tripling the amount of sperm used per insemination and by inseminating the ewes several times. In practice, this would not be feasible because of the small quantities of semen produced by a ram. The problem might be solved by using frozen sperm, yet this technique had still not been developed for sheep. On top of all this, the investigators found that the Flemish ewes used for the crossing experiments at Wageningen University were much more suited to AI than Texel ewes: pregnancy rates of 77 per cent were achieved, and crossbreds did even better.[137]

Evaluating these results, and also taking the costs of hormonal treatment and repeated inseminations into account, investigator Wim van Gemert from the Utrecht veterinary department concluded in 1975 that the chances were slim that AI in Texel sheep would be successful.[138] Agricultural expert P.W. Tol agreed: "Artificial insemination is too expensive and obtaining satisfactory pregnancy rates takes too much effort."[139] Van Gemert repeated his doubts in 1980, ten years after the experiments had ended, and they were echoed by Visscher in his 1982 report on the efficiency of Texel breeding in the Netherlands.[140]

A year later, Visscher had changed his mind. An endemic disease caused by an ovine lentivirus (maedi visna) became a major concern in the sheep sector at the end of the 1970s, mainly as a result of English import restrictions. The disease (called *zwoegerziekte* in Dutch) affected the lungs and other organs, and was ultimately fatal. In 1982, strict measures were taken to separate the flocks that did and did not carry the virus, particularly at shows and during transportation. Uncertified rams could no longer be used in flocks certified to be virus-free.

Visscher realized, however, that if natural mating was replaced by AI, sheep breeders and farmers with a certificate might continue using uncertified rams without jeopardizing their virus-free status, as sperm did not transmit the virus.[141]

A survey among eighty-nine breeders by the Animal Health Service of the province of Gelderland showed that half of them were willing to adopt AI and to accept a pregnancy rate of about 70 per cent.[142] This outcome inspired staff members of the service – AI expert Van Gemert among them – to organize a trip to France to visit AI stations and a company specializing in frozen semen. Some 1,250 ewes were inseminated on a single day at one of these stations; teams of 2 inseminators could handle about 60 ewes per hour. The AI station mainly serviced milk sheep, however, and the Dutch investigators knew from their tests with Flemish sheep that pregnancy rates were much better in milk breeds and that their rams produced more semen. Moreover, ram selection by the French breeders was supported by computerized index calculations, allowing for comparisons across farms. The French had thus succeeded in increasing milk yield in their sheep from 30 to 178 litres in 10 years. Van Gemert and his group were excited about the French results and clearly saw the benefits of AI for the Dutch situation, particularly in light of the lentivirus threat.[143]

Visscher's interest was piqued even more by the French example, as it also demonstrated that the use of AI solved the problem of comparing indexes across farms: with AI, it would be easy to have rams produce offspring on different farms. At the same time, AI would help farmers to speed up genetic progress and improve the organization of the sector as a whole. Visscher suggested that AI stations should be established across the country. Estimating the costs involved on the basis of Van Gemert's earlier experiments, Visscher expected breeders would have to pay up to 46 guilders for an insemination, depending on the quality of the ram. Whereas Van Gemert had obtained pregnancy rates of at best 60 per cent, Visscher ventured that pregnancy rates of about 70 per cent should be possible.[144]

Conspicuously absent from his considerations, however, was the technical side of the matter, which had not changed since Van Gemert's experiments in the 1960s. Texel sheep were not milk sheep, and the results achieved with the two breeds differed considerably. In the following years, however, progress was made in this respect too, though under controlled conditions. Van Gemert initiated new experiments with AI, using the same techniques he had deployed earlier, and after three years he had succeeded in raising pregnancy rates to 64 per cent. "There just might be an opportunity for sheep-AI in the Netherlands," he suggested.[145] In 1986, the technique was indeed made available to the sheep farmers. Thanks to a supporting grant from a Dutch bank, breeders could have their pick from a selection of Texel breeding rams for 25 guilders per insemination. Semen from Swifter and Flemish rams was also on offer. It was expected that sheep AI would be self-supporting by 1992.[146]

But this would never happen. After the funding stopped, Dutch sheep AI collapsed, for several reasons. First and foremost, the breeders' opinion on what constituted an excellent breeding ram differed fundamentally from that of the investigators controlling the AI program. This became clear immediately during the first demonstration day of AI rams at a newly established AI station in Stroe, in the province of Gelderland, in September 1986. The twenty-one rams on display were rejected outright by the hundred or so breeders who visited the station that day. Whatever the rams' purported hereditary qualities, the farmers did not like what they saw: "It is such a hotchpotch," seemed to be the overall sentiment.[147] Obviously, the rams had been chosen by the scientific experts on the basis of their indexes. "Because the growth rate of the lambs is important," they explained, "we incorporated the requirement that the ram should be in the weighing program and have an index of at least 105" – 100 being the population's average.[148] The rams also had to have proven to cope well with the technique of semen collection. To procure such animals had been hard enough. In fact, only four of the rams presented met all the criteria – the others had merely been brought in to offer some variation. In the end, most of the breeders willing to participate in AI were interested in only a single ram out of the twenty-one available at the Stroe station.[149]

This was to be the pattern for the following years; the breeders remained very particular about the type of the rams they wanted. In 1987, all interested breeders in the province of Overijssel had their sights set on the Texel rams bred by top breeders Kikkert and Commandeur.[150] In 1988, four rams from the island again monopolized the breeders' attention.[151] Since semen was a limited resource, not all breeders could use the ram they preferred, and often they were not prepared to use another one.[152] An experiment started by Visscher in 1990 to incorporate the use of AI into the weighing program did not help to resolve the conflict between the breeders' preference for rams that met the criteria of their breeder's eye and the scientists' view that indexes should prevail over conformation.[153] In February 1993, the funding was spent, and with only ten breeders signed up, Dutch sheep AI ceased to exist, leaving a deficit of 80,000 guilders.[154]

There were other, more practical reasons for this fiasco. While pregnancy rates in the late 1980s approached 60 per cent, there was a lot of variation between farms.[155] In 1985, for example, success rates varying between 27 and 100 per cent were recorded. Some AI rams performed marvellously on one farm but not on others. In 1988, when the inseminators achieved an average of 68 per cent, 6 participating farms scored below 50, and 4 of them even below 40 per cent. No satisfactory explanation for such differences was found. The peculiarities of the Texel also depressed the results: rams from other breeds and crossbreds performed better, both in pregnancy rates and in sperm production.[156] The low pregnancy rates made it necessary for the farmers to have a ram of their own as well, since the AI program only provided a single insemination per ewe. It should be added, though, that there is no indication that the farmers found the total costs of AI prohibitive as such.

Even though the better results achieved with crossbreds would suggest that AI might have been successfully implemented in crossing programs involving Swifters and Flemish sheep, it was in fact the interest of the crossbred breeders that was the first to wane.[157] An unexpected complication was mainly responsible for this. To facilitate AI, the PMSG hormone was used to synchronize the ewes' oestrus. Yet besides inducing ovulation, the hormone also increased the birthrate. This directly interfered with one of the Swifter society's principal breeding goals: to increase birthrate by selecting rams from highly fertile mothers. The use of PMSG made it impossible to independently assess the hereditary merits of a ram. The issue gave rise to frequent discussions among the members of the society. The use of PMSG was never explicitly forbidden, but it had to be reported, and thus it hampered the marketability of Swifter rams. As a consequence, the Swifter breeders were among the first to lose interest in AI.[158]

Finally, the ovine lentivirus problem – a major incentive for many farmers to join the AI program – was largely resolved by 1990. In the late 1980s, the NTS even claimed that the Texel was lentivirus-free.[159] The virus had temporarily tipped the balance in favour of AI in the early 1980s, yet when it receded into the background, the delicate interconnection of factors on which the program rested began to fall apart.

**What's in a Breed?**

The creation of the Texel and its crossbred relative, the Swifter, illustrates the various functions and purposes of the notion of a breed. Having its origin in a local type without fixed characteristics, the Texel was not transformed into a breed because the added value of purity was self-evident. On the contrary, when breeders started to devote serious attention to improving their animals in the second half of the nineteenth century, they believed the best results were to be expected from crossbreeding with English rams. The mainland breeders would even continue their crossbreeding experiments until well into the twentieth century. While it seemed plausible in theory that the North Holland breeders might produce heavier and more profitable lambs on their fertile soils by crossbreeding, they ran into insurmountable difficulties in practice. In the end, they followed the example of their island colleagues and adopted purebred breeding as a more effective alternative. The breeders on the island had come to this conclusion several decades earlier. Their soils were poorer and therefore less suitable for raising heavier lambs. Moreover, their flocks were larger, providing ample opportunity to use mass selection to improve their sheep.

The upshot was that by the 1920s both island and mainland breeders had sided with the agricultural experts, who had propagated a focus on purebred breeding as the most reliable starting point for stock improvement from the early 1900s onwards. The scientists followed the same maxim in chicken and pig breeding, and it seems not too far-fetched to suggest that this was also the hidden agenda of Nobel's involvement with the mainland breeders' efforts to find the best crossbreeding combination.

Once established, the Texel's purebred status became the hallmark of its quality. As in cattle breeding, purity guaranteed uniformity and consistency in production, and some of the Texel's distinguishing features became brand characteristics. Commercially speaking, the top breeders considered such traits to be nearly as important as the Texel's productive qualities. Texel breeder Dijt's interest in Hagedoorn's Mendelian approach, for instance, was motivated by the desire to "purify" the Texel's brand features. The Swifter breeders' insistence on a more detailed conformation standard, once they had turned their original crossbreds into a breed, had a similar background.

While scientists might denounce the breeders' preoccupation with branding as hobbyism – they had similarly accused the breeders of the Modern Friesian of breeding for the show ring – and while breeders might indeed be inclined to exaggerate brand features, economic considerations would ultimately prevail. Cattle breeders switched to Holsteins when higher milk yields appeared necessary to stay in business, and the Texel breeders gave up their luxury type when its signature points began to pose a serious threat to its functionality. In making the necessary adjustments, however, the breeders saw to it that the distinctive qualities of the Texel were not entirely lost. A small group of breeders apparently valued the type of their Texels and the joy they derived from breeding eye-catching stock more highly than monetary returns, as the establishment of the new breeders' society TES demonstrates. Then again, perhaps they too were driven by commercial considerations after all, for by 2015 the society had grown to ninety-five members, suggesting there was still a sizeable market for the old type.

When Bekedam reintroduced crossbreeding in the 1970s and showed that the method effectively increased the birthrate, a fair number of breeders were interested. But now it was they who realized that Bekedam's crossbreeding scheme would be too complicated in practice, especially considering the small size of the Dutch flocks. They turned the Swifter into a breed and used Texel rams as a terminal sire to produce lambs for slaughter. As a result, and also because of the sudden popularity of the Swifter, standardizing the breed's conformation became almost as important for them as it was for the Texel breeders, meaning that evaluating animals in the show ring became part and parcel of their breeding culture. They did monitor the productive qualities of the Swifter very carefully, though, as is illustrated by their conflict with Bekedam over the fertility requirements for the mothers of breeding rams.

The breeders' constant concern over brand features was also partly responsible for the eventual failure of the scientific programs developed to increase the productivity of the sheep sector. Although the breeders initially welcomed the plans to calculate growth indexes and introduce AI into sheep breeding, their support was short-lived. Bekedam, Visscher, and Van Gemert had to overcome many technical and practical obstacles to make these techniques work; in particular, the Texel sheep themselves long resisted the attempts at replacing their natural mating process by artificial insemination. If milk sheep had been involved, the story might have been different, as the French example suggests. Even when all the barriers had been removed, successfully implementing the new technologies still depended on factors that were beyond the scientists' control. For a long time, AI seemed too complicated and expensive, yet, as in cattle and pig breeding, an infectious disease opened a window for its introduction. Ten years later, however, the disease was under control, and an important cornerstone of the program disappeared. Growth index calculation also faced many challenges, yet in the eyes of the experts it was feasible. To become really useful, however, it was crucial that the grandparent indexes be available. This turned out to be the Achilles heel of the program: the data required for the calculation of these indexes were not forthcoming.

Again, the reasons the breeders left the scientists in the lurch had much to do with the defining features of the Texel type. Breeders preferred the rams of the top breeders from Texel and North Holland, because these rams were closest to the ideal Texel conformation. More often than not, however, these rams came without indexes, because the top breeders saw no benefit in the weighing program. At the same time, these rams rarely qualified for the AI program, which required them to have a growth index. This further reduced the attractiveness of AI for the breeders – they showed little interest in the rams the scientists selected for them. Swifter breeders also dropped out, because the hormones used to induce ovulation in the ewes distorted the results of the breeders' selection for litter size. Considering that the growth index and AI programs had been a house of cards from the beginning, it is hardly surprising that they were unable to survive this chain of setbacks.

The scientists' ambition in developing their programs was to modernize Texel breeding along the lines of dairy cattle breeding. A quantitative approach, supported by AI, it was thought, would help farmers make faster genetic progress. While the scientists saw their ambition thwarted, the intended results were nevertheless achieved, by and large: the Texel was given a makeover that alleviated its birth problems and resulted in faster-growing lambs. The breeders deployed the traditional instrument of the breeder's eye to accomplish this: what the weighing program had been unable to achieve, the breeders realized by means of selection on the basis of conformation. This was a remarkable achievement, all the more so since the breeders had in fact set themselves an even more difficult task than the scientists had: improving the Texel's growth rate while at the same time preserving its typical characteristics. Unsupported by any quantitative data on the many confounding factors, and without the help of statistics and computers, their breeder's eye guided them unfailingly to select precisely those animals whose hereditary qualities needed to be passed on to realize the new breeding goal.

The scientists had ignored at their peril that marketability depended not only on productivity, but also on finely honed branding. Whatever the merits of breeding by numbers, the Dutch sheep breeding world continued to go by the adage that what you see is what you get. Commercial breeding trumped scientific breeding in this case. As the websites of today's Texel breeders show, however, they do not consider the result any less modern for it: they advertise the new type as the Modern Texel.[160]

# 5 From Farm Horse to Riding Horse: The Dutch Warmbloods

In the 1950s, tractors began to replace horses in Dutch agriculture on a significant scale. At first, horse breeders' societies did not expect the horse to disappear completely from the farm and the field. Most farms in the Netherlands were small and tractors were considered useful and profitable only on larger farms. Moreover, it was believed that horses would continue to be more efficient for the lighter chores on the farm.[1] By the mid-1960s, however, when the scaling up of farms began to be seen as a precondition for their survival, the breeders' societies acknowledged the possibility that the tractor would not just supplement horsepower in agriculture but replace it. This implied that the Dutch draft horses, mostly Warmbloods of the Gelderlander and the Groninger types, might disappear – unless they were given a new purpose.[2] At the time, horseback riding was becoming more and more popular, and it was obvious to fervent Warmblood breeders what needed to be done to rescue the type: they set themselves the task of transforming their working horses into saddle horses.

By the mid-1980s, this mission had been completed, and quite successfully: the Warmblood riding horse and the Dutch Warmblood Horse Studbook Society were at the beginning of their rise to international prominence in equestrian sports. Today the society is one of the leading sport horse breeding organizations worldwide. Dutch show jumping and dressage horses in particular play a prominent role in top-level equestrian events.[3]

This chapter analyses how the Dutch working horse was transformed into a riding horse. The Dutch case lends itself particularly well to a study of this kind. Compared with other European countries, where the transformation of the farm horse had started several decades earlier, the process in the Netherlands took place within a short time span, between 1960 and 1985. Unlike Great Britain, Germany, and France, the Netherlands had no noteworthy tradition in equestrian sports before the 1960s. Horse racing (with Thoroughbreds or trotters), and show jumping and dressage (with Warmbloods) were marginal sports. Except among young farmers, horseback riding as a leisure activity was not widespread either.[4] Racing would continue to be an insignificant sport in the Netherlands, but leisure riding and show jumping became increasingly popular from the 1960s onwards, to be followed by dressage in the 1980s. Warmblood breeders made a concerted effort to produce a good Dutch saddle horse in these decades, and their discussions on how to go about this have been documented in detail in *In de Strengen*, the official journal of the Warmblood breeders' society, which was published and mailed to all members every two weeks. Besides reports on meetings and shows, *In de Strengen* featured numerous articles on breeding issues by board members, studbook inspectors, scientific breeding experts, and breeders. Naturally, debates on the best way to create a riding horse took centre stage in the journal in this period. As will be shown, the methods employed by the breeders were a continuation of methods that had been well known since the late eighteenth century. Still, scientific views on breeding had a significant influence on the Warmblood breeders' methods in this period.

Another salient aspect of the Dutch case is that until the late 1970s, the government was hardly involved in horse breeding, in contrast to Germany, where several of the *Länder* (states) had their own state studs, and France, where the government controlled the national *Haras* (stud farm) system. Before the Second World War, the Dutch government maintained a policy of neutrality and thus had a small army and no need for government controlled studs. Horse breeding, including stallion selection, had been in the hands of private breeding societies since the early twentieth century.[5] However, this situation seemed on the brink of change at the end of the 1970s, when the government attempted what, in the perception of the Warmblood society, amounted to a hostile takeover of the horse-breeding business. The government's stated intent was to modernize horse breeding by turning it into a collectively organized, science-based, and more profitable enterprise. The way the ensuing controversy between the Warmblood society and the government played out illustrates in detail how the interactions between policymakers, scientists, and breeders influenced the society's breeding aims and methods.

As it turned out, the government's plan for reforming the organization of horse breeding was largely subverted by the breeders' fierce opposition. Nevertheless, scientific methods started to make inroads into Warmblood breeding at the time, when the society adopted the instruments provided by quantitative genetics to rationalize its methods of selective breeding. Thus, it might seem as if, in the end, the breeders did fall into step with the government's campaign for scientific modernization. Yet neither the logic of modernization nor that of the scientific method explains how and why the breeders were persuaded to embrace the scientific approach. For this, the breeders' reactions to economic and political pressures and the particulars of Warmblood breeding culture have to be taken into account.

## Gelderlanders and Groningers

Confronted with the challenge of turning their farm horses into riding horses, the Dutch Warmblood breeders' societies – until 1970 there were separate societies for the Groninger and the Gelderlander types – took courage from the fact that the versatility of Warmbloods had ensured their enduring popularity over the centuries. After originating in central Europe as a middleweight horse type, distinct varieties of the Warmblood were created from the eighteenth century onwards, especially in Germany. The Dutch Gelderlander and Groninger took shape in the second half of the nineteenth century. While the heavy and slow Coldblood draft horse was especially suited to demanding hauling and ploughing jobs, the Warmblood was used as a multipurpose farm horse and carriage horse, while the lighter ones found their way to the military as saddle horses. From the 1920s onwards, when the influence of motorization began to be felt, the Warmblood lost ground as a carriage horse. At the same time, it became more popular as a riding horse among young Dutch farmers, who organized themselves in rural riders' associations.[6]

The Groninger type was used on the heavier soils in the north of the Netherlands and had a rather stocky build. The Gelderlander type was lighter and was therefore preferred by the rural riders' associations (Figure 5.1). The difference between the two types was not sharp though. Like all Warmbloods, the Gelderlander and the Groninger were not distinct breeds but performance types that were not bred pure. Breeders of Gelderlanders, for instance, often used Groninger stallions to prevent their type from becoming too light and thus unfit for farm work. And the breeders of both types used various German and French Warmblood sires whenever they felt it would benefit their stock.[7]

Evidently, breed purity did not matter to the breeders of the Dutch Warmblood. Their selection criteria were performance, conformation, gaits, and a compliant character. For a mare or stallion to be

Figure 5.1. The Gelderlander: farm horse, carriage horse and riding horse. From *In de Strengen* 16, no. 10 (1954): 4.

admitted to the studbook – the Gelderlander and the Groninger societies administered their own studbook registers – they had to be judged according to these criteria by the studbook inspectors. Because the Warmbloods were working horses, the emphasis on performance and character is self-evident. Until the 1930s, these traits were simply tested in daily practice – farmers had no use for horses that did not perform. From the 1940s onwards, however, pulling and endurance tests were gradually introduced as part of the procedure for admittance to the studbook. For breeding stock, a well-formed body and sound gaits were also deemed essential by the inspectors. Some breeders professed that conformation was even more important than performance, since a sound body was a necessary precondition for working ability. It was a topic that generated much debate throughout the whole of the twentieth century. Finally, seemingly irrelevant characteristics such as beauty and charisma were considered significant too, as horses were more than just a source of power for many farmers. The horse that worked the fields also transported its owners to church or to visit friends and family, and therefore it had to be both strong and good-looking, and it should move gracefully in harness. Many farmers bred their horses as an extra source of income, and horse shows and prize competitions were organized to advertise the qualities of both mares and stallions. For showing purposes, an attractive conformation and elegant gaits were essential.[8]

Whereas the number of working horses in the Netherlands had reached its postwar height with 268,000 individuals in 1947, ten years later their number had dropped to 163,000, making it clear to both the Groninger and the Gelderlander breeders that a change of course was necessary.[9] Initially, the breeders' societies believed that a number of minor modifications of its characteristics would suffice to make the Warmblood more suitable for riding.[10] The rural riders' associations agreed, as they were interested in riding horses that remained suitable for farm work. By then, some of these associations had even started to import horses from abroad, because good saddle horses were scarce in the Netherlands.[11]

Although Warmblood breeders had always supplied the mounts for the Dutch military, and even though farmers also used their Warmbloods for riding, the Gelderlanders and even less so the heavier Groningers were anything but typical riding horses. They had a high-stepping trot – with neck upright and head held high – which made for graceful moving in harness, but not for pleasurable riding. Their galloping qualities also needed improvement. Furthermore, being built for pulling in harness, they had a rather square frame and lacked the well-developed withers and long, slanted shoulder of the saddle horse – characteristics that enable comfortable riding. So the question was how to introduce such riding-horse qualities into the Dutch Warmblood.

To begin with, there was a tension between enhancing the Warmblood's riding characteristics and its suitability for carriage driving, as breeders were quick to point out. As noted, the carriage horse was a trotter with high knee action. In the early twentieth century, Gelderlander breeders had even used British Hackney sires to enhance the showy trot of their animals. Riding horses, on the other hand, needed smooth gaits with little knee action. Acknowledging the incompatibility of these requirements, the Gelderlander breeders' society decided that the harness horse and the saddle horse should be bred as two distinct types of Warmbloods. From then on, the carriage horse (*Tuigpaard*) would be kept by a small but dedicated group of enthusiasts, for recreation and sport (Figure 5.2).[12] In what follows, I will focus on the creation of the most important and popular type: the riding horse.

Figure 5.2. The Dutch *Tuigpaard*. From *In de Strengen* 47, no. 4 (1980): cover illustration.

## Introducing "Hot Blood"

In theory, several options were available for turning the Warmblood into a riding horse. The fastest solution would of course have been simply to sell the horses of the old type and buy horses of the desired new type. This option was not realistic, however. It would have resulted in a complete collapse of the market for the old type – that was already very weak – and in skyrocketing prices for the new type. Another option was sustained selection within the Warmblood population for riding horse qualities. However, according to the Warmblood breeding experts this was not a feasible approach either, since it would take too long in a slow-breeding animal like the horse.[13] A more realistic technique was breeding up, a method well known among breeders of all kinds of livestock. It was used by the dairy cattle breeders, for instance, when they switched from dual-purpose cows to dairy specialists: the Dutch Friesians were turned into Holsteins by using American sires to mate with them for a number of generations.

Breeders were unanimous that some form of breeding up with riding horse sires was required to turn the Gelderlander and the Groninger into riding horses. Since there were successful examples to follow, they also agreed on what the first step should be. The quickest result would come by using a "hot-blooded" riding horse sire – either an English Thoroughbred or an Arabian – to impregnate the Gelderlander and Groninger mares. In the past, Dutch breeders had produced mounts for the military in this way.[14] Moreover, breeders in some German states, France, and other European countries had not only crossed Warmblood mares with Thoroughbred and Arabian sires to produce saddle horses for the military, but also for sports, since at least the nineteenth century.[15] The Dutch breeding societies decided to follow suit.

Given its racehorse conformation, stamina, superior galloping qualities, and eagerness to perform, the breeding experts felt that the English Thoroughbred in particular would be a suitable breed to infuse riding horse characteristics into the Dutch Warmblood. In 1962, studbook inspectors approved the use of Thoroughbreds as sires by breeders of Gelderlanders and Groningers. Their crossed offspring would be included in the studbook, albeit in a separate sport register.[16]

Many, but by no means all, Dutch breeders followed this advice. Especially in the earlier years, when there was still hope that the Warmblood would continue to be needed on the farm, some breeders, especially of the Groninger type, feared that breeding with Thoroughbreds might result in too much of a good thing. Thoroughbreds were called hot-blooded for a reason, and they might destroy, in a single generation, the equable temperament that was typical of the Dutch Warmblood. Moreover, Thoroughbreds were specialized racers, smaller and lighter than the Dutch Warmblood. Would their offspring still have enough mass and height to serve as both comfortable riding horses and capable farm horses?[17]

Breeders who entertained such worries preferred to breed their mares with riding horse sires that were themselves crosses of Warmbloods and Thoroughbreds, and thus less hot-blooded. Progress would be slower in this way, depending on the percentage of hot blood – simply called "blood" by the breeders – that a stallion carried, but it would also be safer. Given that the transformation from draft to riding horse had started earlier in Germany and France, crossed sires from German and French studs with varying percentages of Thoroughbred blood were used for this purpose. For instance, the German Holstein stallion Amor and the Anglo-Norman stallion l'Invasion, whose pedigrees showed more distant Thoroughbred influences, were to have a considerable influence in Dutch Warmblood breeding; they can still be found in the pedigrees of numerous Dutch-bred Warmblood horses today.[18] The Dutch offspring of such sires – provided they had been approved by the inspectors first – were entered into the studbook too. Nearly half of the breeders would follow this more cautious approach.[19]

The first generation of crossed horses initially raised eyebrows at shows, because they lacked the square body shape the breeders were used to.[20] Yet many of them proved to be of surprisingly good quality. They were judged to be excellent riding horses, and some of them developed into outstanding sport horses, particularly in show jumping, which was becoming popular in the 1970s. Their qualities were said to reside in particular in their docility and robust conformation.[21] Many of the crossed animals combined the conformation and the temperament of their Warmblood mother with the smooth gaits, the stamina, and the willingness to perform of their Thoroughbred or crossed father. By the early 1970s, the best of them were much sought after by jumping riders in the Netherlands and abroad. For instance, the well-known German breeder and show-jumper Alwin Schockemöhle bought two first-generation crosses from a Dutch breeder in 1968, and eight more a year later.[22]

Despite these quick successes, the mission of turning the Dutch draft horse into a riding horse was anything but complete. The big question was what to do next. Experienced breeders knew that the results of breeding with crossbreds, or "half-bloods," were unpredictable due to Mendelian recombination of the variability present in the original parental stock. So what were breeders to do next, once they had performed the first-generation cross?

## Finding the Right Mix

Initially there was a broad consensus among the breeders and the societies' breeding experts that the original population of Warmbloods should be carefully maintained as a basis to breed from, if only because until the early 1960s there was still a need for good farm horses. Moreover, they argued, crossed animals and their descendants should remain capable of farm work too. For this purpose, first-generation crosses might be bred back to the original Warmblood type, resulting in animals that were 75 per cent Warmblood (if a Thoroughbred had been used to produce the first generation). Breeders felt that introducing more blood into the second generation would not only make the animals unfit for farm work, but also too unruly for the average rider. So that left only the option of breeding with half-bloods to be considered, which, as indicated, was the most difficult one because the results from such combinations were hard to predict. As breeder Piet Meinardi expressed it: "It is really hard to say how we should proceed. Half-blood with half-blood, is that it? I don't know. It is very difficult ... Our breeding stock has become very diverse. There are many uncertainties."[23]

To keep variability in the second generation within bounds, breeding experts, after careful deliberation, considered it advisable not to have a first-generation crossed mare inseminated by a first-generation crossed stallion, but rather by a sire whose riding horse qualities had been consolidated by judicious crossing for several generations. Initially, such stallions were of course scarce in the Netherlands, but German riding horses such as Holsteins or Hanoverians, which many breeders had already used to produce the first generation, again provided an alternative. If a crossed mare was still too much of the draft horse type, a sire with more blood needed to be used. Also, if a sport horse was required, more blood was to be added. On the other hand, a sire with a higher percentage of Warmblood blood should be used to even out too much fervour.[24] Inbreeding was another method to reduce variability and preserve desirable characteristics. The method was not without risks, however, which was probably the reason it was rarely mentioned in *In de Strengen*. Yet in practice, inbreeding was routinely applied by Warmblood breeders, as appears from analyses of pedigrees.[25]

Clearly, decisions on what characteristics the animals used to produce the second and consecutive generations had to be made on a strictly individual basis and would depend on the type of horse that was required. According to studbook inspector A.J. Vermond, breeders had to decide for themselves which sire would be best to combine with a particular mare.[26] The Utrecht veterinarian and future society president Gerrit van der Mey acknowledged that, rather than Mendelian crossing schemes, the breeder's experience in finding the right mix was essential.[27]

By the end of the 1960s, it could no longer be denied that there was no future for the Warmblood as a farm horse. "The battle is over," was how breeder J.F. Eysink expressed his resignation, "[T]he car, the truck and the tractor have won."[28] The Warmblood could only survive as a riding horse, the breeding societies acknowledged. As a result, prospects for the original Groninger Warmblood were dim. Its heavy build made it less suitable for riding than the Gelderlander, and there was little reason for maintaining it as a distinct type. The Groninger would indeed for the greater part be amalgamated with the Gelderlander and its crosses, and the Gelderlander and Groninger breeding societies were finally merged into a single studbook association, the *Warmbloed Paardenstamboek Nederland* (WPN), in 1970.[29]

The Gelderlander also faced difficulties. There was a prolonged and animated debate within the WPN as to whether it would continue to be needed for breeding purposes or not.[30] A group of breeders clung to the type, arguing that the Gelderlander was foundational to the successes of the Dutch Warmblood as a riding horse. The first-generation crosses were of proven quality, and some breeders felt they were even superior to any other combination that had been tried. The original type should therefore be maintained, perhaps in slightly "modernized" form. The WPN board acceded to this request to the extent that it allowed the enthusiasts to establish their own sub-society within the WPN for what was variously called the "multipurpose" or the "basic" Gelderlander horse.[31]

However, when a breeder of this type demanded that the WPN should focus exclusively on producing first-generation crosses of basic Gelderlanders with Thoroughbreds, thus implying that the first generation should not be bred from at all, the board rejected this option as unrealistic.[32] Irish Warmblood breeders had followed this approach, and it had proven to be unsustainable, the WPN officials argued. A great number of breeders would be needed to maintain the Gelderlander population, but how many breeders would be prepared to do so? Gelderlanders were less suitable for riding and would therefore have to be kept for breeding purposes only, which was too costly. Producing good stallions seemed especially problematic. Only a small percentage of them would be approved as sires, so many breeders ran the risk of raising males that in the end would turn out to be almost worthless. For a breeder, producing riding horses from riding horses was much less risky and more profitable. The Irish breeders had soon run out of good draft horse parent stock, because hardly anyone was interested in maintaining them.[33] As expected, the same was to happen in the Netherlands: a drastic decrease in the number of "basic" horses was reported in *In de Strengen* in the late 1970s. Like the Groninger, the Gelderlander is now a rare breed.[34]

In the 1970s, with the days of the farm horse over, WPN inspectors concurred that the society's goal should be to create a distinct Dutch riding horse that retained some of the characteristics of the original Warmblood, such as its size and mass, and its pleasant appearance and disposition. Once the Dutch type had been consolidated, foreign input would become unnecessary and the sport horse register might be closed.[35] This goal was not meant to imply, however, that a uniform type or even a breed should be aimed for. For one thing, there was no standard of what a riding horse should ideally look like, even less so since differently built horses were used for different purposes, such as show jumping, dressage, or eventing. Moreover, it was not at all clear what a horse's ideal conformation for each of these different purposes might be – even some horses with seemingly obvious defects performed very well in sports.[36] A further complicating factor was the influence of training and of the rider, which could make or break a horse.[37] Still, the WPN continued to set great store by judging mares and stallions on the basis of conformation, as it had always done. The intention was to examine the animals for correctness of build and movements, and to exclude individuals with diseases or hereditary defects, rather than to compare them to a narrowly defined breed standard.[38]

Before long, even the aim of breeding exclusively with Dutch-bred horses had to be reconsidered. In the late 1970s, breeders had begun to use fewer Thoroughbreds as sires: whereas Thoroughbreds had initially accounted for about half the matings, percentages dropped to about 15 per cent in the early 1980s.[39] Yet when confronted with the disappointing results of this trend, WPN inspectors concluded that the Thoroughbred continued to be needed to enhance stamina and galloping power – possibly even in the long run.[40]

Preferences in terms of blood percentage were also influenced by external factors. In the 1980s, for instance, animal welfare considerations brought about a change in show jumping, beginning with the Olympic equestrian events in Los Angeles in 1984. It had been customary until then to build courses with ever higher and broader obstacles that tested the horses to the utmost of their physical capabilities. The new approach was to design courses with fences that were not as high and were less dangerous. Instead, they required swiftness and well-planned strides and turns. Agility and speed thus replaced extreme jumping power, and horses with more blood appeared to be better suited for this purpose.[41] This again shows that the WPN could not set a fixed standard for the Dutch riding horse, nor did it wish to do so. Some inspectors preferred to talk about a European riding horse, which was certainly more in line with the multinational descent of most of the WPN-bred animals.[42]

A final change in the WPN's breeding policy came in the early 1980s, and its implementation was anything but smooth. The revision exposed a profound conflict between the breeding society and the government, and it set the stage for science to play a lasting role in the WPN's breeding practices.

## The Government Intervenes

In the mid-1970s, the Ministry of Agriculture and Fisheries commissioned a discussion report on Dutch equine husbandry.[43] Unlike most other sectors of animal husbandry, particularly the cattle, pig, and poultry industries, the horse business had remained relatively free from government interference until then.[44] The report appeared in 1977 and sketched a pitiful image of the sector. Although it had grown considerably in the preceding decade, many of those engaged in it – such as owners of riding schools, riding instructors, horse trainers, and breeders – hardly managed to earn a decent income. Most breeders were hobbyists whose objectives did not even include making a profit. The vast majority were farmers, and the report emphasized that they in particular should aim to turn their breeding activities into a profitable sideline. To this end, the report recommended making breeding practices more scientific.

For Warmblood breeders, the situation sketched in the report was aggravated by the economic recession that gripped the Netherlands in the second half of the 1970s. Horse sales stagnated and after 1974 the number of newborn foals dropped steadily. By 1978, the number of inseminations had fallen by 30 per cent and when the market finally stabilized in the mid-1980s, inseminations were down by 50 per cent.[45] Since most mare owners were hobbyists, their livelihoods were not threatened by the economic downturn. However, it was more serious for the stallion owners: even though very few of them depended on their horses for their living, most sought to earn extra income through providing stud services.[46]

The WPN reacted to the report by announcing in early 1978 that it would partner in a study with the Ministry and other equestrian organizations, to gauge the need for and viability of a national horse-breeding centre that, among other things, would promote national and international sales of Warmblood horses.[47] Soon after, however, the minister of agriculture, Fons van der Stee, a farmer's son and an avid rider himself,[48] and Theo Vos, also a farmer's son and the Ministry's deputy director general, decided to take matters into their own hands. Vos in particular would put his stamp on the ensuing course of events. In a previous job, as an animal scientist at Wageningen Agricultural University, he had played a major role in the transformation of dairy cattle breeding in the Netherlands. Vos had assisted animal breeding professor Rommert Politiek in introducing index breeding in Dutch dairy farming in the early 1970s. Horse breeding should take a similar course, Vos argued in two articles in the breeding journal *In de Strengen* and at several WPN meetings. In the poultry industry, he expounded, commercial companies had taken over the business of breeding completely by following a strictly scientific approach, and the same would have happened in pig breeding, had the pig breeders' societies not changed course in time by also adopting scientific breeding methods. It was not too late for the horse breeders' societies to awaken from their slumber and to give up – in Vos's words – their manifest aversion to measuring and calculating their animals' performance. The time-honoured sire-selection method based on quality of conformation had to be replaced by systematic progeny testing and selection for performance.

The WPN should take the dairy cattle breeders as an example, Vos continued. They had managed to keep control over bull breeding thanks to their high level of organization in cooperative breeding associations. Horse breeders had never been organized into cooperatives, but now was the time to catch up. Progeny testing was a costly procedure, and only by establishing cooperatives could small breeders muster the necessary means to implement it successfully. Another crucial element in scientific breeding, again as demonstrated by the cattle breeders, was the use of artificial insemination, which enabled the use of the best sires on a worldwide scale. In this respect especially horse breeding lagged behind, as AI had only just begun to play a role in it.[49] Underlining the necessity, the inevitability even, of the proposed reforms, Vos professed: "Horse breeding will not be able to avoid what has happened in chicken, pig and cattle breeding. This development cannot be reversed, and neither can the use of AI."[50]

The WPN board, now led by the veterinarian Gerrit van der Mey, responded to Vos's call to action by initiating talks with the Ministry. The tone was positive at first, and the board applauded the government's intent to stimulate the sector. They again discussed the idea of a national horse-breeding centre, in which the WPN and other equestrian organizations would participate. But the atmosphere soured when it appeared that the Ministry had also begun consultations with Léon Melchior, a Maastricht millionaire who had earned his fortune as a contractor and developer, and who owned a large stud farm named Zangersheide.[51]

In Vos and Van der Stee's opinion, Melchior's breeding methods were exemplary. At Zangersheide, he closely followed the dairy cattle breeding system by subjecting his stallions to rigorous progeny testing. When a promising young stallion was sexually mature, at the age of two or three, he was to inseminate a limited number of about twenty mares. Then he was put on hold, so to speak: until data became available about the quality of his offspring, he was not to mate with any more mares. In the meantime, he was used as a sport horse, which also provided information about his qualities as a sire. When he had reached the age of eight or nine, the merits of his offspring became decisive in determining his future as a stud horse.[52]

Vos and Van der Stee felt that, implemented on a national scale, this system would transform Dutch horse breeding into a science and give it a rational foundation as a commercial enterprise. In consultation with Melchior, they developed plans for an experiment station and a stud farm in which the government, Melchior, and, hopefully, the WPN breeders would participate to improve the Dutch riding horse and its marketability. Melchior was to bring a couple of excellent sires and some 400 mares into the joint enterprise. (In comparison, Dutch breeders at the time owned fewer than two mares on average.)[53] Furthermore, facilities were envisaged for rearing, training, and selling horses, and for scientific research on artificial insemination, nutrition, grassland management, and the like.[54] The WPN breeders were invited to become partners in the breeding program.

President Van der Mey and the WPN were unpleasantly surprised by the government's course of action. In their view, despite protestations to the contrary by Minister Van der Stee, the partnership with Melchior implied that the government would become a competitor in the field of Warmblood breeding.[55] The WPN breeders, particularly the stallion owners – about eighty – would be pushed out of business if the plans were put in effect. Horse breeding had always been a small-scale, private activity, in which profit had been subordinate to the pleasure some 10,000 mare owners derived from their hobby. The ministerial plans, according to Van der Mey, were too centralist and went against the grain of what really mattered in the Warmblood breeding world. The board was still willing to cooperate, but stated firmly that the WPN would end negotiations if the government were to become a competitor of the stallion owners.[56]

Van der Stee, Vos, and Melchior pressed on, however. Another impetus for their plans derived from Van der Stee's vision of a wider initiative to stimulate employment in an economically weak region, the southern part of the province of Limburg. Besides the breeding station, Van der Stee also planned the construction of a racecourse in the province, with stables and training and other facilities for racehorses and their owners. Horse racing and betting on horses had never enjoyed great popularity in the Netherlands, yet Van der Stee believed that the sport had the potential to develop into a profitable business. It might improve regional employment and bring in revenues to finance the projected equine breeding and research station.[57]

Misgivings about these plans were not only voiced by WPN breeders. The president of the federation of Dutch equestrian sports organizations (*Nederlandse Hippische Sportbond*) also criticized them for being centralist and for focusing on the commercial aspects of horse breeding, failing to acknowledge that horseback riding was, first and foremost, a recreational sport. The *Landbouwschap*, the national agricultural board, warned that establishing a state stud farm might force out many small studs. This would jeopardize the availability of the wide variety of bloodlines that was needed for breeding riding horses.[58] After the minister's intentions had been detailed in a policy document in early 1980, members of Parliament also began to question them. They heckled the minister about what they saw as an undesirable intrusion into the private business of horse breeding. Furthermore, they felt that the plans' vagueness precluded an assessment of their financial soundness.[59]

Meanwhile, the WPN consulted its members in the regional branches of the society about the ministerial plans.[60] Newspapers reported about heated meetings of stallion owners, with one headline in a national newspaper proclaiming that the horse breeders were at war with the Ministry.[61] Stallion owners also voiced their concerns in *In de Strengen*.[62] The unfair competition implicated by the partnership with Melchior and the threat to their independence formed the core of their grievances. Their agitation only grew when it was suggested that Melchior might establish his own studbook if the WPN refused to register the horses to be bred at the Limburg experiment station.[63] It did not help either that Melchior was unwilling to subject his stallions to the regular WPN sire-approval procedure; in his view, rigorous exterior evaluation was superfluous.[64] The dispute reached its climax on 19 June 1980, when the WPN organized a protest rally at the *Binnenhof*, the Dutch parliament building, where President Van der Mey read a petition that emphasized that horse breeding should remain the domain of small-scale private enterprises (Figure 5.3).[65]

As a result of the opposition, a new round of parliamentary consultations on the Limburg project was scheduled for early September. It

Figure 5.3. WPN members demanding more scope for their hobby at the *Binnenhof*, the Dutch parliament building. From *In de Strengen* 47, no. 13 (1980): extra pages, II.

was forestalled, however, in early July 1980 when Melchior announced his withdrawal from the partnership with the government, saying that he was sick and tired of being kept in suspense.[66] This necessitated a major revision of the Ministry's plans. By then, Van der Stee had been succeeded by Gerrit Braks as minister of agriculture, who took a different view of the subject.[67] Acknowledging that horse breeding should remain a small-scale activity, he presented a new version of his predecessor's plans in which the government would restrict its involvement to research, education, and information – the regular instruments to support agriculture. The goal would remain to help the horse-breeding sector to escape from its marginal position, but there would be no state stud. Instead, Braks opted for an experiment station for equine husbandry, which would conduct research on subjects such as artificial insemination, equine diseases, stable design, and nutrition. He also planned a rearing and training centre as well as facilities to promote the export of sports horses. Funding would have to be partly provided by the stakeholders in the horse industry, as was also customary in other sectors.[68]

This resolved the main issue that had provoked the WPN's opposition to the government. There was some further wrangle over three stallions the government had bought from Melchior, which WPN breeders were invited to use, but after some time peace was restored in the horse-breeding world.[69] In the end, Van der Stee's original project was to be realized only to a very limited extent, because lack of funds forced Minister Braks to scale down his reduced plan even further. The experiment station (*Dienstencentrum Proefbedrijf Paardenhouderij Nederland*) was indeed established in Merkelbeek, in the province of Limburg, and the projected research on AI quickly gained momentum there.[70] Also, a start was made with offering rearing accommodation for young stallions. Yet the proposed extension to include training, information, and sales facilities was not realized; neither the breeders nor businesses had shown sufficient interest in participating.[71] On top of it all, the racecourse that was part of Van der Stee's wider project for the region and that opened in 1980 proved unprofitable. After a hopeful beginning, the public's interest dwindled rapidly, and the revenues never lived up to expectations. Ultimately, after years of accumulating deficits, it had to be closed down.[72] Thus, the betting revenues expected to support the experiment station never emerged, and its activities had to be scaled down.

The only activity that generated some returns was the AI station, where researchers collected data by making the stallions bought from Melchior available to WPN breeders. Even though his semen was twice as expensive as that of an average stud, mare owners happily made use of the insemination services offered by Ramiro Z, a Holsteiner sire of proven quality whose offspring showed their mettle in both show jumping and dressage. When the experiment station was scaled down in 1982, these services were suspended and two years later Ramiro was transferred to a private stallion station elsewhere in the country, where he continued his services. He was to have a long-lasting influence on the WPN breeding program.[73]

While it may appear that the Ministry's initiative to stimulate horse breeding had only a very limited effect, its indirect effect was more significant. Between 1979 and 1981, the years of the Melchior affair, the WPN board announced a number of what were called "historic" adjustments to its breeding strategy and methods. Most of these had been under consideration for quite some time, but their implementation was hastened by the pressure the government put on the WPN.

## Scientific Breeding

In the 1970s, after the WPN had once and for all given up on preserving the farm horse, it had defined producing good saddle horses as its new breeding goal. Besides the traditional inspection of stallions on the basis of their conformation, gaits, and character, their performance as riding horses was given increasing weight, while other characteristics, such as pulling capacity, lost their usefulness. After extensive deliberation, a new testing procedure was adopted in 1978, which included a 100-day period of training and testing of three-year-old stallions. Core components of the evaluation were soundness of conformation and gaits, talent for jumping and dressage, willingness to work, and docility. Selection for conformation and movements was intense: less than 10 per cent of the stallions offered for inspection were admitted to the 100-day test after the external examination. Stallions that passed the test were, after a final examination by the inspectors, entered into the studbook, yet only for a restricted time. Sport performance data that became available over the years, both on the sires themselves and on their offspring, were taken into account during periodical reassessments of their stud-worthiness.[74]

Sport data were not yet collected systematically in the Netherlands, in contrast to France and Germany. Therefore, such assessments remained rather haphazard. In 1978, however, at the time when Vos was presenting his views on scientific breeding to the WPN breeders, discussions in *In de Strengen* generally acknowledged the need for systematic recording of sport data.[75] For instance, in a debate over whether precedence should be given to either conformation or performance, one of the most influential figures within the WPN, Piet van Binsbergen, the chairman of the stallions inspection committee, stepped forward and stated his opinion that, even though conformation and comportment were important, stallions should ultimately be judged on the basis of their performance.[76]

Five years before, in 1973, consultations had begun between the WPN and the federation of Dutch equestrian sports organizations, NHS, to link the studbook data of all stallions to their own and their progeny's performance in sports by computer.[77] Initially, the project came to nothing. Even though the Ministry of Agriculture had offered financial assistance, the costs of the operation were deemed prohibitive, and the initiative was shelved, much to the Ministry's dismay.[78] In June 1979, however, the WPN announced that new consultations with the NHS had been successfully completed, and that a computer had been acquired to store and process performance data.[79] In early June 1980, just when the controversy with the Ministry was nearing its climax, the

WPN formally declared that breeding for performance would henceforth be the society's breeding goal. The computer began operating in December 1980 and the first data on WPN breeding sires and their progeny were published in 1983.[80] A few years later, the Utrecht animal scientist Huub Huizinga converted the data into indexes quantifying the stallions' breeding value.[81]

While the WPN's decision to evaluate stallions on the basis of their performance was the final piece in the society's recent reform of its testing procedure, it was also an acknowledgement of Vos's critique that a focus on performance rather than conformation was needed to rescue horse breeding from its marginal economic position. In his yearly report, President Van der Mey indeed underlined that stallion owners should set their sights on quality of performance to overcome the difficult period they were experiencing.[82] Quality paid, *In de Strengen* affirmed: even in times when overall sales were low, the truly good WPN horses remained in high demand on the international market.[83]

On top of this change in breeding policy, the WPN board introduced an optional selection system, in which a stallion, after a restricted number of test matings, was not to be used for breeding until data about his progeny became available.[84] This system by and large was a copy of Melchior's breeding method, the only difference being that the WPN retained exterior and character evaluation as key elements of the testing procedure. As it turned out, however, WPN breeders showed no interest in this option, and it never got off the ground. The system's downside had in fact been pointed out by the WPN board itself during the altercations over Melchior's breeding method: during his waiting period, a stallion brought in less money, and when the results of his progeny finally came in, they might make an eight- or nine-year investment almost worthless.[85] Raising a colt was expensive enough, two stallion owners explained in *In de Strengen*, and the waiting period would simply be unaffordable for small breeders.[86]

Another development that was already under way but was clearly facilitated by the government's intervention was the introduction of artificial insemination. While breeders had occasionally experimented with the technique since the late nineteenth century, its use remained marginal until the 1980s. AI in horses faced numerous complications. There was considerable variability in sperm quality and quantity between stallions; fresh semen was short-lived and therefore difficult to transport; preparing frozen semen was complicated; determining the right moment for inseminating a mare required much experience; and in the end, success percentages, especially with frozen semen, were much lower than in dairy cattle breeding.[87]

Until the 1980s, most stallion owners saw little reason to adopt the technique. They had the same reservations as their colleagues in Thoroughbred breeding, who continue to prohibit the use of AI today, purportedly to prevent excessively using a small number of top stallions. Yet, obviously, economic considerations play a major role: the limited availability of a top sire's semen keeps the prices of both the animal and its semen high.[88]

The WPN never considered such an absolute ban on AI, yet their regulations were strict. For instance, a veterinarian had to perform the insemination; natural service was no longer permitted for AI stallions; and in 1979, the WPN board limited the number of yearly inseminations per stallion to 250, a number a fertile stallion could also realize by natural service.[89] A calculation in *In de Strengen* in 1982 suggested that, given the limitations and regulations, natural mating was still more efficient, economically as well as practically, than artificial insemination.[90] Moreover, bringing the mare and the stallion together rarely posed problems in a small country such as the Netherlands. Overall, there was little incentive for the use and technical improvement of AI in the Dutch context.

Again, the government's dealings with Melchior prepared the ground for a turnaround. The state-stallions that the government had bought from Melchior were available to WPN breeders for AI only. Inseminations with semen from Ramiro Z proved to have an especially high success rate and, as noted, breeders eagerly seized the opportunity to make use of this excellent sire's services. Researchers at the Merkelbeek equine experiment station, in collaboration with veterinarians from Utrecht University, investigated how best to collect, dilute, freeze, and transport horse semen, and they learned how to obtain satisfying success rates. In 1984, when Ramiro Z was transferred to a private AI station, WPN stallion owners began to feel they might miss the boat. In the same year, veterinarian Hans Uwland, a pioneer of AI in dairy cattle, and three stallion owners set up an AI station in Lexmond, in the province of Gelderland, an event described in *In de Strengen* as a "milestone in the history of horse breeding."[91]

While the number of stallion owners who embraced AI began to grow, mare owners were hesitant to follow suit. Apparently their interest in Ramiro Z did not imply an interest in AI as such. On top of this, the private stations found it difficult to match the success rates the experienced AI researchers at Merkelbeek had obtained with Ramiro Z semen. The station in Lexmond was not a commercial success and had to close its doors after two years. The situation changed suddenly in 1987, however, when the extremely contagious venereal disease CEM (contagious equine metritis) was diagnosed for the first time in the Netherlands.[92]

AI became the spearhead of the veterinary program set up to contain the spread of this disease. The regulations for its use were relaxed and the costs reduced, resulting in mare owners swiftly adopting AI. By 1993, AI accounted for 80 per cent of all inseminations in the Netherlands.[93]

A final development within the WPN on which the government's intervention had a catalyzing effect was the society's reorientation from catering to the needs of the national market of leisure riders to those of the international market for sport horses. In the 1970s, the society saw recreational riders as the principal target market; they were estimated to account for about 80 per cent of the horses sold at the time. Sport horses, making up about 5 per cent, were difficult to select for as long as pedigree and performance data were not linked; they were seen as a by-product.[94] When the WPN redefined its breeding goal as breeding for performance, however, it redirected its focus to the production of sport horses, for which demand exceeded supply, nationally and internationally. Now recreational horses became the by-product, although they would continue to constitute the majority of the horses bred, because only a small percentage of them had the talent to make it as a sport horse. By focusing on breeding for performance, the WPN clearly hoped to get the best of both worlds: a better chance for the stallion breeders to profit from the rising international market for sport horses, as well as better horses for the leisure riders.[95]

This reorientation signalled the beginning of the WPN's rise to international prominence as a sport-horse breeding society. It entailed increasing specialization, in that dressage horses and jumping horses became separate breeding lines. It also resulted in an ever closer cooperation with animal scientists, whose methods for quantitative assessment of performance and index calculation enabled the specialization. As in cattle breeding, the evaluation of conformation ultimately also came under the regime of quantitative assessment.[96]

The WPN's new breeding policy would in due course be accompanied by a major change in the social background of the society's membership, as breeding would cease to be a predominantly agrarian activity. The international world of competitive horse breeding and sports is now dominated by affluent people from outside agriculture, among whom, not coincidentally, Léon Melchior was a major figure until his death in 2015. There is no indication that the WPN foresaw this development in the period discussed here, and it was certainly not intended by Theo Vos and the Dutch government, whose principal objective had been to develop horse breeding into a profitable sideline for farmers.

In the early 1980s, when all this was still far away, the WPN board confidently declared in *In de Strengen* that its mission to transform the

Dutch farm horse into a riding horse was complete. The result was not, nor had it been planned to be, a uniform new breed. Like the Gelderlander and the Groninger, the Dutch saddle horse was a performance type. There continued to be much variability among the mares: some of the classical Gelderlanders were still around, many were half-bloods, and an increasing number had varying percentages of Thoroughbred blood. Therefore, a wide variety of bloodlines was needed when it came to the sires, and they had to be chosen individually by the mare breeders. The Thoroughbred remained indispensable for consolidating the riding horse characteristics of the population as a whole. Thus, if anything, flexibility was a defining characteristic of Dutch Warmblood breeding, and finding the right mix was the secret of breeding a good horse.[97] The WPN switched to breeding for performance, yet the society held on to judging prospective sires on the basis of some of the typical characteristics of the farm horse: soundness of conformation and movement, and tractability.

## Balancing Practical and Scientific Methods

As we have seen, "purity" became the hallmark of successful breeding in cattle, chicken, pig, and sheep breeding in the early twentieth century. Purity implied uniformity: the offspring produced by purebred breeding stock were of predictable quality, and Mendelism explained why this was so. In Warmblood breeding, however, there was no such focus on purity. The versatility of purpose that was gained by judicious crossing was deemed more important than uniformity. Breeding was a balancing act, and Mendelism was of no help in making breeding decisions.

Ideas on purity in livestock and pets were linked to conceptions of class and race in humans, as many authors have shown in detail. To give an example pertaining to horse breeding: Phillip Thurtle has argued that, in reaction to aristocratic Thoroughbred breeders for whom purity was sacrosanct, self-made American businessmen in the Gilded Age bred their trotters for performance only; their selection method was based on competition, not pedigree, and it epitomized a new definition of social excellence.[98] The cultural contingency of such connections is highlighted by the fact that many Dutch Warmblood breeders, being farmers, also kept purebred dairy cows: while they strongly adhered to the ideal of purity in cattle breeding, they did not care for purity in their farm horses. Then again, the only Dutch purebred horse, the Friesian, was created in the province that was also the cradle of the purebred black-and-white dairy cow, and both breeds became icons of Friesian regional identity.[99]

When scientists entered the field of Warmblood breeding in the Netherlands, the transformation of the farm horse was, by and large, complete. As with other livestock species, scientists assisted famers in rationalizing the breeding process by means of AI, progeny testing, and index calculations. The WPN's response to the Ministry's plan for a scientific overhaul of Warmblood breeding shows, once again, that the agency of the farmers was an important factor in shaping the practical effects of the government's agricultural modernization project. Minister Van der Stee and Deputy Director General Vos's initiative illustrates how agricultural scientists and the Dutch Ministry of Agriculture worked together to bring this modernization about. After graduating from Wageningen University and having worked as a staff member in Politiek's animal science department for seven years before entering the Ministry in 1977, Vos would ultimately return to his alma mater in 1990 as president of the executive board. He thus exemplifies the strong personal ties that cemented the discourse coalition between the university and the Ministry.[100] For both Van der Stee and Vos, the idea of modernization through science had an intrinsic logic. In their view, it was inevitable that scientific methods such as progeny testing and AI would be introduced in horse breeding, if not by the WPN, then by commercial companies. Vos in particular was convinced that what had happened in dairy cattle, pig, and poultry breeding, would and should also take place in horse breeding.

Convincing the breeders of the inevitability of scientific modernization was more difficult than Vos had imagined, however. "Oh boy, have I underestimated the resistance that Melchior would evoke," he sighed, looking back on the episode in a later interview.[101] Seen from the farmers' perspective, however, the reasons for this resistance were obvious. For one, the establishment of a state-sponsored stud farm was considered unfair competition. Even more important, Vos's avowed model for his reform plan was dairy cattle breeding, in which the bull breeders had been pushed out of business by farmers' cooperatives. Unsurprisingly, the Warmblood stallion breeders were unwilling to take part in a scheme that threatened to undermine part of their livelihood. Contrary to Vos's prediction, however, the stallion owners were not destined for the same fate that had befallen the bull breeders: they successfully repelled the attack on their small-scale enterprises.

Van der Stee and Vos similarly misjudged the willingness of the mare owners to form cooperatives. There had never been cooperative horse breeders' associations. The main reason, I suggest, was the absence of a common breeding goal. In dairy cattle breeding it made sense to collectively exploit a bull, since cattle were bred pure and there were clear-cut standards for a good bull. Warmbloods, on the contrary, were produced by mixing blood, and for the mare owners the availability of a wide variety of stallions took precedence over the advantages of collectivization. Furthermore, the dairying crisis of the late sixties put the dairy cattle farmers under severe pressure. Their economic survival was at stake, and increasing milk production seemed an absolute necessity to rescue their business. Collectively testing bulls for performance and index breeding, as propagated by animal scientists, offered them a way out of their predicament. Mare owners experienced no such urgency, because they did not depend on their horses for their living. Their voices were hardly heard during the Melchior episode, and they seem to have resigned themselves to just sitting out the adverse economic circumstances of the late 1970s.

Mare owners were similarly unimpressed by Vos's insistence on the necessity of AI. Until the mid-1980s they saw no pressing need for it, as it appeared to offer no advantages over natural service. When they began to adopt AI in the late 1980s, it was not for breed improvement, but to fight a highly contagious disease. There is a parallel with cattle breeding here: dairy farmers massively embraced AI in the 1940s, when venereal diseases spread by natural mating had become a major threat. Only in the 1970s would AI become important as a breed improvement technology in dairy cattle.

Because of its timing – at the peak of the Melchior affair – the WPN's endorsement of breeding for performance can partly be seen as a genuflection to the Ministry's urging in favour of scientific breeding. The WPN thus professed to show that it was already practising what the Ministry preached and therefore could do without its intervention. At the same time, the WPN's change of breeding strategy was an acknowledgement of the economic pressure that the stallion owners were under: the market was at a low ebb, but good sport horses continued to be in high demand. Furthermore, it should be kept in mind that the WPN had not been averse to making use of performance data in the 1970s, and it was already moving in this direction of its own accord, as the efforts to link pedigree and sports performance data in these years show. Finally, the WPN did not relax its selection for conformation and gaits, as a result of which only about 10 per cent of the stallions submitted for admittance to the studbook were actually tested for performance. So in its practical effects, the change in breeding strategy was not as dramatic as it might seem at first glance.

Similarly, the WPN's decision to allow its members to test stallions by means of the waiting system deployed by cattle breeders was obviously prompted by the Melchior affair. However, one may wonder whether this was anything but a token gesture, as the board had earlier pointed out that it was too expensive for the average breeder. The stallion breeders indeed remained singularly uninterested in this option.

In sum, the reactions of the WPN breeders to the government's campaign for scientific breeding cannot be said to have been dictated by the suggested logic or necessity of modernization through science. The breeders reacted to specific pressures, economic or otherwise, rather than to the call to modernize their practices. Nor can it be said that the government enforced its modernization policy on the farmers. As we have seen, the WPN made its own decisions and successfully warded off unwanted interventions. All this is not to deny, however, that science-based breeding technologies became an important factor in the reorientation that the WPN underwent from the early 1980s onwards. Once the WPN was able to systematically link pedigree and sports data, breeding for performance could be rationalized using index calculation, for which quantitative genetics provided the tools. Indexes, in turn, enabled specialization: on the basis of their performance, show jumpers and dressage horses could be specifically selected for, which had been well-nigh impossible on the basis of conformation only. Similarly, AI technology in horses was researched with government support at a time when the breeders showed little interest in it, and it was ready for use when the breeders were compelled to adopt it to fight contagious equine metritis. Once it had become the default reproduction method, and after frozen sperm technology had been improved, AI would also become a breeding tool that enabled the worldwide use of the best sires.

There was no sign among the breeders of a dislike of calculating, as Vos had put it, or of scientific methods more generally. Breeders welcomed new technologies if they fit into their breeding practices and if the advantages were clear to them. The reason for their opposition was the government's intrusion into their breeding culture, which did not lend itself to being restructured along the lines of the cattle-breeding model, and in which other considerations, besides making a profit, played a role. Horse breeding practices would in the end become scientific, yet the tenets of agricultural "modernization" are of little help to understand how this came about.

# Conclusions

In a 1975 review of pig breeding methods, the Danish animal scientist Per Jonsson noted: "It is a well-known fact that the animal geneticist Jay L. Lush has developed the biometrical methods to maximize the improvement in practical animal production through breeding ... The story of the trend in pig improvement through breeding in the European countries is, therefore, related to the extent to which the pig industries in the different countries in Europe were ready to utilize these tools to maximize the improvement of their products through breeding." Commercial pig breeders saw things differently, Jonsson continued: "[They] will claim that pig improvement through breeding is a skill." However, they were mistaken: in Jonsson's view, the maximization of pig improvement depended on "(1) the ability of the industry to define its market demands (product traits); (2) the ability of the breeding authorities to utilize the breeding theory to improve these production traits; and (3) the ability of the breeders to follow the directions of their authorities."[1]

Not even geneticist Arend Hagedoorn, the determined champion of the scientific approach to breeding, would have contrasted traditional breeding and scientific breeding in such stark terms. Hagedoorn readily acknowledged that the breeders' practical skills and experience were an indispensable starting point for scientists to develop effective breeding strategies. On the other hand, he would doubtlessly have agreed with Jonsson that real progress was only to be made on the basis of scientific insight and that scientists should take the lead in livestock breeding. Hagedoorn's colleagues in animal breeding science would have concurred.

It is beyond dispute that quantitative genetics has changed the face of animal breeding; it formed the foundation for the tremendous growth in production that most sectors of livestock husbandry saw in the second half of the twentieth century. Nevertheless, this book has shown that the story was not nearly as straightforward as Jonsson purported and as Hagedoorn would have liked. For one thing, as the chapter on sheep breeding has shown, the quantitative approach did not always work. Breeding by numbers is predicated on the numbers being available in sufficient quantities, which the Dutch sheep sector was not prepared to deliver. Second, even if the quantitative approach did work, it did not necessarily satisfy all parties involved. Durk Minkema's decision to focus on improving meat quality in pigs worked out well for the slaughterhouses, yet the multipliers were much less pleased with the results, because they were more interested in enhancing their pigs' fertility. Jonsson's claim that market demands should determine the direction of breeding ignored these conflicts between the interests of the sector as a whole, from which Minkema had taken his lead, and those of the breeders. We encountered a similar example in dairy cattle breeding: Rommert Politiek's campaign to preserve the red-and-white dairy cow as a dual-purpose type to safeguard the national beef supply fell on deaf ears among the breeders, who had every reason to believe they could make more money by turning their red and whites into specialized milk producers. Third, the animals themselves posed limits to what quantitative genetics could accomplish: meat quality and fertility cannot be simultaneously selected for in chickens and pigs, and neither can meat and milk production in dairy cattle.

The idea that market demands should guide the direction breeding was to take is problematic for another reason as well: such demands might conflict with breeding goals. In the 1950s and 1960s, it was crystal clear to Politiek that dairy farmers should strive to increase both the production and the productivity of their cows, implying that the principal criterion for the evaluation of bulls was their hereditary capacity for milk production. Yet the breeders had different criteria for a good breeding bull, which did not include passing on a high hereditary potential for milk production. Consequently, Politiek's advice was ignored by the breeders for many years. Leading Texel sheep breeders similarly valued the particulars of a ram's conformation more highly than his growth index. And horse breeders rejected the government's plan for the economic reinvigoration of their sector because they did not accept the assumption underlying it: that a standard of excellence could be defined for stallions. In their view, a stallion's suitability as a sire depended as much on the mare's characteristics as his own.

In the case of dairy cattle and Texel sheep, the disagreement over breeding goals was directly related to the breeders' concern with what I have called brand features. In the period investigated here, most scientists showed themselves to be strikingly insensitive to this concern.

From their perspective, brand characteristics were nothing more than show points if they had no relation to an animal's merit in terms of production. Breeding for show could easily deteriorate into hobbyism, Hagedoorn stressed time and again. Scientists thus largely ignored the commercial significance of branding. For the breeders, however, the typical features of their animals were the tell-tale signs of quality, no matter how contingent the relation between such characteristics and productive traits might be. The aesthetic qualities of their best animals were no mere luxury: they paid off on the market for breeding stock. This explains why the tendency to exaggerate typical characteristics was second nature to many breeders, yet we have also seen that economic considerations prevailed in the end. In dairy cattle as well as Texel sheep, the trend towards sturdier-looking animals was reversed when their peculiarities of conformation were no longer seen as contributing positively to their market value.

While Texel breeders were aware that some of the distinguishing features of their sheep came at a cost – lambing problems, for instance – beauty of conformation was not just a marketing issue for the dairy farmers. The Friesian black and whites' characteristic traits were seen as causally related to their productive qualities. A beautiful cow was a good cow, because aesthetic qualities reflected the constitution of their animals and thus the qualities the farmers valued most. Breeding was a long-term endeavour whose guiding principles were the safeguarding of disease resistance, easy maintenance, and reliable production. Cows that met these requirements looked decidedly more robust than high-bred milk specialists, and their well-marked conformation was the visible expression of their productive value.

This is not to say that there was no element of hobbyism to breeding at all. While almost all scientific experts used the term in a derogatory fashion, Politiek's predecessor Wieger de Jong acknowledged that many farmers derived their joy in farming from breeding animals that did well in shows; breeding might even lose its attraction without this incentive. Therefore it was acceptable to reserve some selection space for show points, according to De Jong. Breeding for beauty was a form of creative expression and a source of professional pride for the breeders, and owning eye-catching animals lent prestige to the famers, who were willing to pay extra to acquire them. The line between hobby breeding and commercial breeding was thin indeed in some cases. The breeding of riding horses was in fact both, mare owners being more on the hobby side, stallion breeders more on the commercial side. Thus, the Ministry's plan to turn horse breeding into a profitable sideline held little appeal for the mare owners, yet it did help to speed up the breeders' society's plans to calculate indexes for the stallions' performance in sports. In Texel breeding, commercial interests were more important, yet smallholders predominated in the sector, and for some of them the hobby aspect prevailed, as demonstrated by the small group of breeders who established their own society to preserve the "luxury type."

James McAllister has argued that ideas on "beauty" in science find their origin in functionality: what is found to be functional or useful is likely to become perceived as aesthetically appealing.[2] A similar mechanism can be seen in breeding practices. For instance, the well-rounded Modern Friesian that was developed to remedy the constitutional weakness of the earlier dairy type became an icon of "nobility." And while Dutch breeders at first found the gawky Holsteins downright ugly, they began to appreciate the well-marked dairy-type features of the American cows once they had embraced them for their greater productivity. Beauty might even acquire a cultural and commercial value of its own that gained precedence over functionality. Even though the breeders of the Modern Friesian and the luxury Texels became increasingly aware of the drawbacks of their extreme types, they would not change their breeding goals as long as their animals sold well. The breeders thus negotiated functional, commercial, and aesthetic considerations in making their breeding decisions.

Most scientists were not only indifferent to issues of branding and breeding for show, they also framed the debate on the value of conformation in different terms: for them, the dispute was first and foremost over breeding methods, in which the breeders' traditional methods entered the lists against the experts' scientific methods. Yet methods were not the principal issue for the dairy cattle breeders. Although their rhetoric in defence of their breeding culture sometimes suggested otherwise, they did not object to quantitative methods as such and used them whenever they saw the benefits – for instance, milk recording was successfully introduced in the early twentieth century. They had a different breeding goal, however, and they considered their skills and experience in evaluating conformation to be essential in maintaining the type that served their purposes best. The situation was similar in horse and sheep breeding. Mare owners saw no advantages in the dairy cattle model of index breeding that the government tried to impose on them, because they had a different idea of what constituted a good stallion. A number of the sheep breeders were willing to give the quantitative approach a try, yet they did not like the conformation of the animals produced by the index and AI programs. While they agreed with the experts that some of the Texel's type characteristics had disadvantages, they lost confidence in the scientific program to remedy them and showed that their own approach, based on the breeder's eye, could successfully accomplish the task without compromising the Texel's defining features.

Only in this last example can a traditional breeding method be said to have competed with the quantitative scientific approach. Generally speaking, however, the scientists' tendency to juxtapose art and science in breeding does little justice to the actual changes that took place in twentieth-century livestock breeding. Breeders adopted new scientific techniques if the advantages were clear to them. In most sectors, farmers readily embraced AI as an effective remedy against contagious diseases. They were much more hesitant to deploy AI as a breed improvement technology, because conflicts between breeding goals might arise. Dairy farmers and horse breeders saw no need for AI as long as it failed to deliver the kinds of animals they preferred. The multipliers in pig farming initially saw no benefits in AI either, since the AI boars were not selected for fertility. When they did adopt the technique in the mid-1970s, it was for reasons of management rather than breed improvement. The pig and chicken breeders proper, on the other hand, willingly embraced AI as an aid to improving their stock.

Furthermore, practical breeding methods, such as external evaluation, in which the breeder's eye played a prominent role, cannot be said to have been supplanted or superseded by scientific approaches. In all sectors of livestock breeding, the evaluation of conformation remained an indispensable first step in the selection of potential breeding stock. Functional criteria – a well-built frame, absence of defects, and sound gaits – came to prevail more and more, but they had always been important. While various point systems to objectify external evaluation were introduced from the early twentieth century onwards, qualities such as "soundness," "general appearance," or "gaits" had an indelibly subjective component, and their evaluation required the skills, experience, and talent encompassed by the breeder's eye. New tools, such as the backfat measurement device for pigs and conformation indexes, supplemented the judges' verdict but could not replace it. For instance, less than 10 per cent of the stallions that were signed up annually for the 100-day performance test made it to the actual test; the rest of them were rejected on the grounds of insufficient quality of conformation.

The word "method" was used by scientists as well as breeders in a rather indiscriminate way in the context of breeding practices. It might refer to technical tools such as AI, milk recording, and point systems, but also to the different mating systems breeders deployed in selective breeding, such as purebred breeding, inbreeding, crossing, hybrid breeding, and breeding up, and finally to the various forms of selection, such as individual selection, mass selection, and progeny testing. The loose use of the term is understandable. Quantitative genetics, for instance, is often based on progeny testing – a selection method – but it also characteristically provides mathematical and statistical tools to make selection more efficient. And some form of selection is involved in all "methods" to improve a population of farm animals. It is important, however, to unravel what was meant by "the scientific approach" and "scientific methods" if we want to assess what it was, exactly, that scientists contributed to animal breeding practices.

Selection had of course been used by breeders – intentionally and unintentionally, as Charles Darwin rightly noted – for centuries. Progeny testing was explicated in detail by Robert Bakewell in the late eighteenth century, but the principle had been known for a long time. The mating systems deployed by breeders had also been in use since at least the late eighteenth century. Bakewell "purified" his animals by breeding them in-and-in, and the method of purebred breeding was firmly established by the mid-nineteenth century. Experienced breeders were familiar with the heterosis effect that emerged in crossbreds, and they also knew how to breed up their herd to a different variety, or how to create a new variety by using crossbreeding, inbreeding, and selection.

Scientists introduced new combinations and refinements of such mating systems. Hybrid chicken and pig breeding did not involve fundamentally new breeding principles but combined inbreeding, crossing, and the heterosis effect in a new way. So did reciprocal recurrent selection, which linked hybridization to progeny testing, while avoiding inbreeding. These approaches reflect the increasing collaboration between science and business in breeding: the time and resources that the complicated hybrid methodologies required were beyond the means of individual breeders. The incentive for breeding companies to explore hybridization techniques was that they created a biological lock that made it commercially attractive to invest in the development of new varieties of animals and plants. Hybrid-corn experts did claim that hybridization represented a fundamentally new Mendelian breeding method. As we have seen, however, there was little that was Mendelian about hybrid-corn breeding, and it was certainly not a method for obtaining predictable results. If the Dutch saying "breeding is gambling" (*fokken is gokken*) is applicable anywhere, it is in hybrid-corn breeding, because trial and error is an essential constituent of the method. For the scientists involved, Mendelism was no doubt a source of inspiration, and the rationality of some aspects of the method could be explained by pointing to the Mendelian rules of heredity. The rationale of the method itself, however, did not follow from Mendelism – rather, the reverse was true: as critics have pointed out, Mendelian principles predict that the same, possibly even better results, can be obtained by purebred breeding.

Mendelian principles had a similar explanatory function in other areas of livestock breeding. For example: purebreds are reliable producers because of their homozygosity; inbreeding is not deleterious as such, but it increases the chances of deleterious allele combinations; and breeding from crossbreds results in highly variable offspring as a consequence of recombination. In practical terms, breeders had known all this long before 1900, yet Mendelism's explanatory capacity supported scientists in their campaign for rational breeding practices.

Generally speaking, however, the role of genetic theory in breeding practices was small. The productive traits of livestock animals are of the quantitative kind, and Mendelism is of no help in improving them. Qualitative characteristics are amenable to a Mendelian approach in principle, yet when several such characteristics or multiple alleles are involved – as is usually the case – factor analysis quickly becomes too complex to handle. Farmer Dijt and geneticist Hagedoorn probably ran into this problem in their attempts to "purify" the Texel sheep. Conventional mass selection therefore remained indispensable, and experienced breeders had been using it successfully long before geneticists entered the field of livestock breeding. The quantitative approach that was required when productive traits were involved starts from the premise that both parents contribute about equally to the hereditary make-up of their offspring, an assumption that had not gone uncontested in previous centuries, yet that was accepted by many breeders in the nineteenth century. Apart from this, quantitative genetics involves no theoretical suppositions about hereditary particles and their behaviour.

Scientists certainly did introduce various new "methods" to livestock breeding, such as AI and frozen sperm technology, mathematical and statistical tools, and weighing and measuring programs. All these innovations were instruments to make breeding, particularly selection and progeny testing, more efficient, and I would argue that their successful implementation constituted scientists' most important contribution to the improvement of livestock breeding. In other words, the extraordinary increase in production that was achieved in several sectors of livestock farming was mainly the result of the scientific rationalization of farmers' breeding practices. Weighing, counting, measuring, and calculating, as well as systematically executed trial and error, enabled scientists to find the best breeding stock, and AI and frozen sperm technology (and, in a later phase, embryo transfer and cloning) served to make optimal use of the best animals.

The new technique of genomic selection, introduced in the 2000s, fits into this picture. While farmers in the early twentieth century judged the productive qualities of their animals on the basis of their external qualities, genomic selection similarly uses the principle of correlation to evaluate productive qualities on the basis of DNA comparison. The technique is based on a quantitative comparison of similarities in DNA structure between, for instance, a newborn bull calf and a reference group of breeding bulls whose productive performance is known. The aim is to establish statistical correlations; the genes involved and their specific effects remain unknown.

Looking below the surface of scientific breeding in the twentieth century thus evokes the sensation that David Edgerton has called "the shock of the old."[3] Scientific breeding started from principles that had been known and in use long before 1900. Scientists combined these methods in new ways but added no fundamentally new breeding principles or insights into heredity. Their forte was the rationalization of the farmers' breeding practices.

In the early twentieth century, purebred breeding rapidly became standard practice in most sectors of livestock breeding. Historians have shown how the concept of purity was linked to notions of race and social class. In the early nineteenth century, for instance, gentlemen farmers began to create breeds that allegedly, like their owners, stemmed from ancient, "uncontaminated" and hence noble ancestral lineages. Such sentiments can also be found among the Friesian breeders of black and whites, who cherished the long pedigrees and "nobility" of their cattle and gave them an iconic role in expressions of their regional identity. Several famous Friesians, such as Dirk 4 and Sunny Boy, were immortalized as bronze statues, testifying to both their cultural and economic significance. Even more revealingly, a life-size bronze true-type model of a Friesian cow, commissioned by a group of Friesian breeders in the 1950s, was given the name Ús Mem, our mother (Figure C1). It is equally significant that the only purebred Dutch horse is the Friesian, whose lineage is believed to go back to medieval times. When the Friesian capital Leeuwarden was elected European capital of culture 2018, a plan was made to have an artist sculpt a statue of a Friesian horse, 25 metres high, as a symbol of the province.[4] Texel sheep also figure prominently in the history and iconography of the Isle of Texel, and the island breeders were the most ardent defenders of the Texel's distinguishing features. The emphasis on history and lineage in breeders' conceptions of purity clearly indicates that more was at stake than is encapsulated by the Mendelian idea of purity.

Figure C1. Bronze type model of a Friesian cow in Leeuwarden (Friesland). From the archives of the cattle breeders' journal *Veeteelt*. © Veeteelt (CRV Holding BV).

Social and cultural connotations of this kind did not, however, predominate in the trend towards purity that can be seen in most sectors of livestock breeding after 1900. The switch to purebreds was mainly motivated by pragmatic considerations. The pigs, chickens, and sheep of the late-nineteenth-century farm were a mixed lot, as a result of a century or more of haphazard crossbreeding with breeds from all over the world. The pig farmers' scientific advisers knew from the Danish example that systematic crossing made sense: first-generation crossbreds did better than their parents. Yet they decided against this because it would require farmers to maintain at least two breeds in pure form, which was deemed too complicated for most Dutch farmers, who only kept pigs as a sideline. Sheep breeders did try to make crossbreeding work until the 1920s, only to find that, in practice, purebred breeding worked better. The same pragmatic considerations induced chicken breeders to concentrate on a few pure breeds. Dairy farmers had undertaken some crossing experiments in the mid-nineteenth century, without success, and had been keeping their herds in fairly pure form since then. Yet even they did not bother to "purify" their many-coloured herds until their American buyers began to show a preference for a uniform, black-and-white colour pattern. Finally, the horse breeders, who bred horses for diverse purposes, simply had no use for the purebred system and continued to breed several performance types on the basis of "mixing blood."

That purity was not sacrosanct is also evidenced by developments later in the twentieth century. Once regulations to prevent chaos were in place, the ban on crossbreeding in pig and chicken breeding was lifted, and after the Second World War it was the commercial companies in particular, which had the resources to do so in an organized manner, who began to explore the benefits of heterosis and the hybrid-corn method. Sheep breeding expert Bekedam ventured to reintroduce crossbreeding in the sheep sector, yet now it was the breeders who considered the system too complicated for their small holdings: for them it was much more expedient to turn Bekedam's Swifter into a pure breed. Purebred breeding, in short, was often the result of practical considerations, and other systems were tried if they were deemed both advantageous and feasible.

Pragmatism goes a long way as an explanation for the farmers' breeding decisions in general. On the one hand, they might be hesitant about new scientific approaches if the advantages were insufficiently clear to them; on the other hand, they might adopt them for fear of missing out well before the scientists had experimentally confirmed the benefits. The dairy farmers' decision to switch to Holsteins – which Politiek considered premature but which worked out well – is a case in point, and so is the pig farmers' adoption of the Duroc as a crossbreeding sire – which turned out to have been too rash. Scientific arguments or the rhetoric of modernization were never enough to sway the farmers to adopt new approaches. The agricultural ministry's claim that the dairy cattle model of index breeding would inevitably take over horse breeding too failed to make an impression on the farmers, and the pig- and horse-breeding experts' insistence on the necessity of AI was similarly ignored. Commercial farmers made their decisions on the basis of expected economic returns, and values of a different nature might be decisive in breeding cultures in which commercial gains mattered less. Thus, the claim that farmers were forced to modernize by the "expert system" does no justice to their agency in the development of animal breeding. Closer inspection of the breeders' decisions reveals contingency rather than necessity or coercion.

This is not to deny that farmers were put under enormous pressure to modernize, that is, to scale up, mechanize, intensify, and specialize their holdings, nor that science played an increasingly significant role in animal husbandry and livestock breeding, especially in the second half of the twentieth century. After the establishment of the EEC and the opening up of the European markets, farmers in all sectors had to increase their productivity to compensate for falling prices and rising labour costs. While it had been the Ministry of Agriculture's intention to keep farmers' incomes on par with those in industry, this soon turned out to be unrealistic, and more and more farmers were confronted with the dilemma of having to either modernize or give up their farms. Agricultural scientists worked hand in glove with the government to implement the policy of modernization, and they actively offered their services to farmers or were invited to do so by the farmers themselves. As a consequence, production and productivity, as well as the involvement of scientists, increased across the board.

Historian Abigail Woods has pointed to a teleological element in histories of twentieth-century agriculture. In her view, they present linear accounts that consider the development of an efficient and productive modern agriculture to be a self-evident process requiring no explanation, whereas changes that do not fit into the general trend are ignored. In a reaction to this criticism, historian Paul Brassley has argued that the industrialization of sectors such as pig and chicken husbandry cannot reasonably be questioned. Taking pig and poultry breeding in the UK as his example, he has argued that there was an indisputable trend in which the myriad small-scale farms of the past, with relatively few animals, were replaced by specialized, intensive, mechanized, and large-scale holdings with much larger numbers of animals. "Teleology or not," he concludes, "that was what happened."[5]

These views are not really incompatible, in my view. The trend towards industrialization in postwar Dutch pig and poultry breeding is obvious too, and more or less successful attempts at modernization were undertaken in all sectors. In dairy cattle breeding, the number of cows per farm quadrupled in a few decades; they were turned into specialized milk producers, and the diversity of traditional breeders was replaced by a single breeding and herd-book organization. In horse breeding, performance indexes and AI were in the end adopted by the breeders. Even in Dutch sheep breeding, farmers sought scientific advice to increase the productivity of their sheep, and scientists succeeded in convincing farmers of the potential of crossbreeding, which resulted in the creation of the Swifter. Thus, a seemingly teleological trend can indeed be discerned in the development of most sectors of livestock. This is neither mysterious nor surprising, however, as the changes in breeding practices underlying it were fully intended and actively promoted by both agricultural policymakers and scientists.

Clearly, this does not imply that modernization was "inevitable," as the coalition of experts and policymakers believed. However inescapable the demands of the market may have seemed to them, the market economy is not a natural given: it is a moral economy that prescribes how actors should behave rather than how they unavoidably must and will behave. Only as long as its tenets are not questioned can the demands of the market determine the general direction of change. In the postwar period, both scientists and farmers did firmly believe that they had to follow market demands, and it is also clear that breeders made their most important reform decisions under heavy economic pressure. It was accepted, by scientists and farmers alike, that there were only two options in response to such pressure: to modernize or to give up farming.[6] The "industrial ideal," as historian Deborah Fitzgerald has called it, was forcefully promoted in postwar Dutch farming. It did not merely shape farmers' ideas on how to run their farms, it was also translated into policies that stimulated its realization in practice.[7] Guaranteed prices and other support measures, for instance, were geared to what experts considered to be the needs of "viable" farms, and farmers with insufficient prospects for modernization were advised to give up their holdings. Until the late twentieth century, other options, such as organic farming or diversified farming systems, were not considered feasible alternatives by the vast majority of the farmers, and they received scant, if any, attention in the breeding journals until the 1990s. As we have seen, most farmers who had the resources to stay in business were willing to try scientific approaches, if only to help them out of their predicament under adverse economic circumstances. And in many cases, science delivered what it was expected to deliver, if not sooner, then later. Modernization came at a dramatic cost, to be sure, for simultaneously a "silent revolution" took place in the countryside: the route to modernization was open only to a select group of farmers, while an overwhelming majority felt compelled to throw in the towel.[8]

Obviously, however, this is not the whole story. "Modernization" had different meanings in different periods and in different sectors, and the outcomes were diverse. The Dutch government began to invest in agriculture and agricultural science around 1900, and the increase in productivity that would characterize the twentieth century as a whole set in in its early decades. Yet until the Second World War, Dutch ideas about efficient farming differed markedly from the industrial ideal. Small-scale mixed farming was the norm, and the government intended to keep it that way, not to curb the modernization process but as a part of it. As historians Johan Schot and Dick van Lente have rightly noted, the small farm was considered a reliable source of income for hundreds of thousands of families on the less fertile soils in the east and the south of the Netherlands.[9] To be sure, the dairy farmers in the clay provinces were specialists, in the sense that dairying was their mainstay. Yet after 1900, as we have seen, they replaced their specialized cows with the dual-purpose type, which was believed to be more efficient in the long run, not only by the farmers themselves, but also by their scientific advisers. Until the 1960s, dairy farmers had a different idea of what modern farming entailed, as is perfectly illustrated by the name they gave to the new dual-purpose type: the Modern Friesian. The criticism Politiek levelled at the dairy farmers' "unscientific" breeding methods after the war was also a critique of their conception of modern farming.

It should also be noted that, while the emphasis was on efficiency, the government tried to protect the farmers from the exigencies of the market in various ways, both before and after the Second World War. It introduced price protection and restrictions on growth to help farmers overcome the crisis years, and guaranteed prices for several products and import restrictions were also a central element of Mansholt's post-war agricultural policy, to protect European farmers from the volatility of the world market. Furthermore, and remarkably, the Dutch government tried to preserve the small scale of the poultry sector even after the Second World War, to keep the mixed farmers in business. It was the decision to join the EEC and its open internal markets that made the scaling up of the sector seem "inevitable."

When modernization came to be conceived as intensification, specialization, and increase in scale after the war, we find no uniform, linear development either. Scientific solutions that worked well in one sector might not work in others, and it was not the logic of the scientific method or of modernization that compelled the farmers to adopt new approaches. They were willing to consider new options, but they weighed the benefits against other values within their breeding cultures and made their decisions on pragmatic grounds. Pigs and chickens can be kept in large numbers, produce ample offspring, and have a short generation interval. Thus they were most amenable to the industrial ideal of scaling up, specialization, and intensification. Scientific approaches came to dominate in both sectors, albeit in different ways – pigs are not chickens. In all the sectors we have discussed, the trajectory of scientific change was anything but straightforward. As we saw, for instance, scientists propagated the use of AI as a breeding tool, yet in practice disease prevention was a much more compelling reason for breeders to adopt it. If it became a breeding tool, it was only in a later phase. Scientific experts believed that the horse breeders' adoption of the dairy cattle model of collective index breeding was essential for the survival of equine husbandry. Yet this model made no sense to the breeders, and they managed to survive without collectivization. The turnabout in dairy cattle breeding around 1970 is perhaps the most ironic example of the contingencies of the modernization process. The dairy farmers did not switch to scientific breeding because they finally accepted the logic of modernization, but rather because Mansholt's modernization policy was on the brink of collapse, as a result of overproduction and the soaring costs of price protection. The "logic" in this case was that because prices dropped as a consequence of surpluses, farmers had to produce ever more, just to stay in business. Finally, the small-scale sheep breeding sector was least amenable to scientific breeding programs. Scaling up was not an option for most farmers, as sheep husbandry was a sideline and dairying was more profitable on larger farms. Marten Bekedam's intention was to make the benefits of crossbreeding available to sheep breeders, but his efforts ultimately resulted in the creation of a new purebred, the Swifter. Its greater manageability easily weighed up against the loss of hybrid vigour – a déjà vu, considering how the Texel had come to be established as a breed in the 1920s. The Texel's distinguishing features and the sector's small scale proved to be unsurmountable obstacles for Bekedam and Visscher's attempts to introduce AI and index breeding. Sheep farmers certainly felt the need to increase the productivity of their animals, and they did succeed in doing so. However, it was the breeder's eye that accomplished the task, after the scientific approach had failed. Tellingly, again, the breeders advertised their improved breed as the Modern Texel.

Scientists had no compelling theory to offer of how livestock should be bred, and although scientists and the government worked closely together in the period investigated here, there is no reason to consider the scientific approach as intrinsically or inevitably bound up with the policy of modernization or the industrial ideal. It can of course – with equal chances of success – be applied to other goals. Some years ago, AI was introduced in organic cattle farming in the Netherlands, and index breeding may just as well be put at the service of sustainable breeding and welfare-friendly production methods.[10] For instance, Wageningen researchers recently developed a quantitative breeding program to select for shorter tails in sheep, so that they no longer need to be docked for hygienic reasons. A similar scheme was devised to make for easier calving in double-muscled beef cattle, to bring down the number of caesarians.[11] Science is not finicky about the ends for which it provides the means. It is up to us to decide what these ends should be.

# Notes

**Introduction**

1 Attenborough, *Charles Darwin*.
2 Theunissen, "Practical Animal Breeding."
3 Trow-Smith, *A History*; Clutton-Brock, *A Natural History*; Russell, *Like Engend'ring Like*; Ritvo, *The Animal Estate*; Derry, *Bred for Perfection*; Wood and Orel, *Genetic Prehistory*.
4 For my analysis of Darwin's views on breeding, see Theunissen, "Darwin and His Pigeons."
5 Social worlds can be defined as "groups with shared commitments to certain activities, sharing resources of many kinds to achieve their goals, and building shared ideologies about how to go about their business. Social worlds form a fundamental building block of collective action ... Social worlds are the principal affiliative mechanisms through which people organize social life ... Society as a whole, then, can be conceptualized as consisting of a mosaic of social worlds that both touch and interpenetrate" (Clarke, "Social Worlds," 131). For expositions of the theory, see Strauss, "A Social World Perspective"; Clarke and Star, "The Social Worlds Framework." The sociological theory of social worlds has been an inspiration for my study, but my approach is historical.
6 Anon., *Proceedings of the Animal Breeding and Genetics Symposium*, iii.
7 Sebright, *The Art of Improving*.
8 The College became Wageningen Agricultural University (*Landbouwuniversiteit Wageningen*) in 1986. For a history, see Van der Haar, Faber, and De Ruiter, *De geschiedenis van de Landbouwuniversiteit*.
9 Woods, "Rethinking the History."

**1. Breeding for Nobility or for Production? Friesian Dairy Cattle**

Earlier versions of parts of this chapter were published as Theunissen, "Breeding without Mendelism," Theunissen, "Een mooie koe," and Theunissen, "Breeding for Nobility."

1 Stapel, *Rundveefokkerij*; Strikwerda, *Melkweg*; Bieleman, "De georganiseerde rundveeverbetering"; Van der Wiel and Zijlstra, *Paradijs*.
2 See, for instance, Hengeveld, *Het rundvee*.
3 Bieleman, *Boeren in Nederland*, 271–95; Broekema, "Rundveeteelt"; Knibbe, *Agriculture*; Van Zanden, "De economische ontwikkeling."
4 Strikwerda, *Een eeuw*, 65–80.
5 Minderhoud, *De Nederlandse landbouw*, 126.
6 For the history of dairy cattle breeders' societies in the Netherlands, see for instance Löhnis, *Veefokkerij*; Tukker, *Rundveehouderij*; Van Adrichem Boogaert, *De ontwikkeling*; Strikwerda, *Melkweg*; Bieleman, "De georganiseerde rundveeverbetering." Facts and figures illustrating the involvement of the government can be gleaned from Directie van den Landbouw, *Staatszorg*.
7 I will refer mainly to *De Veldbode*, a widely read weekly established in 1903, that appeared between 1902 and 1965 (from 1933 onwards as *De Nieuwe Veldbode*) and reported on all important events and discussions related to dairy cattle breeding. Its full title was *De Veldbode, Geïllustreerd Weekblad voor Land- en Tuinbouw, Pluimvee- en Konijnenfokkerij en Bijenteelt*.
8 Stanford, *British Friesians*, 61.
9 The name Holsteins was a misnomer, as Holstein is a region in Germany; black and whites from Holstein were also widely known for their productivity, which may partly explain the mistake. For the history of the Dutch black and whites in America, see, for instance, Prescott and Price, *Holstein-Friesian History*; Mansfield, *Progress*.
10 Wood and Orel, *Genetic Prehistory*, 45–6, passim.
11 Orland, "Turbo Cows," 173–4.
12 Thus it was difficult to compare their performance to that of the Friesians in the Netherlands. The latter were fed far less concentrate and barn-fed only during the winter housed period; see for instance Van den Bosch, *De fokkerij*.
13 I.G.J. van den Bosch, "Stierhouderijen en fokvereenigingen," *De Veldbode* 4 (1906) 585–8, 597–8, 633–4. Pott developed his views in reaction to what was called "Formalismus," i.e., selection for phenotypic traits with no demonstrable relation to production; see Pott, *Der Formalismus*; Comberg, *Die Deutsche Tierzucht*, 122, 336–9.
14 Kroon, *De tegenwoordige richtingen*, 95–9; Löhnis, *Veefokkerij*, 28, 46. In the decades after 1900, animal husbandry specialists A.A. ter Haar, Aryen

van Leeuwen and Engelbert van Muilwijk constantly warned readers of *De Veldbode* not to be misled by the high milk yields which Friesian farmers were able to obtain on their rich soils. Wageningen agricultural experts concurred with this view; see for instance De Jong and Koenen, "Welke eigenschappen." Animal husbandry textbooks promoted the same message; see for instance Kok, *Handleiding*, 76; Dommerhold, *Veeteelt*, 10, 14–17; Broekema, *Nederlandsche rundveeteelt*, 16.

15 Ter Haar, "Het oordeel," 997.

16 Van Leeuwen, "Invoer"; Van Leeuwen, "Rundveefokkerij." Abbo-Tilstra, *Om de sûnens*, investigates the fight against tuberculosis in cattle and humans in Friesland between 1890 and 1940. For a history of bovine tuberculosis in Britain since 1850, see Atkins, *A History of Uncertainty*.

17 Abbo-Tilstra, *Om de sûnens*, 27, 146–7, 201.

18 The susceptibility of Friesians to tuberculosis was pointed out time and again in agricultural journals and handbooks in the early decades of the twentieth century; see for instance Kroon, *De tegenwoordige richtingen*, 97; Bakker et al., *Gedenkboek*, 133; Timmermans, *Gedenkboek*, 12; Van Leeuwen, "Tuberculosebestrijding"; Dommerhold, *Veeteelt*, 10.

19 See for instance A.A. ter Haar, "Veeverbetering op lichten bodem," *De Veldbode* 17 (1919): 489–90; Ter Haar, "Roodbont vee," *De Veldbode* 21 (1923): 875; Kroon, *De tegenwoordige richtingen*, 107.

20 E. van Muilwijk, "De Friesche richting een gevaar voor de Zuidhollandsche fokkerij," *De Veldbode* 17 (1919): 881–2, 924; E. van Muilwijk, "De Dirk IV-stam," *De Veldbode* 23 (1925): 312–14. Together with the veterinarian Van Leeuwen, Van Muilwijk promoted the Hoornaar type in *De Veldbode* for years.

21 Timmermans, "Zuiden vooruit."

22 I.G.J. van den Bosch, "Stierhouderijen en fokvereenigingen," *De Veldbode* 4 (1906): 597–8.

23 Stanford, *British Friesians*, 50.

24 Kronacher expressed his views at a national dairy show in the Netherlands in 1928; see Anon., "De nationale tentoonstelling IV. Het oordeel van de Duitsche deskundigen," *De Veldbode* 26 (1928): 863–5.

25 Abbo-Tilstra, *Om de sûnens*, 330.

26 On the role of conformation in evaluating dairy cattle, see Grasseni, "Skilled Vision"; Grasseni, "Designer Cows"; Pawley, "The Point of Perfection"; Holloway and Morris, "Viewing Animal Bodies."

27 Strikwerda, *Een eeuw*, 317–33; Strikwerda, *Melkweg*, 96.

28 Strikwerda, *Een eeuw*, 64, 96–7, 253–7, 261.

29 Stanford, *British Friesians*, 186–7. This is not to say that the Modern Friesian was accepted uncritically in Britain. The hereditary qualities of a group of fifty-seven bulls exported to Great Britain in 1950 gave rise to heated

discussions. Nevertheless, Dutch Friesians were very popular in Britain, generally speaking; see Anon., "Uit de Britse zwartbontfokkerij," *De Keurstamboeker* [*KS*] 3 (1955) 521–2, 547–9; Mingay, *British Friesians*, 176–99.

30 Hofman, "Het succes."

31 The national cattle breeders' society, the NRS, decided in 1954 that it was no longer necessary to judge female cattle from different soils in separate categories at shows, as had been customary until then; see Anema and Jepma, *Veeteelt-I*, 116.

32 See for instance J. Jepma, "Enkele gedachten over de veefokkerij," *KS* 2 (1954): 274–5; J. Jepma, "Gedachten over veefokkerij," *KS* 5 (1957): 314; Anon., "De fokwaardebepaling van stieren van de praktische kant gezien," *KS* 3 (1955): 204–5; Anon., "Het keuren van rundvee en wat daarmee samenhangt," *KS* 5 (1957): 79–80; Anon., "Naschrift," *KS* 5 (1957): 580–1. See also Grasseni, "Skilled Vision"; Grasseni, "Designer Cows."

33 Van der Ploeg, *De virtuele boer*, 57–106. See also Spahr van der Hoek, *Geschiedenis*, vol. 1, 204–54, 437–80.

34 Strikwerda, *Een eeuw*, 81–6; Van der Wiel and Zijlstra, *Paradijs*, 32–5.

35 Derry, *Bred for Perfection*, 156–61. Conversely, when the German, English and American markets were being closed for live cattle around 1900, the breeders' societies experienced a crisis; see Löhnis, 1901.

36 Derry, *Bred for Perfection*, 48–102; Ritvo, *The Animal Estate*, 82–115; Ritvo, *The Platypus and the* Mermaid, 104–20; Pawley, "The Point of Perfection."

37 For a history of the NRS, see Dekker and Stapel, *Honderd jaar*.

38 Although this was later denied by FRS officials, there were a few cases of Friesians born outside Friesland that had been registered in the herd book in the early years of the FRS; see Strikwerda, *Een eeuw*, 144. For histories of the FRS, see Zwart, *Tachtig jaar*; Strikwerda, *Een eeuw*.

39 Derry, *Bred for Perfection*, 9.

40 Berge, *Die geschichtliche Entwicklung*, 131–4; Comberg, *Die Deutsche Tierzucht*, 106ff; Wood and Orel, *Prehistory*, 244–6, 264–6.

41 Strikwerda, *Een eeuw*, 31–6, 109–22. See also Dekker and Stapel, *100 jaar*, 256–67.

42 The belief of an ancient origin of domestic breeds was widespread in the nineteenth century; see Trow-Smith, *A History*, 235–6. Charles Darwin, as we saw in the introduction, also believed that the most important breeds must have had a long history; see Theunissen, "Darwin and His Pigeons."

43 The agriculturist Bakker (*Die Niederländische Rindviehzucht*) contested this view and argued that the original Friesians had been red and whites. The black and whites, he believed, had been imported from Denmark after the ravages of the rinderpest epidemics in the eighteenth century.

44 Interestingly, a century earlier Dutch bulls were imported into England to improve the Shorthorn's milk yield (Thirsk, *The Agrarian History*, 54).

45 See, for instance, Strikwerda, *Een eeuw*, 109–16.
46 A. van Leeuwen, for instance, campaigned against the depreciation of animals with spotted legs for years on end in *De Veldbode*; see for instance his "Consequenties van de zwarte-vlekjes-vervolging," *De Veldbode* 10 (1914): 98–121.
47 A.D. Groneman, "De vlekken-kwestie," *De Veldbode* 10 (1912): 805–6.
48 Dog and horse breeding provide similar examples; see Derry, *Bred for Perfection*, 158, passim.
49 Wood and Orel, *Genetic Prehistory*, chapters 3 and 4. See also Russell, *Like Engend'ring Like*.
50 See, for instance, Hoogland, *Een studie*.
51 Strikwerda, *Een eeuw*, 317.
52 Some famous bloodlines were described in monographs; see for instance Van Muilwijk, *De Jacob-Ruiter-Frans-Max-Stam*.
53 For the history of cattle breeding in North Holland see Kroon, *Onze zwartbonte*; Van der Wiel and Zijlstra, *Paradijs*.
54 On Hugo de Vries, see, for instance, Stamhuis, Meijer, and Zevenhuizen, "Hugo de Vries." For the scientific and societal motives underlying his research, see Theunissen, "Closing the Door"; Theunissen, "Knowledge Is Power." For his views on agricultural plant breeding, see De Vries, *Plant-Breeding*.
55 See for instance Hagedoorn, *Oordeelkundige zaadteelt*; Waardenburg, *Het Mendelisme*; Giltay, *Het principiële*; Lotsy, *Grondbeginselen*; Reimers, *Die Bedeutung*.
56 A. van Leeuwen, "De standvastigheid van het roode haar," *De Veldbode* 10 (1912): 98, 121.
57 For Arend Lourens Hagedoorn (1885–1953), see Theunissen, "Practical Animal Breeding."
58 A.L. Hagedoorn, "Schapenfokkerij op Texel," *De Veldbode* 9 (1911): 595–6; Kroon, *De kruisingen*, 43.
59 Reimers, *Die Bedeutung*, 2, 27; Hagedoorn, *Oordeelkundige zaadteelt*, 5–6.
60 Reimers, *Die Bedeutung*, 27, 37–8, 78; Hagedoorn, *Oordeelkundige zaadteelt*, 83.
61 A.L. Hagedoorn, "De toepassing van wetenschap, in het bijzonder van erfelijkheidswetenschap," *De Veldbode* 25 (1927): unpaginated Christmas issue. Hagedoorn, *Animal Breeding*, 19.
62 C. Broekema, "De gehouden wedstrijd betreffende de organisatie en werking van fokvereenigingen," *De Veldbode* 11 (1913): 963–5; A. van Leeuwen, "Veeteeltkundige snufjes," *De Veldbode* 21 (1923): 801–2; Anon., *Compte-rendu*, 53–8; E. van Muilwijk, "De moderne erfelijkheidsleer en de praktische fokkerij," *De Veldbode* 26 (1928): 1025–7; Overbosch and Van der Plank, "Een bijdrage." For a similar assessment with respect to

the role of classical genetics in horse and dog breeding, see Derry, *Bred for Perfection*, 12–13.

63 Kroon, *De tegenwoordige richtingen*, 71, 121; Kroon, *De kruisingen*, 24.

64 Van den Bosch, *Kort overzicht*.

65 Kroon, *De tegenwoordige richtingen*, 102; Hagedoorn, Oordeelkundige zaadteelt, 57–64; Lotsy, *Grondbeginselen*, 15–17, 33; Reimers, *Die Bedeutung*, 95; D.L. Bakker, "Over het wezen en de betekenis van inteelt," *De Veldbode* 24 (1926): 766–7; Hagedoorn, *Handboek*, 54, 87–95.

66 Reimers, *Die Bedeutung*, 89; Hagedoorn, *Oordeelkundige zaadteelt*, 47–8; Van der Plank, "Stamboomstudie."

67 See notes 51, 52, 67.

68 Van Popta, *Geschiedenis*.

69 Reimers, *Die Bedeutung*, 81, 93; Hagedoorn, *Ooordeelkundige zaadteelt*, 48; Hagedoorn, *Handboek*, 130–7.

70 In 1940, for instance, the registration costs of an animal were 5 guilders; a farm hand at the time earned about 15 guilders a week (Kroon, *Onze zwartbonte*, 118).

71 Wibbens, "Welke gegevens"; Anon., *Compte-rendu*, 51–3.

72 Russell, *Like Engend'rin Like*, 35, 196–215; David L. Wykes, "Robert Bakewell (1725–1795) of Dishley: Farmer and Livestock Improver," *Agricultural History Review* 52 (2004): 38–55; Ritvo, "Possessing Mother Nature," Ritvo, *Noble Cows*, 157–74. For a general history of conceptions of heredity, see Müller-Wille and Rheinberger, *A Cultural History of Heredity*.

73 Hagedoorn, *Oordeelkundige zaadteelt*, 47–8; 86, 88; Hagedoorn, *Handboek*, 63. See also, for instance, Van Krimpen, *Verbetering*, 13; Reimers, *Die Bedeutung*, 79, 92–3; Kroon, *De tegenwoordige richtingen*, 99.

74 The situation in the Netherlands shows many similarities to that in the UK, as described by Wilmot, "Between the Farm."

75 J. Timmermans, "Naar aanleiding van de centrale stierenkeuring te Roermond," *De Veldbode* 18 (1920): 615–16; Strikwerda, *Melkweg*, 67.

76 See, for instance, A. van Leeuwen, "Verplichte stierenkeuring," *De Veldbode* 2 (1904): 804–5; H. Wibbens, "Eenige koeien van het roodbonte Maas-Rijn-IJssel-veeras," *De Veldbode* 5 (1907): 243–5; Löhnis, *Veefokkerij*, 46.

77 Van der Wiel and Zijlstra, *Paradijs*, 57–61.

78 Löhnis, *Veefokkerij*, 3; Van Adrichem Boogaert, *De ontwikkeling*, 303–5.

79 Nobel, *Veefokkerij*, 10–11; Van der Wiel and Zijlstra, *Paradijs*, 99–109, 145–6.

80 This happened in North Holland, for instance; see Van der Wiel and Zijlstra, *Paradijs*, 146.

81 Löhnis, *Veefokkerij*, 46; F.A.F. Groneman, "Herinneringen en ervaringen II," *KS* 4 (1956): 34–7.

82 Strikwerda, *Melkweg*, 114.
83 A.L. Hagedoorn, "Rationeele fokkerij," *De Nieuwe Veldbode* 8, no. 33 (1941): 10–13; H.W. Kuhn, "Rationeele fokkerij. Een wederwoord," *De Nieuwe Veldbode* 8, no. 43 (1941): 11–12.
84 Anon., "Over verandering van principe bij de rundveestamboeken," *De Nieuwe Veldbode* 8, no. 44 (1941): 8–10; R.G. Anema, "Enkele bemerkingen betreffende de beschouwingen van dr. Hagedoorn inzake rationeele veefokkerij," *De Nieuwe Veldbode* 8, no. 52 (1941): 16–17.
85 For an overview of the technological "modernization"of the Netherlands in the twentieth century, see, Schot, Lintsen, and Rip, *Technology and the Making of the Netherlands*; for a history of Dutch agriculture (1500–2000), see Bieleman, *Boeren in Nederland*; for the postwar "modernization" of agriculture, see for instance Karel, *De maakbare boer*, Karel, *Boeren tussen markt en maatschappij*; for the developments in agriculture described here, see in particular Maris, Scheer and Visser, *Het kleine-boeren vraagstuk*; Anon., *De Nederlandse landbouw*; Le Mair, "Typering van een tijdvak"; Van den Hoek, "De ontwikkeling van de landbouw"; Van der Molen and Douw, "Een bedrijfstak in ontwikkeling"; Molegraaff, *Boeren in Brussel*; for the developments in dairying, see Bieleman, De georganiseerde rundveeverbetering"; Anon., *Problematiek en perspectief*; Cleveringa, "De ontwikkeling"; R.D. Politiek, "Verleden, heden en toekomst in de rundveehouderij en -fokkerij," *KS* 14 (1966): 91, 129, 170–2; for Mansholt, see Goldstone Rosenthal, *The Men*; Van Merriënboer, *Mansholt*.
86 Maat, *Science Cultivating Practice*, 7–9. On discourse coalitions, see Hajer, "Discourse Coalitions," 47.
87 The three directors active in the period under investigation (Theo Kees Rijssenbeek, Bertus Geessink and Theo Vos) were Wageningen graduates and had begun their careers as animal husbandry advisers or researchers. Vos would later return to Wageningen as president of the board.
88 Politiek, *Doel en streven*, 13.
89 Van den Hoek, "De ontwikkeling," 142–3; Strikwerda, *Melkweg*, 16–17.
90 Sijbrandij, "De verhoging"; Politiek and Vos, "Veranderingen"; Van Adrichem Boogaert, *De ontwikkeling*, 125; Strikwerda, *Melkweg*, 47.
91 *Jaarverslag K.I. 1956*, 10–12.
92 Adrichem Boogaert, *De ontwikkeling*, 141.
93 Th. de Groot and M. Bekedam, "De melkproductievererving van Friese stieren," *KS*, 5 (1957): 138; Politiek, *Doel en streven*, 7; Politiek and Vos, "Veranderingen."
94 Siebenga, *Kunstmatige inseminatie*. For the development of AI in the Netherlands, see Strikwerda, *Revolutie*. For a general history, see Foote, "The history."
95 Hagedoorn, *Animal Breeding*; Van der Plank, "Fokwaardebepaling."

96 Strikwerda, *Revolutie*, 20–1; Van Adrichem Boogaert , *De ontwikkeling*, 129–34. British pedigree breeders entertained similar doubts about AI: see Wilmot, "From 'Public Service,'" 416–20.
97 S.N. Kingma, "Fokkerservaringen en fokkersinzichten," *KS* 9 (1961): 121–3, on p. 122; see also B. Hemmink, "Wetenschap en praktijk over exterieurbeoordeling," *KS* 12 (1964): 272–3.
98 Anon., "Het nieuwe N.R.S.-gebouw te Den Haag,"*De Friese Veefokkerij* [*FV*] 3, nos. 16–17 (1953–4): 12–14, on p. 13. See also Anon., "Het getal in de rundveefokkerij," *FV* 8 (1957–8): 184–8; and W.B. Hijlkema, "De boer als fokker," *FV* 8 (1957–8): 190–1.
99 Anon., "De moderne Friese melkkoe," *FV* 3, nos. 14–15 (1953–4): 7–8.
100 Editorial, *KS* 5 (1957): 580–1, on p. 181.
101 Strikwerda, *Een eeuw*; Strikwerda, *Melkweg 2000*.
102 Th.C.J.M. Rijssenbeek, "25 Jaar geleden werd de Nederlandsche Zoötechnische Vereniging opgericht," *KS* 4 (1956): 6–8.
103 Stapel, *Rundveefokkerij*, 42, 67.
104 De Jong, "Productie," 116; De Jong, *Een halve eeuw*.
105 Dekker and Stapel, *100 Jaar*, 315–16.
106 De Jong, "Productie"; De Jong, *Een halve eeuw*; W. de Jong, "Geluk, ervaring, wetenschap," *KS* 5 (1957): 109–11; Th.C.J.M. Rijssenbeek, "Foktechnisch beleid in K.I. verenigingen," *KS* 11 (1963): 381–2, 405–6.
107 De Jong, "Productie."
108 A.L. Hagedoorn, "Rationeele fokkerij," *De Nieuwe Veldbode* 8, no. 33 (1941): 10–13.; A.L. Hagedoorn, "Over kruising," *De Nieuwe Veldbode* 8, no. 44 (1941): 10–12; P. Hoekstra, "De waarde der exterieurkeuring voor de Nederlandse rundveefokkerij," *KS* 6 (1958): 342–3, 370–1; P. Hoekstra, "De betekenis van het type voor de rundveefokkerij en de rundveehouderij," *KS* 15 (1967): 124–7; Hoekstra, "Kentering."
109 Th.C.J.M. Rijssenbeek, "Foktechnisch beleid in K.I. verenigingen," *KS* 11 (1963): 381–2, 405–6; Minkema, "Bespiegelingen"; 237–44; Minkema, "Het effect"; Bekedam, "Selectie en gebruik"; Politiek, "De praktische betekenis."
110 Politiek, "Evolutie"; *Jaarverslag K.I. 1968*, 7; *Jaarverslag K.I. 1969*, 5. To be precise, the average was 12,000 *first* inseminations; about a third of the cows had to be inseminated more than once. In 1951 the number of AI associations had reached its maximum of 160; in 1960 there were 131 (*Jaarverslag K.I. 1954*, 27; *Jaarverslag K.I. 1960*, 28). Britain followed a different model: AI was organized and controlled by the Milk Marketing Board; see Wilmot, "From 'Public Service,'" 426–30.
111 *Jaarverslag K.I. 1956*, 14; *Jaarverslag K.I. 1959*, 25. There were also mundane reasons for associations to remain independent. Opposition from board members for whom the financial compensation for their services was important, was one of the reasons that induced a small association in

Friesland to reject all merging plans until the late 1970s; interview with Piet Scheer, former secretary of the Friesian union of AI associations, 5 March 2008.

112 Strikwerda, "Persoonlijke ervaringen."

113 *Jaarverslag K.I. 1969*, 5; Adrichem Boogaert, *De ontwikkeling*, 144.

114 See, for instance, Anon., *Knelpunten*; Anon., *Kanttekeningen*; Th. Stegenga, "Het afstammelingenonderzoek en de selectie van stieren op vererving," *KS* 13 (1965): 393–5; R.D. Politiek, "Verleden, heden en toekomst in de rundveehouderij en -fokkerij," *KS* 14 (1966): 91, 129, 170–2; H. Vos and R.D. Politiek, "Het aankoopbeleid van k.i. stieren in 1967," in *Jaarverslag K.I. 1967*: 23–34; Politiek, *Problematiek en perspectief.*

115 Hoekstra and Van der Mey, "De betekenis," 59.

116 *Jaarverslag K.I. 1965*, 30–2.

117 A few of the farmers" scientific advisers continued to defend the focus on conformation as well. For instance, in 1962 animal husbandry adviser Jetze Jepma published a spirited defence of the concept of nobility and the ideals of good farming discussed above; see J. Jepma, "Gedachten over veefokkerij. Nogmaals: de fokrichting," *KS* 10 (1962): 251–3; see also Cazemier, "Over het "historisch" meningsverschil." For an analysis of Jetze's position, see Theunissen, "De Fries-Hollandse zwartbonte."

118 Anon., "Melkkontrole en melkproduktie," *FV* 13 (1962–3): 146–56; J.M. Dijkstra, "De melkproductie in Friesland," *FV* 14 (1963–4): 231–5.

119 Strikwerda, *Melkweg*, 94. A new point system for the evaluation of pedigree animals was introduced in which functional characteristics (udder, legs and hooves) were given more weight: Anon., "Het nieuwe keuringsrapport," *KS* 13 (1965): 326–8.

120 In reaction to this policy change, the Friesian pedigree breeders joined forces with their antipodes, the AI associations, to help them find the most promising Friesland-bred young bulls. Nothing much was achieved by this new approach, however, due to the small size of the associations and to the fact that most of the chosen test bulls had untested fathers; see J. Keestra, "Vereniging Veefokkerijbelangen Friesland," *FV* 8 (1967–8): 414–17; P.L. Scheer, "Vereniging Veefokkerijbelangen Friesland 7-4-66–1-11-69," *FV* 20 (1969–70): 182–8.

121 L. de Vries, "Over de oorzaken van verschillen in de fokkerij tussen Noordholland en Friesland," *KS* 2 (1954): 71–2. For a history of cattle breeding in the region, see Van der Wiel and Zijlstra, *Paradijs*.

122 H. Schaap, "De fokkerij, nu en in de toekomst," *FV* 18 (1967–8): 684–5; R.D. Politiek, "Mogelijkheden van samenwerking tussen individuele fokkers en de k.i. bij rundvee: Eendracht maakt macht," *KS* 17 (1969): 826–7; P.L. Scheer, "De foktechnische ontwikkeling bij de Friese k.i.," *FV* 20 (1969–70): 308–14.

123 For the economic developments described here, see note 84; see in particular Van der Molen and Douw, "Een bedrijfstak"; Molegraaff, *Boeren in Brussel;* Goldstone Rosenthal, *The Men behind the Decisions;* Merriënboer, *Mansholt.* For the EEC's agricultural policy, see Ackrill, *The Common Agricultural Policy.*
124 For instance, in 1968 a Dutch farmer received 5.8 guilders for a kilo of butterfat, while the price on the world market was 3 guilders.
125 Strikwerda, *Melkweg,* 16–17, 124.
126 For instance, the dairy farmer Minne Fokkema baulked at the huge investment of 350,000 guilders involved in building such a cubicle house; it made him "extremely nervous" for some time, he said. Yet in the end he decided that scaling up was the only way to stay in business; see Molema and de Haan, *De boer,* 56–7, 62.
127 E.F. Geessink, "De gewenste fokrichting van het Nederlandse vee," *FV* 21 (1970–1): 314–19.
128 J. Veer in *FV* 20 (1969–70): 581; see also Anon., *De Nederlandse landbouw,* 61, 83, 85.
129 *Jaarverslag K.I. 1980,* 19–20.
130 Strikwerda, *Melkweg,* 182; Strikwerda, *Revolutie,* 122; https://www.crv4all.nl/; accessed 7 December 2018.
131 P.L. Scheer, "Het fokkerijbeleid bij de Friese k.i.," *FV* 19 (1968–9): 408–14; P.L. Scheer, "De betekenis van een goede productie-afstamming," *FV* 19 (1968–9): 718–24; P.L. Scheer, "Perspectief voor de Friese rundveehouderij en fokkerij," *FV* 20 (1969–70): 454–8, 514–20, 562–8, 616–23.
132 W. Bosma in *FV* 20 (1969–70): 381.
133 Van der Wiel and Zijlstra, *Paradijs,* 218, 223, 230–2, 376–8; R.D. Politiek, G. Nijboer, and H. Vos, "Het aankoopbeleid van zwartbonte proefstieren in 1973," *KS* 55 (1973): 842–5. The difference in popularity can also be illustrated by export data: in 1972, for instance, half (268) of the bulls sold to foreign buyers were bred in North Holland; only a single one was from Friesland; *KS* 55 (1973): 63.
134 *Jaarverslag K.I. 1968,* 21; *Jaarverslag K.I. 1970,* 5; *Jaarverslag K.I. 1975–1976,* 8; *Jaarverslag K.I. 1980,* 19.
135 *Jaarverslag K.I. 1966,* 14; *Jaarverslag K.I. 1980,* 19. The new priority in breeding was also reflected in the farmers' participation in AI. About 60 per cent of the farmers had participated in the early 1960s; by 1980 participation was almost 72 per cent (*Jaarverslag K.I 1960,* 14; *Jaarverslag K.I. 1970,* 7; *Jaarverslag K.I. 1980,* 19).
136 Anon., *Rapport van een werkgroep,* 12–13; *Jaarverslag K.I. 1974,* 8, 28.
137 Strikwerda, *Revolutie,* 48, 91, 121–2, 135; M.P., "Hoe kijken afgestudeerde LU-ers terug," *Veeteelt* (1988): 872–3.
138 R. Strikwerda, "Discussie over foktechnisch beleid in Friesland," *FV* 21 (1970–1): 20, 48–9.

139 Interview with Piet Scheer, 5 March 2008. See also the report on a meeting about the use of Holstein genetics organized by young Friesian farmers: Anon., "Amerikanen in het licht van de Friese fokkerij," *FV* (1973): 24–7.
140 C. Kroon in *FV* (1973): 424; Maso, *Rood en zwart*, 76.
141 P.J. Koster in *FV* 19 (1968–9): 418; H. Heemskerk in *FV* 21 (1970–1): 300.
142 W. Jonkers, "Een enquête over het gebruik en de stieren in Drenthe," *KS* 61 (1979): 278–9; J.W. Meerdink, "Ontwikkelingsactualiteiten in Gelderland," *KS* 61 (1979), 562; A.A. van Gent and I. Hamming, "Een rendabele koe ... is een mooie koe ...!" *Veeverbetering* 64 (1982): 356–9, on p. 359.
143 After Utrecht animal scientist Van der Plank had drawn attention to the relevance of quantitative genetics for cattle breeding in 1948 (Van der Plank, "Fokwaardebepaling"), two of his colleagues introduced Jay Lush's work to Dutch scientists: Vogel and Werkman, "Progeny-testing." Another incentive was provided by a workshop on quantitative genetics organized by the Dutch Zootechnical Society in 1951. Ivar Johansson was one of the speakers, and he would return to the Netherlands in 1960 as a visiting professor in Wageningen; see Boer and Strikwerda, "Zestig jaar," 16, 21.
144 Politiek, *The influence*.
145 Interview with Rommert Politiek, 13 February 2007; for biographical information, see Strikwerda, "Professor Rommert Politiek"; M.P., "Hoe kijken afgestudeerde LU-ers terug." Another early Dutch investigator of quantitative genetics was the agricultural expert Durk Minkema.
146 The Wageningen agricultural scientists called themselves population geneticists rather than quantitative geneticists; see for instance J. Stigter, "Gesprek met Prof. Politiek (veeteeltwetenschappen)," *KS* 61 (1979): 499–601. Internationally, however, the term population genetics is customarily used when particular genes and their behaviour are studied; quantitative genetics studies the effects of unknown genes.
147 His book *Animal Breeding Plans* gave step-by-step descriptions of how to execute breeding programs: Lush, *Animal Breeding Plans*. For the development of quantitative genetics, see Lush, "Genetics and Animal Breeding"; Derry, *Masterminding Nature*, 71–128.
148 E. Parmalee Prentice, *Breeding Profitable Dairy Cattle* (Boston, 1935): 155–75. See also Freeman, "C.R. Henderson," 4046.
149 Politiek, "De productieverervingsbepaling"; Politiek and Vos, "Publikatie en interpretatie"; R.D. Politiek and M.P.M. Vos, "De melk-, vet- en eiwitindex van stieren en de praktische betekenis voor de fokkerij," *KS* 13 (1965): 39–41.
150 El Shimy, *The Hereditability*.
151 Politiek's pupil Piet Scheer was among the first to point this out: P.L. Scheer, "Enkele aspecten van de Utrechtse fokkerij," *KS* 13 (1965): 222–3.
152 This method was based on the system used by the British Milk Marketing Board. It also compensated for management differences. See Anon.,

"Productievererving van stieren volgens de DB-methode," *KS* 55 (1973): 399; J. Dommerholt, "Gebruik van productiegegevens voor de fokkerij," *KS* 55 (1973): 435–7.

153 In 1971, Friesland was the first province to electronically integrate the processing of data gathered by the FRS and the milk recording and AI associations; Strikwerda, *Melkweg*, 102.

154 Freeman, "C.R. Henderson."

155 Anon., "Een nieuwe fokwaardeschattingsmethode voor melkproductiekenmerken van stieren: De stier-index." *Veeverbetering* 63 (1981): 387–9.

156 For the earlier work, see for instance Smith, "A Discriminant Function"; Hazel, "The Genetic Basis." See also Derry, *Masterminding Nature*, 109–12.

157 J. Dommerholt, "De productievererving van stieren in netto melkgeld," *FV* (1979): 106–8; H. Wismans, "Klasse-indeling van de stieren volgens netto melkgeld," *Veeverbetering* 63 (1981): 24.

158 R.D. Politiek, "Welke koe voor de toekomst," *FV* (1976): 226–31.

159 W.G.M. Wismans, "Omrekening van de fokwaardeschatting voor melkproductie uit de Verenigde Staten en Canada voor Nederland," *Veeverbetering* 63 (1981): 102–5.

160 For the situation in North America, see for instance Derry, *Ontario's Cattle Kingdom*.

161 Th.C.J.M. Rijssenbeek, "Indrukken van de F.R.S.-tentoonstelling," *FV* 4, nos. 15–16 (1954–5): 10–11; and R.D. Politiek, "De selectiemogelijkheden van ons rundvee op de productie van vlees," *FV* 15 (1964–5): 155–62.

162 For the Dutch views on the American Holsteins up to the late 1960s, see Van den Bosch, *De fokkerij*; Anon., "Iets over de veefokkerij in de Verenigde-Staten van Noord-Amerika," *KS* 1 (1953): 172–3; De Jong, Leignes Bakhoven and Hoogland, *De veeteelt*; H. Bouwma, "Praktische ervaringen met Holstein Friesians in de Verenigde Staten," *FV* 13 (1962–3): 273–7; W.F. Gerhardt, "Amerikanen thuis en bij ons," *FV* 21 (1970–1): 152–61.

163 Stegenga, "De Noordamerikaanse zwartbonte"; Ernst, "Vergleichende Untersuchungen"; Stegenga, "De rundveehouderij," 160–1.

164 R. Strikwerda, "A. Oosterbaan: Amerikaanse reis deed waardering voor eigen vee stijgen," *FV* (1972): 22–4.

165 H.A. Boersma and J. Zijlstra, "Indrukken van de zwartbontfokkerij in de Verenigde Staten en Canada," *KS* 53 (1971): 735–7, 776–82; D.C. Aanen et al., "Verslag van een verkenning in Canada en de Verenigde Staten," *KS* 57 (1975): 450–3.

166 C. van Bruggen, "De melkveehouderij in Californië," *KS* 17 (1969): 362–7.

167 See, e.g., J. Leenheer (president of the NRS), "De rol van het stamboek bij verdere versteviging van de economische basis van de veeteeltproductie," *KS* 54 (1972): 16–17.

168 Facilities for scientific animal breeding experiments were created in the Netherlands only after the Second World War. Earlier attempts to create such facilities, undertaken by geneticist Hagedoorn and others, had failed. In 1952 a government institute for animal husbandry research, the IVO (*Instituut voor Veeteeltkundig Onderzoek*) was established that was the first to have animal breeding on its research agenda. Rommert Politiek, at the animal sciences department at Wageningen Agricultural College, acquired his first experimental farm for breeding and selection experiments in 1960. More extended facilities were created in the late 1960s and 1970s; see Anon., *IVO 25 jaar*.

169 The initiative to form a working group was taken by the agricultural scientist Y.T. Bakker of the *Instituut voor Moderne Veevoeding Schothorst*, a government institute for feed research. Also involved was the *Zoötechnisch Instituut* of Utrecht University; see D. Minkema, "Proef met sperma van Noordamerikaanse zwartbonte stieren in Nederland," *KS* 57 (1975): 568–9.

170 The experiments included two other dairy breeds: British Friesians and Dutch red and whites.

171 Strikwerda, *Melkweg*, 118; Anon., "Voorlichtingsavond over de Holstein Friesian fokkerij," *FV* (1972): 208–11.

172 Interview with Piet Scheer, 5 March 2008; see also P.L. Scheer, "Verslag van een studiereis naar Noord-Amerika," *FV* (1972): 370–8.

173 *FV* (1974): 260.

174 *KS* 55 (1973): 373; Strikwerda, *Melkweg*, 84.

175 P.K. ter Veer, "Rassenstrijd," *KS* 54 (1972), 74; J. Chardon, "Koeien te fokken die de grens verleggen van wat we menen dat een koe kan," *Veeverbetering* 63 (1981): 227–8.

176 R. Strikwerda, "Groep Friese fokkers weert Holsteinbloed," *FV* (1972): 264.

177 R.D. Politiek and H. Vos, "De rundveeselectieproef op het P.L.F.," *KS* 55 (1973): 8–10, 40–2, 823–5.

178 *FV* 21 (1970–1), 359, 605; FRS annual report for 1972, *FV* 21 (1970–1): 282–6.

179 Report of the general meeting of the FRS on 26 April 1978, *FV* (1978): 230–7.

180 Strikwerda, *Melkweg*, 85.

181 For the main results of the experiments see J.K. Oldenbroek, J. de Rooy, and H.A.J. Laurijsen, "Vergelijking van Holstein Friesians, Nederlandse zwartbonten en Nederlandse roodbonten," *KS* 56 (1974): 890–1; D. Minkema, "Proef met sperma van Noord-Amerikaanse zwartbonte stieren in Nederland," *KS* 57 (1975): 568–9; H. Vos, R.D. Politiek, and J. de Rooy, "Proef met sperma van Noord-Amerikaanse zwartbonte stieren in Nederland," *KS* 57 (1975): 612–14, 634–7; J.K. Oldenbroek, Vergelijking

van Holstein Friesians, Nederlandse zwartbonten en Nederlandse roodbonten," *KS* 58 (1976): 740–5; H. Vos and R.D. Politiek, "De rundveeselectieproef op de Minderhoudhoeve," *KS* 59 (1977): 194–6; H. Vos and J. de Rooy, "Kruisingsproeven met sperma van Noord-Amerikaanse zwartbonte stieren in Nederland," *KS* 59 (1977): 405–7; J.K. Oldenbroek, "Vergelijking van Holstein Friesians, Nederlandse zwartbonten en Nederlandse roodbonten," *KS* 61 (1979): 236–8.

182 Vos, *Het meten*; M.P.M. Vos, "Niet alleen melk maar ook vlees is belangrijk bij de Nederlandse zwartbonten," *FV* (1972): 8–13. See also E.F. Geessink, "De gewenste fokrichting van het Nederlandse vee," *FV* 21 (1970–1): 314–19.

183 For a short discussion of "hybrid cow breeding" see *Veeverbetering* 64 (1982): 263. On hybrid corn, see Fitzgerald, *The Business of Breeding*; Kloppenburg, *First the Seed*; Berlan and Lewontin, "The Political Economy." I will return to hybrid corn breeding in the chapter on chicken breeding.

184 P.L. Scheer, "Gedachten omtrent de introductie en het gebruik van HF-bloed in de Nederlandse zwartbontveestapel," *FV* (1977): 92–7; A.N. Osinga, "Inleiding tot de algemene ledenvergadering van de Bond K.I.," *FV* (1978): 256–61; Strikwerda, *Melkweg*, 87–8.

185 J.A.P. Chardon, "De zwartbontfokkerij in de V.S.," *KS* 59 (1977): 342–6.

186 *Jaarverslag K.I. 1978*, 39. Holstein bull Nienrode was the most frequently used bull in Friesland in 1976; *FV* (1977): 152.

187 *FV* (1976): 665; *FV* (1977): 216, 419.

188 Strikwerda, *Melkweg*, 159, 161; Betteridge, "A History."

189 Strikwerda, *Melkweg*, 47, 168, 171; *Veeverbetering* 64 (1982): 46.

190 H. Vos, "Vergelijking van tien populaties zwartbonten in Polen," *KS* 62 (1980): 334–6, 406–8; ibid., 64 (1982): 14–16; H.A. Jasiorowski, M. Stolzman, and Z. Reklewski, "International FAO."

191 Strikwerda, *Melkweg*, 184.

192 J. Stigter, "Gesprek met Prof. Politiek (veeteeltwetenschappen)," *KS* 61 (1979): 499–601.

193 I. Hamming, "Met melk meer mans?" *Veeverbetering* 63 (1981), 196–8; and H.J.J. Oudenampsen, "Perpectieven voor MRIJ-fokkerij inzake vleesproductie," *Veeverbetering* 63 (1981): 264–5.

194 That the farmers and the national economy's interests did not run parallel in this matter was recognized in other European countries too; see Politiek and Bakker, *Livestock Production in Europe*, 116, 125.

195 Politiek, "Verleden, heden en toekomst," 78–9; Anon., "Bezinning op de positie van het MRIJ-veeras thans en naar de toekomst, alsmede de mogelijke opzet van een praktijkproef met gebruik van RHF-HRF-bloed," *Veeverbetering* 63 (1981): 532–53; Strikwerda, *Melkweg*, 158–9.

196 J.K. Oldenbroek et al., "Kan de kalfsvleesproductie van MRIJ-vee verbeterd worden door selectie?" *Veeteelt* (1986), 236–9; J.K. Oldenbroek

et al., "Dubbeldoelproef: De vleesproductie van MRIJ-vee kan duidelijk verbeteren door selectie," *Veeteelt* (1987): 160–3.

197 Strikwerda, *Melkweg*, 187. According to breeding adviser Frans Kuijpers (interview 26 September 2008) the fact that Politiek's pupil Guus Laeven became director of the most important breeding unit of MRIJ associations in 1986 played an important role in this. Laeven was a Holstein adept and had worked with Piet Scheer in Friesland.

198 Strikwerda, *Melkweg*, 187.

199 A. Hamoen, "Het roodbont dubbeldoel vraagt aandacht op weg naar nieuwe perspectief," *Veeteelt* (1989): 752–4; J.K. Oldenbroek et al., "Gecombineerde selectie op melk en vlees bij MRIJ levert geld op," *Veeteelt* (1990): 300–2.

200 Strikwerda, *Melkweg*, 189. Only the red colour was retained, because red-and-white calves, even though they carried varying percentages of Holstein genes, still brought in better prices than black-and-white calves; the slaughterhouses found it too cumbersome to assess the quality of red-and-white calves one by one.

201 See, for instance, R. Zijlstra, "Fokdoel en zuivelbeleid," *Veeverbetering* 63 (1981): 6–9; and R.D. Politiek, "Moet het fokbeleid aangepast worden aan een productiebeperking?" *Veeteelt* (1984): 102–5.

202 Strikwerda, *Melkweg*, 154, 166.

203 Strikwerda, *Melkweg*, 89.

204 R. Strikwerda, "Genetische trends bevestigen Nederlands fokkerijsukses," *Veeteelt* (1994): 582–4; Anon., "Sperma-export," *Veeteelt* (1995): 1004; and W. Koopman, "Spermahandel in beweging. Marktleider Verenigde Staten krijgt Europese konkurrentie," *Veeteelt* (1995): 1226–8.

205 Strikwerda, *Melkweg*, 190–1, 194.

206 Derry, *Bred for Perfection*, 156–61.

207 See for instance *Veeverbetering* 70 (1988): 1145; *Veeverbetering* 72 (1990): 1213.

208 M.P.M. Vos, "Niet alleen melk maar ook vlees is belangrijk bij de Nederlandse zwartbonten," *FV* (1972): 8–13.

209 Van der Ploeg, *De virtuele boer*, 260–5.

## 2. "The Most Efficient Chickens in the World"

An earlier version of this chapter was published as Van der Waaij and Theunissen "De meest efficiënte kip."

1 Mulder, "Met pijn in het boerenhart," 30.

2 Knibbe, "De opkomst," 60.

3 For historical overviews of poultry farming in the Netherlands in the nineteenth and twentieth centuries, see Janssen, Broos and Renders, *Handboek*; Westerink, *De pluimveeteelt*; Ketelaars, *Historie*; Knibbe,

"De opkomst"; Bieleman, "De legkippenhouderij"; Frankenhuis, *Over het ontstaan*; Schippers, Simons, and Borst, *Kippen*. See also Frost, *Die Holländische Landwirtschaft*.

4 Knibbe, "De opkomst," 67–73. Compare Derry, *Art and Science*, 68–73; Sayer, "His Footmarks."

5 Ketelaars, *Historie*, 60–2.

6 For a description of this development in North America, see Derry, *Art and Science*, 128–53.

7 Knibbe, "De opkomst," 63; Bieleman, "De legkippenhouderij," 156; Thurlings and Meulenberg, "De betekenis van de pluimveehouderij," 946–50.

8 Ketelaars, *Historie*, 23–56; Westerink, *De pluimveelteelt*, 26–9. The journal was entitled *Het Nuthoen. Officieel Orgaan der Eerste Ned. Coop. Bond voor Hoenderfokker. Geïllustreerd Maandblad Gewijd aan de Ned. Hoenderteelt en Eierenhandel.* The breed descriptions were published in V.P.N, *Nuthoenderstandaard*.

9 Some of the serious fanciers published illustrated handbooks; see for instance Maitland, *Hoenderboek*; Houwink, *De hoenderrassen*.

10 Westerink, *De pluimveeteelt*. There was more tension between fancy breeders and farmers who bred their animals for utility in Britain and North America. Unlike their Dutch colleagues, fancy breeders in North America continued to exert considerable control over the direction of breeding in the early decades of the twentieth century. The situation in the United States was complicated by debates over the usefulness of the Standard of Perfection and the Record of Performance, two instruments for assessing the quality of individual chickens that were used in combination in North America, thereby blurring the distinction between breeding for beauty and breeding for utility; see Derry, *Art and Science*, 39–73. No such standards or records were in use in Dutch poultry farming.

11 Ketelaars, *Historie*, 121–4, 129–33; Schippers, *Kippen*, 118–21, 150–3, 174–7, 238–41.

12 Ketelaars, *Historie*, 126–8.

13 Hagedoorn, *Handboek*, 138; Hagedoorn, "An Improved Method." The random sampling test suggested by Hagedoorn was implemented in the USA in the 1950s; see Derry, *Art and Science*, 108–18.

14 Cooke, "From Science to Practice."

15 Ketelaars, *Historie*, 133–6.

16 Maris, Scheer, and Visser, *Het kleine-boeren vraagstuk*.

17 Ketelaars, *Historie*, 88–95; Ford, *Netherlands: Surplus Producer*.

18 For histories of hybrid-corn breeding, see Crabb, *The Hybrid-Corn Makers*; Kloppenburg Jr, *First the Seed*; Fitzgerald, *The Business of Breeding*; Kimmelman and Paul, "Mendel in America"; Kingsbury, *Hybrid*, 219–50. For Wallace, see Schapsmeier, *Henry A. Wallace*.

19 Sebright, *The Art*; Darwin, *The Effects*, 16–18. See also Zirkle, "Early Ideas."
20 Tegetmeier, *The Poultry Book*, 51; Derry, *Art and Science*, 59–68; Matz, "Crossing"; Paul and Kimmelman, "Mendel in America," 288–90.
21 Darwin, *On the Origin of Species*, 20.
22 Shull, "Duplicate Genes," 127; Shull, "What is Heterosis."
23 For a review, see Gowen, *Heterosis*.
24 An additional hypothesis that has been suggested to overcome this problem is that some genes that are relevant for the heterosis effect may be situated closely together on the same chromosome: they are linked, meaning that they are transmitted to the next generation together. If the dominant (beneficial) allele of one of these genes is linked to the recessive (deleterious) allele of another gene, the two genes' dominant alleles will never appear together in a single pure line and can only be brought together by crossing the two lines that carry them.
25 Crow, "Anecdotal, Historical and Critical Commentaries," 926–7.
26 Berlan and Lewontin, "The Political Economy of Hybrid Corn." For the history of intellectual property rights in living animals, see for instance Kevles, "Patents"; Kevles, "New Blood"; Gaudillière, Kevles and Rheinberger, *Living Properties*. Derry analyses the role of herd books in protecting the work of livestock breeders; see for instance the chapter on Shorthorns (*Bred for Perfection*, 17–47).
27 Mangelsdorf, *Donald Forsha Jones*, 137.
28 Comstock, Robinson, and Harvey, "A Breeding Procedure"; Havenstein, H&N – A Brief History; Derry, *Art and Science*, 183.
29 A.L. Hagedoorn, "De nucleus-methode in de pluimveefokkerij," *De Bedrijfspluimveehouder* [*BPH*] 27, no. 24 (1949) 2; Hagedoorn and Sykes, *Poultry Breeding*, 61–6.
30 Skaller, "The Hagedoorn Nucleus-System"; Anon., "De fokkersvergadering te Utrecht," *BPH* 29, no. 25 (1951): n.p.
31 Crow, "Anecdotal, Historical and Critical Commentaries," 924–5; Mangelsdorf, *Donald Forsha Jones*, 137.
32 For reviews of chicken breeding methods, see Hartmann, "From Mendel to Multi-National"; Crawford, *Poultry Keeping*, 987–1009.
33 Hy-Line Nederland, *Hy-Line hybridekippen*; Crabb, *The Hybrid Corn-Makers*, 301–18.
34 Sprague and Tatum, "General vs. Specific Combining Ability."
35 Freeman, "C.R. Henderson," 4048–9; Derry, *Masterminding Nature*, 111–12.
36 For the development of AI in chickens in the Netherlands, see Strikwerda, *Revolutie*, 210–15.
37 For an analysis of intellectual property protection in chicken breeding, see Bugos, "Intellectual Property Protection."
38 Crabb, *The Hybrid Corn-Makers*, 301–18; Hy-Line Nederland, *Hy-Line hybridekippen*.

39 Anon., "Hybrids on the nest," *Wallace's Farmer*, 16 October 1948.
40 A.L. Hagedoorn, "Bastaardhennen voor de leg," *BPH* 10, no. 38 (1932): 1–2.
41 Hirschfeld, "Voor- en nadelen"; Van Albada, *Evolutie*; Ketelaars, *Historie*, 136–7.
42 Anon., "De fokkersvergadering te Utrecht," *BPH* 29, no. 25 (1951): n.p.
43 Van der Plank, "Theoretische grondslagen."
44 P.J. Wijk Pzn, "Zuivere rassen of bedrijfskruisingen," *BPH* 30, no. 24 (1952): 1.
45 Smith, "The History of Euribrid."
46 Interview with Theo Peters, former employee of Euribrid, 22 December 2015; Smith, "The History of Euribrid."
47 Courtney P. Allen, former employee (from 1950) of Hy-Line Poultry Farms, personal communication via email, 5 September 2015. Allen was present at several meetings between Henry B. Wallace and Guust van den Eynden in 1951–4.
48 Interview with Theo Peters, former employee of Euribrid, 22 December 2015; Bläsing, *Op het spoor van de Körver*, 45, 198, 273; Ketelaars, *Historie*, 143–4; Anon., "Miscellaneous."
49 Smith, "The History of Euribrid."
50 Interview with Theo Peters, former employee of Euribrid, 14 January 2016. Peters did not witness the events described here personally; Smith, "The History of Euribrid"; Lefever, *Wel en wee*, 38–9.
51 Smith, "The History of Euribrid."
52 Bläsing, *Op het spoor van de Körver*, 45, 198, 273; Ford, *Netherlands: Surplus Producer*.
53 Hendrix had by then obtained trademarks for several other European countries, which were transferred to Hy-Line Poultry Farms; Smith, "The History of Euribrid"; Courtney P. Allen, former employee (from 1950) of Hy-Line Poultry Farms, personal communication via email, 5 September 2015.
54 Smith, "The History of Euribrid." The company also had a pig breeding division; more on this in the next chapter.
55 M.P.G. van den Eynden, "Enkele gegevens over praktijk-ervaringen met Amerikaanse hybriden," *BPH* 35, no. 10 (1957): 13.
56 Hy-Line Nederland, *Hy-Line hybridekippen*.
57 Advertisement in *BPH* 35, no. 19 (1957): 11.
58 A., "De Hy-Lines in aantocht," *BPH* 34, no. 9 (1956): 2.
59 De V., "Het zijn de kruisingen, die de boerenpluimveebedrijven bevolken," *BPH* 34, no. 20 (1956): 1–2.
60 Afdeling Pluimveeteelt, Hendrix" Pluimvee- en Veevoederfabriek Boxmeer, "Enige theoretische beschouwingen over het combinatievermogen bij de kippenfokkerij," *BPH* 30, no. 3 (1952), 2.

61 De V., "De fokkerij blijft de belangrijkste pijler van onze pluimveehouderij," *BPH* 35, no. 13 (1957): 1–2.
62 Anon., "Fokkerijproblemen," *BPH* 34, no. 19 (1956): 2.
63 Stichting voor het fokkerijwezen bij de pluimveehouderij, *50 jaar pluimveetoetsen*; Ketelaars, *Historie*, 137–41.
64 De V., "Het zijn de kruisingen die de pluimveebedrijven bevolken," *BPH* 34, no. 20 (1956): 1–2; Anon., "Meer zekerheid bij aankoop van kuikens," *BPH* 35, no. 10 (1957): 8–9.
65 Anon., "Fokkerijproblemen," *BPH* 34, no. 19 (1956): 2.
66 Anon., "Enkele mededelingen over de pluimveefokkerij en de taak in deze van het Coöperatief Pluimveefokkers-Instituut," *BPH* 35, no. 13 (1957): 5; Ketelaars, *Historie*, 141–3.
67 After a buy-out of its Belgian partner in 1971, CPI became the single owner of Hypeco; Smith, "The History of Hypeco CPI Bovans."
68 Lefever, *Wel en wee*, 48.
69 Ketelaars, *Historie*, 141–3.
70 Ketelaars, *Historie*, 159–63; for examples of the frequent discussions about the issue in *De Bedrijfspluimveehouder*, see Anon., "De gevolgen van de EEG-verordening voor onze pluimveehouderij," *BPH* 41, no. 14 (1963): 371, 375; Anon., "Nederlandse eierexport ernstig bedreigd, kwade trouw bij Fransen, verdachtmaking door Duitsers, naar hogere eierprijzen," *BPH* 43, no. 6 (1965): 225; Anon., "Inkrimping van onze pluimveehouderij voor eierproduktie gevolg van E.E.G.-verordening," *BPH* 44, no. 2 (1966): 37; R. Brons, "De legsector het kind van de rekening in de EEG-landbouwpolitiek," *BPH* 48, no. 9 (1970): 341.
71 Bieleman, "De legkippenhouderij," 169.
72 For a discussion of the pros and cons of the new regime for the smallholders, see De V., "Is de afschaffing van de pluimveeregeling een pluimveehoudersbelang?," *BPH* 38, no. 17 (1960): 3.
73 Tukker, "E.E.G. en pluimveehouderij"; Speight, "The effects of the EEC," 50.
74 For the introduction of battery cages, see Ketelaars, *Historie*, 170–1, 220–2; Bieleman, "De legkippenhouderij," 168–73. Compare Sayer, "Battery Birds."
75 De V., "Ook de pluimveehouderij moet zich aanpassen," *BPH* 39, no. 18 (1961): 413–15. On the postwar rise of the broiler industry, see Horowitz, "Making the Chicken."
76 Anon., "Bovans-kuikenbroeders vergaderen: spreker C.A.S. Zwetsloot over het structuurprobleem in de pluimveehouderij," *BPH* 42, no. 22 (1964): 755.
77 See https://opendata.cbs.nl/statline/#/CBS/nl/dataset/81302ned/table?ts=1544197283496; accessed 7 December 2018.

78 Ketelaars, *Historie*, 209–26; Anon., "Integratie in de pluimveehouderij," *BPH* 47, no. 1 (1969): 4; Anon., "Eerste eierring in ons land dateert van 1961," *BPH* 47, no. 7 (1969): 209–10.
79 Interview with Frans van Sambeek, director R&D of ISA, Hendrix Genetics, 22 December 2015.
80 Anon., "Naar concentratie en integratie bij de Nederlandse fokkerij?," *BPH* 41, no. 4 (1963): 75.
81 Anon., "Nog ruim 70 fokbedrijven in ons land," *BPH* 43, no. 17 (1965): 573.
82 Ibid.; Anon., "Een derde minder fokkers door vrijwillige sanering," *BPH* 41, no. 19 (1963): 467; Anon., "Door vrijwillige sanering 100,000 hennen minder op fokbedrijven," *BPH* 41, no. 19 (1963): 473.
83 Interview with Gerard Albers, director of innovation at Hendrix Genetics, 30 March 2016; Anon., "Fokkersdag 1965: Problemen rond de commercialisatie van kippenfokprodukten," *BPH* 43, no. 19 (1965): 691.
84 Anon., "Bovans slaat de vleugels uit," *BPH* 43, no. 6 (1965): 229.
85 Interview with Frans van Sambeek, director R&D at ISA, Hendrix Genetics, 22 December 2015; Smith, "The History of Hypeco CPI Bovans."
86 Anon., "Fokkersdag 1965: Problemen rond de commercialisatie van kippenfokprodukten," *BPH* 43, no. 19 (1965): 691.
87 Anon., "De fokbedrijven," *BPH* 42, no. 12 (1964): 383.
88 Anon., "Fokkersdag 1965: Problemen rond de commercialisatie van kippenfokprodukten," *BPH* 43, no. 19 (1965): 691.
89 Interview with Koos van Middelkoop, former director of breeding at Hypeco, 20 January 2016.
90 Interview with Gerard Albers, director of innovation at Hendrix Genetics, 30 March 2016.
91 Interview with Frans van Sambeek, director of R&D at ISA, Hendrix-Genetics, 22 December 2015. For American examples of the trend towards globalization of the breeding business, see Derry, *Art and Science*, 180–2.
92 Interview with Theo Peters, former employee at Euribrid, 22 December 2015.
93 Ibid.; interview with Frans van Sambeek, director of R&D at ISA, Hendrix Genetics, 22 December 2015.
94 Interview with Theo Peters, former employee at Euribrid, 22 December 2015.
95 Cited by Derry, *Art and Science*, 188.
96 Interview with Theo Peters, former employee at Euribrid, 22 December 2015. "'Hisex wit' – witte leghornhybride van Euribrid. Euribrid maakt snelle ontwikkeling door," *BPH* 48, no. 16 (1970): 565.
97 Interview with Addie Vereijken, former employee at Hybro, later at Hendrix Genetics, 14 January 2016.

98 Ibid.; interview with Theo Peters, former employee at Euribrid, 22 December 2015; interview with Frans van Sambeek, director R&D at ISA, Hendrix Genetics, 22 December 2015.
99 Groenen et al., "A Consensus Linkage Map."
100 Haley and Knott, "A Simple Regression Method."
101 Interview with Gerard Albers, director of innovation at Hendrix Genetics, 30 March 2016.
102 Ibid.
103 By analogy with Gould, *Cats Are Not Peas.*
104 Derry, *Art and Science*, 97–127.
105 Paul and Kimmelman, "Mendel in America," 288–90, 298, 301; Fitzgerald, *The Business of Breeding*, 23, 29, 43.
106 See, for instance, Palladino, "Wizards and Devotees"; Harwood, "The Reception of Genetic Theory"; Bonneuil, "Mendelism." For an excellent overview of recent work on this issue, see Harwood, "Did Mendelism Transform Plant Breeding?"
107 Paul and Kimmelman, "Mendel in America," 298; Crabb, *The Hybrid Corn-Makers*, 42.
108 Mulder, "Met pijn in het boerenhart," 31–3.
109 Derry, *Art and Science*, 195–6.

### 3. Breeding a Pig for All Parties

This chapter uses material from Van der Laan, *Een varken voor iedereen.*

1 Bieleman, *Boeren in Nederland*, 273–80, 398–410; Knibbe, *Agriculture*, 262.
2 For histories of Dutch pig breeding, see Löhnis, *Varkenshouderij*; Kroon, *Die Schweinezucht*; Slaghuis and Van der Berg, *Van everzwijn tot vleesvarken.* See also Reens, *De vleeschexport.* For the UK, see Wiseman, *The Pig*; for Germany and the USA, see Matz, "Crossing." For an analysis of pig breeding in the context of the rise of European fascism, see Saraiva, *Fascist Pigs.*
3 See for instance A. van Leeuwen, "Varkensfokkerij en geen einde," *De Veldbode* 5 (1907), 181; T.H., "Van twee varkensrassen," *De Veldbode* 10 (1912): 108–9; Kroon, *De tegenwoordige richtingen*, 181.
4 H.M. Kroon, Rapport omtrent de vraag: is het mogelijk en gewenst om met de varkensfokkerijen den weg op te gaan dien men in Denemarken gevolgd heeft? Nationaal Archief, Den Haag 2.11.05–22. For the Danish pig industry and its influence on Dutch pig breeding, see Slaghuis and Van der Berg, *Van everzwijn tot vleesvarken*, 29–39; Jonsson, "Methods," 2–5.
5 Löhnis, *Varkenshouderij*, 15–33.
6 G. van Blaricum, "Ingezonden stukken. Onze varkensfokkerij," *De Veldbode* 12 (1914): 667.

7 A. van Leeuwen, "Typen en fokrichtingen," *De Veldbode* 17 (1919): 713–14; J. Timmermans, "Houdt raszuivere fokvarkens!" *De Veldbode* 29 (1930): 158.

8 A. van Leeuwen, "Een interessante erfelijkheids- en rechtskwestie," *De Veldbode* 24 (1926): 773.

9 H.W. Schilt, "Een interessante erfelijkheids- en rechtskwestie," *De Veldbode* 24 (1926), 1047; H. Roest, Een interessante erfelijkheidskwestie," *De Veldbode* 24 (1926): 1133.

10 C.R. van Vloten, "Ten behoeve van de varkensfokkerij," *De Veldbode* 27 (1929): 227.

11 Anon., "Onze vleeschhandel op Engeland," *De Veldbode* 24 (1926) 1131; S. van Zwanenburg, "80ste Nederlandsch Landhuishoudkundige Congres," *De Veldbode* 26 (1928): 811–16.

12 See, for instance, E. Dommerhold, "Zouters," *De Veldbode* 24 (1926): 618–19; A. van Leeuwen, "Het Engelsche bacon-varken," *De Veldbode* 24 (1926): 1335–6.

13 T. Mansholt, "Onze bacon-export," *De Veldbode* 26 (1928): 747–8; Wiseman, *The Pig*, 71–3.

14 For more extensive definitions, see for instance https://beefandlamb.ahdb.org.uk/wp-content/uploads/2013/05/p_cp_glossary_carcase_and_meat_quality_terms031012.pdf; accessed 7 December 2018.

15 Leignes Bakhoven and De Jong, *De varkensfokkerij*. See also R. Anema, "Selectiemesterijen en hun beteekenis voor de varkensfokkerij," *De Veldbode* 28 (1930): 851–3.

16 Slaghuis and Van der Berg, *Van everzwijn tot slachtvarken*, 31–5, 41.

17 Minutes CBV meeting on 18 December 1931, Archives of the Nationaal Veeteelt Museum Beers, k13, 20A box 342; Paridaans, *75 jaar*, 106–7; Broekhuizen and Thijs, "Selectiemesterijen," 60.

18 J.H. Holsbrink, "De toekomst van de stamboekfokkerij," *Maandblad voor de Varkensfokkerij* [*MV*] 31, no. 1 1968): 5.

19 Werkgroep Technisch-Genetische Aspecten van de Varkenshouderij, *Mogelijkheden*.

20 Ibid., passim.

21 Y. Kroes, "Mogelijkheden van de varkensfokkerij in stamboekverband," *MV* 31, no. 9 (1969): 141–2.

22 Bieleman, *Boeren in Nederland*, 463, 515–19. For the effects of the Common Agricultural Policy on the pig industry, see Kenyon, "The Impact of CAP."

23 W. Wisman, "Noodtoestand," *De Boerderij/Varkenshouderij* [*B/V*] 58, 13–18 May (1974): 3; Anon, "Prijsdieptepunt bereikt?" *B/V* 58, 22–7 April (1974): 3.

24 Anon., "Nieuwe CBV-directeur ir. P.C. Reekers: "Stamboeken moeten nieuwe kennis inpassen in fokprogramma,"" *B/V* 56, no. 48 (1972): 9. For Euribrid, see chapter 2.

25 D. Minkema, "Heeft het pwf-systeem voor de varkenshouderij wel zin?" *B/V* 58, 11–16 March (1974), 14–15.
26 Anon., "Het stamboek gaat de "snelweg" op," *B/V* 58, 3–8 June (1974): 10–11.
27 Anon., "Het selectiemesterij-onderzoek," *MV* no. 9 (1975): 12–15.
28 D. Minkema, "Heeft het pwf-systeem voor de varkenshouderij wel zin?" *B/V* 58, 11–16 March (1974): 14–15; G. Ogink, "Vooruitgang in de stamboekfokkerij," *Bedrijfsontwikkeling* 8 (1977): 61–3.
29 Anon., "Nieuw stamboekfokkerijsysteem kan snellere vooruitgang bewerkstelligen," *B/V* 58, 22–27 April (1974): 8–9; P.C. Reekers, "Buitengewone Algemene Vergadering C.B.V. in Utrecht," *MV* 36, no. 1 (1974): 2; Anon., "Wijziging stamboekfoksysteem," *MV* 36, no. 1 (1974): 3.
30 https://opendata.cbs.nl/statline/#/CBS/nl/dataset/71904ned/table?ts=1530740089245; accessed 7 December 2018; Kenyon, "The Impact of CAP." The human population in the Netherlands increased from 10 to 14 million in this period.
31 Bieleman, *Boeren in Nederland*, 479–80, 515–22.
32 See for instance Slaghuis and Van der Berg, *Van everzwijn tot vleesvarken*, 83. See also P. Heijnen, "Integratie en fokkerij," *MV* 35, no. 4 (1973): 52–3; Anon., "Fokkersbijeenkomst voor de stamboekfokkerij," *Varkensfokkerij/Mesterij* [*V/M*] no. 11 (1978): 13.
33 Anon, "Varkensmarkt onder druk," *V/M* no. 12 (1976): 3; Bieleman, *Boeren in Nederland*, 517–18; Kenyon, "The Impact of Cap."
34 Y. Kroes, "De invoering van de E.E.G.-klassificatie van geslachte varkens en de uitbetaling naar kwaliteit," *MV* 34, no. 12 (1972): 197–200.
35 See for instance W. van der Sluis, "Herbezinning fokkerijbeleid nodig," *B/V* 60, no. 7 (1976), 3; W. van der Sluis, "Slachtkwaliteit is niet het enige," *B/V* 61, no. 17 (1977): 3; Anon., "Uitbetaling naar kwaliteit in discussie," *V/M* no. 4 (1977): 12.
36 See for instance, Anon., "Meer dan 11 miljoen slachtvarkens," *MV* no. 2 (1975): 3; Anon., "58% Export en uitbetaling naar kwaliteit," *MV* no. 4 (1975): 3–5.
37 Anon., "Aanpassing selectie-mesterij-index bij de varkensstamboeken. Intensieve selectie op slachtkwaliteit blijft gehandhaafd," *MV* no. 8 (1976): 4–5; Anon., "Nederlandse boer kan niet zonder export," *V/M* no. 10 (1976): 19.
38 H. Reintjes, "Selektie op vruchtbaarheidskenmerken," *V/M* no. 1 (1981): 11.
39 Anon., "Stamboekfokprogramma op de helling," *V/M* no. 1 (1980): 3.
40 W. van der Sluijs, "Het moet anders," *B/V* 66, 13 May (1981): 3; Anon., "Ir. E. Talstra waarschuwt: stamboeken hebben te weinig oog voor beter varken," *B/V* 66, 13 May (1981): 10–11.
41 Anon., "Fokproducten op de Nederlandse varkensmarkt," *V/M* no. 7 (1977): 3; Anon., "Algemene vergadering van het Centraal Bureau voor

de Varkensfokkerij," *V/M* no. 10 (1980): 16–17. The companies that participated in the comparative test were Euribrid, Cofok, Fomeva, and Nieuw-Dalland.

42 C. Kuipers, "Wroetweide: "De billen bloot,"" *B/V* 66, 28 October (1981): 5.

43 P. Knap, "Enkele kanttekeningen bij de resultaten van de merkentoets," *V/M* no. 10 (1981): 20–1; Anon., "Bestuur CBV besluit tot fokkerijmaatregelen," *V/M* no. 11 (1981): 3.

44 W. Cöp, "De praktijk wijst beter uit," *B/V* 66, 28 October (1981): 11; Anon., "Stel nou eens ..." *B/V* 66, 28 October (1981): 9.

45 Anon., "Bestuur CBV besluit tot fokkerijmaatregelen," *V/M* no. 11 (1981): 3.

46 Anon., "Herziening van het stamboekfokprogramma," *V/M* no. 12 (1981): 3; Anon., "Nieuwe definitie voor de sterzeug," *V/M* no. 3 (1982): 9–10.

47 Interview with Chris Willems, 8 November 2014. For a history of AI in pigs in the Netherlands, see R. Strikwerda, *Revolutie*, 160–209. See also Anon., "De varkensfokkerij," 41–4.

48 J. Tijs, "De invloed van de K.I. op de Nederlandse Landvarkenfokkerij," *MV* 29, no. 1 (1966), 5–12.

49 See Wilmot, "From 'Public Service' to Artificial Insemination," 435; Brassley, "Cutting across Nature?," 442–61.

50 See for instance, W.M. Gotink, "Proef met K.I. bij varkens in Overijssel," *MV* 21, no. 8 1958): 71–2; W.M. Gotink, "K.I. bij varkens," *MV* 23, no. 9 (1961): 104–5; Y. Kroes, "De varkensfokkerij en -houderij in 1961," *MV* 24, no. 9 (1962): 103–5; C.M.T. Willems, De ontwikkeling van de varkens k.i. in Noord-Brabant," *MV* 24, no. 9 (1962): 107–8.

51 See for instance P. Zandstra, "Enkele opmerkingen over beerhouderijen," *MV* 25, no. 6 (1962): 73; J. Holsbrink, "Het voor- en nadeel van het houden van een dekbeer voor eigen bedrijf," *MV* 25, no. 7 (1962): 80–1.

52 H. Bakker, "De invloed van K.I.-beren op de resultaten van de selectiemesterij in Drenthe," *MV* 32, no. 6 (1969): 104–5.

53 Before the 1960s, boars were kept by boar keepers, and sows were brought to their stations for insemination. The risks of infection were high, however, and the stations were closed in the 1960s; Slaghuis and Van der Berg, *Van everzwijn tot vleesvarken*, 61–2.

54 J. Holsbrink, Het voor- en nadeel van het houden van een dekbeer voor eigen bedrijf," *MV* 25, no. 7 (1962): 80–1; G. Jansen-Venneboer, "Kan met succes van varkens K.I. worden gebruik gemaakt?" *MV* 35, no. 1 (1972): 3–4.

55 A. Rutgers, "K.I. bij varkens van 1 juli 1962 – 30 juni 1963," *Jaarverslag K.I. 1963*, 26; A. Rutgers, "K.I. bij varkens van 1 juli 1972 – 30 juni 1973," *Jaarverslag K.I. 1973*, 65; Strikwerda, *Revolutie*, 173–4.

56 M. Veenstra, "De varkens K.I.-verenigingen in de vier noordelijke provincies," *MV* 36, no. 3 1973): 38–9. See also Anon., "Varkens k.i. ook voor de productie van mestbiggen," *V/M* no. 12 (1977): 10–11.
57 C. Willems, "De ontwikkeling van de varkens k.i in Noord-Brabant, *MV* 24, no. 9 (1962): 107.
58 Giesen, "200 zeugen per man," 45; Anon., "Varkens-k.i. maakt enorme sprong vooruit," *Boerderij/Varkenshouderij* 60, no. 12 (1976): 5–6; Anon., "Varkens k.i. ook voor de productie van mestbiggen," *V/M* no. 12 (1977): 10–11; Anon., Ontwikkeling van varkens k.i. in Gelderland gaat zeer snel," *V/M* no. 7 (1977): 14.
59 G.J. Mombarg., "Doe het zelf-K.I. Gelderland," *V/M* no. 1 (1981): 19.
60 Slaghuis and Van der Berg, *Van everzwijn tot slachtvarken*, 66.
61 Strikwerda, *Revolutie*, 186–91.
62 Anon., "Bescherming stamboekfokmateriaal," *MV* 36, no. 1 (1974): 6.
63 Anon., "Voorwaarden en algemene regels "doe het zelf" K.I. bij varkens," *V/M* no. 1 (1979): 11.
64 Anon., "Actuele stamboekzaken," *MV* no. 1 (1976): 7.
65 Anon., "Werkwijze en omvang van de fokkerijinstellingen," *MV* 36, no. 5 (1974): 74–5.
66 P.C. Reekers, "Coosta programma gestopt in Cavee-Coveco-werkgebied," *V/M* no. 1 (1984): 5; Slaghuis en Van den Berg, *Van everzwijn tot vleesvarken*, 108.
67 H. van der Steen, "Invloed biotechnologie op KI/fokkerijorganisaties," *Varkens* no. 4 (1989): 26–7.
68 A. Rutgers, "K.I. bij varkens van 1 juli 1969 – 30 juni 1970," *Jaarverslag K.I. 1970*, 56; B. Noordman, "Nederlands Varkensstamboek van start!" *Varkens* no. 1 (1989): 3; Slaghuis and Van der Berg, *Van everzwijn tot vleesvarken*, 122–36; Strikwerda, *Revolutie*, 194–201; http://www.wattagnet.com/articles/19191-topigs-norsvin-merge-into-second-largest-pig-genetics-supplier; accessed 7 December 2018.
69 Slaghuis and Van der Berg, *Van everzwijn tot slachtvarken*, 81–2, 122–4, 135–6; Strikwerda, *Revolutie*, 199–200; Anon., "De varkensfokkerij," 5–10, 30–9.
70 https://www.pic.com/about-us/; accessed 9 August 2019. Other important companies include the Danish Danbred and Next Genetics.
71 Robroek, *Verslag over den landbouw*, 31; W. de Jong, "Uitbetaling naar kwaliteit," *MV* 1, no. 1 (1937): 2–5.
72 P. Labouchère, "Regeling Beerhouderij," *MV* 9, no. 10 (1947): 1–2.
73 See for instance de J., "Varkensfokdagen Heythuizen 14 Mei," *MV* 20, no. 5 (1957): 40–1; Y. Kroes, "De varkensfokkerij en -houderij in 1958," *MV* 21, no. 9 (1959): 81–3.
74 Slaghuis and Van der Berg, *Van everzwijn tot slachtvarken*, 81–2; Anon., "De varkensfokkerij," 11–17.

75 P.C. Reekers, "Hybridefokkerij bij varkens," *MV* 30, no. 2 (1967): 184–5.
76 Ibid.
77 De R. te Z., "Vragen-rubriek. Vraag 89," *MV* 25, no. 8 (1962): 98.
78 P.C. Reekers, "Enkele nieuwe aspecten van de varkensfokkerij in stamboekverband," *MV* 35, no. 7 (1972): 93–5.
79 Y. Kroes and J. Huiskes, "De varkensfokkerij en -houderij in 1968," *MV* 31, no. 9 (1969): 137–40; M. Vos, "De betekenis van de gebruikskruising voor de producent van mestbiggen," *MV* 33, no. 10 (1971): 181–3; Anon., 60 jaar Centraal Bureau voor de Varkensfokkerij, Archives Nationaal Veeteeltmuseum Beers: k13, 14B box 301.
80 P.C. Reekers, "Enkele nieuwe aspecten voor de varkensfokkerij in stamboekverband," *MV* 35, no. 7 (1972): 93–4.
81 P.C. Reekers, "Praktische betekenis der stamboekhybriden voor vermeerderaar en mester," *MV* 36, no. 2 (1973): 18–20; Anon., "Hebben hybridevarkens de toekomst?" *MV* no. 6 (1975), 3.
82 P.C. Reekers, "Commentaar op een artikel in *De Boerderij*," *V/M* no. 10 (1977): 7; Anon. "Ervaringen met het fokken van stamboek hybride varkens," *V/M* no. 9 (1978): 12–13.
83 *Jaarverslag Instituut voor Veeteeltkundig Onderzoek "Schoonoord" in 1976* (Zeist: IVO, 1977), 46.
84 Anon., "Het Duroc varken als derde ras?" *V/M* no. 8 (1979): 5; P. Brascamp, "Het mogelijk nut van Duroc in een stamboek kruisingsprogramma," *V/M* no. 3 (1979): 6–9.
85 W. van der Sluis, "Slachtkwaliteit is niet het enige," *B/V* 61, no. 17 (1977): 3.
86 Anon., "Bestuur CBV besluit tot fokkerijmaatregelen," *V/M* no. 11 (1981): 3.
87 *Jaarverslag Instituut voor Veeteeltkundig Onderzoek "Schoonoord" in 1983* (Zeist: IVO, 1984): 75; Slaghuis and Van der Berg, *Van everzwijn tot vleesvarken*, 105–7.
88 Anon., "GY-ras kan in geen enkel kruisingsprogramma gemist worden," *V/M* no. 6 (1979): 15; Anon., "De vruchtbare Yorkshire-lijn (GY-Z-lijn)," *V/M* no. 6 (1982): 16–17; *Jaarverslag 1982 van het Centraal Bureau voor de Varkensfokkerij en de Bond van Verenigingen voor Kunstmatige Inseminatie van Varkens* (Nijmegen: CBV, 1983): 36–43; Slaghuis and Van der Berg, *Van everzwijn tot vleesvarken*, 125–9.
89 Slaghuis and Van der Berg, *Van everzwijn tot vleesvarken*, 83–6.
90 See for instance Knol, Nielsen, and Knap, "Genomic Selection."
91 A.L. Hagedoorn, "Deensche varkens voor ons land," *De Veldbode* 27 (1929): 441–3.
92 C.R. van Vloten, "De vlekjesziekte bij varkens, een koppige kantoorkwaal," *De Veldbode* 28 (1930): 832.
93 K. Rijssenbeek, "Erfelijkheid in praktijk," *MV* 2, no. 3 (1938): 25–6; K. Rijssenbeek, "Erfelijkheid in praktijk," *MV* 2, no. 4 (1938): 33–5.
94 Dommerhold, *Het uitwendig voorkomen.*

95 Minutes of the CBV meeting of 20 December 1927, Archives Nationaal Veelteeltmuseum Beers: k13, 20A doos 342.
96 Dommerhold, *Het uitwendig voorkomen*, 11.
97 See for instance H. Bakker, "Keuringsimpressie," *MV* 23, no. 8 (1960): 89–90; J. Holsbrink, "Varkensfokdagen en varkensfokverenigingen," *MV* 28, no. 4 (1965): 39–40; Y. Kroes, "Varkensfokdagen. Mheer 3 juli," *MV* 20, no. 5 (1957): 41; Y. Kroes, "Najaarsfokdagen Utrecht," *MV* 20, no. 7 (1957): 54–5; Y. Kroes, "Najaarsfokdagen. Raalte 10 september," *MV* 21, no. 6 (1958): 57–9; Y. Fopma, "Varkensfokdagen. Utrecht," *MV* 27, no. 8 (1964): 92–4. For the introduction of ultrasonic backfat measurement, see L. Brinke, "Voorjaarsfokdagen. Horst," *MV* 31, no. 3 (1968): 40.
98 See for instance B. Alcuïnus, "Voorjaarsfokdagen. Gilze 22 april," *MV* 23, no. 2 (1960): 12; H. Krabbenborg, "Gereglementeerde aankoop van toetsberen, bestemd voor K.I.," *MV* 35, no. 9 (1973): 132–3.
99 The yearly reports on AI *(Jaarverslagen KI)* show that until 1972, insufficient quality of conformation was the reason given for the elimination of 10 per cent of all the AI boars eliminated. In 1975 this had dropped to less than 0.5 per cent.
100 See for instance Anon., "Limburg. Centrale Fokdag nieuwe stijl," *MV* 35, no. 5 (1972): 69; C. Backx, "Provinciale fokvarkensdag te Goes," *MV* 35, no. 6 (1972): 80–1; H. Rietberg, "Aanpassing stamboekfokkerij is een zaak van alle leden," *MV* 35, no. 10 (1973): 143–4.
101 Karel, *De maakbare boer*,5, 190; De Jonge, "Varkensfokkerij en -houderij," 160–1.
102 Anon., "Limburg. Centrale fokdag nieuwe stijl," *MV* 35, no. 5 (1972): 69.
103 H. Reintjes, Demonstratie fokvarkens in Helden (L.)," *MV* 35, no. 7 (1972): 98–9.
104 K. Rol, "Steek wat op van een ander," *MV* 32, no. 6 (1969): 104.
105 Y. Fopma, "Varkensfokdagen. Alkmaar," *MV* 35, no. 8 (1972): 116.
106 Anon., "Limburg. Centrale Fokdag nieuwe stijl," *MV* 35, no. 5 (1972): 69; C. Backx, "Provinciale fokvarkensdag te Goes," *MV* 35, no. 6 (1972): 80–1.
107 H. Reintjes, Demonstratie fokvarkens in Helden (L.)," *MV* 35, no. 7 (1972): 98–9.

**4. Just Not Like Any Other Sheep Breed: The Texel**

This chapter uses material from J. Oldenburger, Nederlandse schapenfokkerij in de twintigste eeuw, PhD dissertation, Utrecht University, in preparation.

1 Numan, *Handleiding*, vol. 1, 35–52, 85–107; Löhnis, *Schapenhouderij*; Kroon, *De tegenwoordige richtingen*, 127–54; Reens, *De vleeschexport*; Van der Vlis, *'t Lant van Texsel*; Bakker, *De Texelaar*, 9–50; Van der Wiel, *Veehouderij*, 157–67; Oldenburger and Theunissen, "Alexander Numan."

For a history of Dutch sheep husbandry in the twentieth century, see Van Bodegraven, *Geschiedenis*. For histories of sheep breeding in the UK, Germany, and Australia, see for example Ryder, *Sheep and Man*; Wood and Orel, *Genetic Prehistory*; Woods, *The Herds*.

2 Numan, *Handleiding*, vol. 2, 291–324.

3 Homburg, *Groeien*, 25–30.

4 Van Bodegraven, *Geschiedenis*, 38–43. In the Netherlands as a whole, the number of sheep dropped from over a million in 1867 to fewer than 900,000 in 1910 (Reens, *De vleeschexport*, 15–16).

5 J. Vullings, "Albert Bruin: "Nationaal wordt schapenvlees niet gewaardeerd," *Het Schaap* no. 7 (1985): 10–11; Bakker, "Voeding in Nederland"; https://www.vlees.nl/faq/waarom-eten-we-nederland-nauwelijks-schapenvlees/; accessed 5 May 2018.

6 Bieleman, *Boeren in Nederland*, 271–95.

7 Reens, *De vleeschexport*, 62–9.

8 Loman, "Het Texels schaap"; Loman, "Gemeente Texel."

9 Anon., "Tentoonstelling Den Haag," *Texelse Courant*, 27 September 1888.

10 Ibid.

11 Dijt's diary is preserved in the Municipal Archives, Texel, located in the Regional Archives, Alkmaar. See also Bakker and Vosjan, "Bewaaïerig weer," 12–17; Bakker, De *Texelaar*, 135–45.

12 Dijt's diary, 27 June 1888.

13 Ibid., 23 May, 2 July, 6 July, 23 July, and 28 July 1888.

14 Ibid., 23 May 1888.

15 Ibid., 28 June 1888.

16 Ibid.

17 Ibid.

18 D.E. Landman, "De schapenhouderij op Texel in verband met de aanstaande groote landbouwtentoonstelling," *Schager Courant*, 30 August 1908; Loman, "Gemeente Texel," 25.

19 D., "Van het eiland Texel," *Nederlandsch Landbouw-Weekblad*, 13 April 1901; J.D., "Van her en der," *Nederlandsch Landbouw-Weekblad*, 18 April 1903.

20 Loman, "Gemeente Texel," 21, 25.

21 Anon., "t Is voor de eer van Texel," *Texelsche Courant*, 13 August 1908; Anon., "Vergadering van de H.M.v.L.," *Texelsche Courant*, 6 August 1908.

22 Speech by H.W. Keesom in Anon., "Landbouwvergadering en tentoonstelling op Texel," *Bijvoegsel van "t Vliegend Blaadje*, 12 September 1908.

23 Anon., "De landbouwtentoonstelling te Den Burg op Texel," *Nederlandsch Landbouw-Weekblad*, 26 September 1908.

24 D.E. Landman, "De schapenhouderij op Texel in verband met de a.s. groote landbouwtentoonstelling aldaar," *Schager Courant*, 23 August 1908.

25 Löhnis, *Schapenhouderij*, 16.

26 A.L. Hagedoorn, "Schapenfokkerij op Texel," *Nederlandsch Landbouw-Weekblad*, 12 August 1911, 10 February 1912, and 2 March 2012; A.L. Hagedoorn, "Ingezonden stukken. Schapenfokkerij op Texel," *De Veldbode* 9 (1911): 595–6; A. van Leeuwen, "Wetenschappelijke schapenteelt," *De Veldbode* 8 (1910): 700–1; Kroon, *De tegenwoordige richtingen*, 154–5. See also Vosjan, "De eerste toepassing."

27 J.S. Dijt, "Schapenfokkerij op Texel," *Nederlandsch Landbouw-Weekblad*, 17 February 1912 and 2 March 1912.

28 A. van Leeuwen, "Schapenfokkerij op Texel," *De Veldbode* 9 (1911): 537–8.

29 C. Nobel, "Schapenfokkerij op Texel," *Nederlandsch Landbouw-Weekblad*, 25 November 2011, 2 December 1911, 10 February 1912, and 24 February 1912.

30 C. Nobel, "Verslag omtrent een onderzoek naar de resultaten, verkregen met het fokken met Lincoln- en Wensleydale-rammen in Noord-Holland," *De Veldbode* 7 (1909): 347–9.

31 Vosjan and Bakker, "Eén van de eerste beschrijvingen"; Jaarverslag der Vereeniging tot Verbetering van de Schapenfokkerij in Noord-Holland over ... 1909, North-Holland Archives, Haarlem, http://noord-hollandsarchief.nl/bronnen/archieven?mivast=236&mizig=210&miadt=236&miaet=1&micode=213&minr=772171&miview=inv2 [NHA]; accessed 20 July 2018.

32 Jaarverslag der Vereeniging tot Verbetering van de Schapenfokkerij in Noord-Holland over ... 1909, NHA.

33 Ibid.

34 *Texelsche Courant*, 19 August 1888, 21 July 1889, 3 November 1889, 29 December 1892, and 22 September 1895; *Schager Courant*, 28 July 1895, 9 February 1896, 2 August 1896, 9 August 1896, 16 August 1896, 11 November 1897, 3 March 1898, 22 May 1898, 18 August 1898, 24 November 1898, 11 June 1899, 24 August 1899, 17 September 1899, 24 September 1899, 1 July 1900, 9 August 1900, 27 September 1900, and 29 September 1901. See also Govers, *50 Jaar wol*, 4–11.

35 *Schager Courant*, 28 July 1895; Govers, *50 Jaar wol*, 9.

36 *Texelsche Courant*, 3 November 1889.

37 Ibid., 22 September 1895.

38 *Nederlandsch Landbouw-Weekblad*, 9 April 1904; *Schager Courant*, 31 August 1905, 24 September 1905, 26 August 1906, and 13 September 1906; C. Nobel, "Verslag omtrent een onderzoek naar de resultaten, verkregen met het fokken met Lincoln- en Wensleydale-rammen in Noord-Holland," *De Veldbode* 7 (1909): 347–9.

39 Jaarverslag der Vereeniging tot Verbetering van de Schapenfokkerij in Noord-Holland over ... 1910, 1911, 1912, 1917, 1918, NHA.

40 Ibid., 1917, 1918, NHA; Govers, *50 Jaar wol*, 16.

41 Bakker, *Grondbeginselen*, 38; Jaarverslag der Vereeniging tot Verbetering van de Schapenfokkerij in Noord-Holland over ... 1917, NHA.
42 *Texelsche Courant*, 27 October 1917.
43 Jaarverslag der Vereeniging tot Verbetering van de Schapenfokkerij in Noord-Holland over ... 1909, NHA; *Texelsche Courant*, 1 January 1910; Jaarverslag der Vereeniging tot Verbetering van de Schapenfokkerij in Noord-Holland over ... 1917, NHA.
44 Jaarverslag der Vereeniging tot Verbetering van de Schapenfokkerij in Noord-Holland over ... 1917, NHA.
45 Ibid. 1923, 1924, 1925, NHA.
46 Van Bodegraven, *Geschiedenis*, 23–9.
47 Timmermans, *Schapenfokkerij*, 13.
48 Bats, *Schapenfokkerij*, 52.
49 Bakker, *De Texelaar*, 159–64.
50 This section discusses the origin of the Swifter sheep, a new breed developed by crossbreeding and selection. Other breeds were created in similar manner at about the same time: the Flevolander and the Noord-Hollander (Van Bodegraven, *Geschiedenis*, 54–5). The Swifter was the most successful of the three.
51 Bekedam, "A Crossbreeding Experiment"; see also Van Bodegraven, 115–16. For Bekedam, see J. Vullings, "Ir. M. Bekedam uit Wageningen: "Economische lamsvleesproduktie dwingt tot kruisen,"" *Het Schaap* no. 3 (1986): 6–7.
52 Bekedam, "Voortplanting en vruchtbaarheid bij schapen," *Het Schaap* 3, no. 4 (1959): n.p.
53 See for instance Donald, Read and Russell, "A Comparative Trial"; Kallweit and Pfleiderer, "Steigerung der Fruchtbarkeit"; Nitter and Fewson "Experimental Designs."
54 Bekedam and Van der Greft, "Vruchtbaarheid."
55 Bekedam, "A Crossbreeding Experiment." Finnsheep were used in the 1970s to produce two new breeds by crossbreeding and selection, the Noord-Hollander and the Flevolander (Van Bodegraven, *Geschiedenis*, 54–5).
56 P. Verhoeven, "Het Vlaamse schaap," *Het Schaap* 4, no. 8 (1980): 38–9.
57 Bekedam, "A Crossbreeding Experiment." The village of Achtmaal is about a kilometre from the Dutch-Belgian border, yet the sheep were born in nearby Nieuwmoer in Flanders. Bekedam called them Flemish sheep, referring to Alexander Numan's *Handleiding* of 1835–6, which included a rather vague description of a Belgian milk sheep variety of that name.
58 Bekedam, "A Crossbreeding Experiment"; M. Bekedam, "Zuivere teelt en kruisingen bij schapen," *Het Schaap* 3, no. 1 (1979): 30–1; M. Bekedam, "Texelaars kruisen met Vlaamse schapen verbetert bedrijfsresultaat,"

*Het Schaap* 3, no. 1 (1979): 32–3; M. Bekedam, "Kruisingsproeven met enkele buitenlandse rassen," *Het Schaap* 3, no. 1 (1979): 34–5.

59 In 1978, Bekedam gave a talk titled "Pure Breeding and Crossbreeding in Sheep" at the annual meeting of the Dutch Zoötechnical Society. A year later he published it in *Het Schaap* (see the previous footnote), and it was this publication that fueled the debate among Texel breeders about his results. See for instance H. Jansma, "Zwoegerziekte en kruislingen," *Het Schaap* 5, no. 3 (1981): 4; Anon., "Ik heb met de kruislingen de juiste weg ingeslagen," *Het Schaap* 4, no. 2 (1980): 20–3; J. Westendorp, "Zwarte schaap is het haasje," *Het Schaap* 3, no. 4 (1979): 4.

60 J. Westendorp, "Zwarte schaap is het haasje," *Het Schaap* 3, no. 4 (1979): 4.

61 For instance A. Douwes, "Vruchtbaarheid bij Texelaars," *Het Schaap* 3, no. 2 (1979): 4–5; Anon., Eendracht maakt macht," *Het Schaap* 3, no. 5 (1979): 3; Anon., "Texel wil schapenhouderij aanpassen," *Het Schaap* 3, no. 3 (1980): 37; W. Kistemaker, "Méér lammeren mogelijk bij Texelaar," *Het Schaap* 4, no. 4 (1980): 11; Anon., "Mag ik me even voorstellen?" *Het Schaap* 4, no. 6 (1980): 6–8.

62 Anon., "De beste maar toch slechts de zevende prijs," *Het Schaap* 4, no. 3 (1980): 26–7.

63 Anon., "Pijpbeenderen vertellen veel over de vleesproduktie," *Het Schaap* 5, no. 1 (1981): 9–11; Anon., "Fokkerij moet hard aan de weg timmeren om niet achterop te raken," *Het Schaap* 5, no. 1 (1981): 18–21; Anon., "Smithfield '80: slachtkwaliteit is niet aan exterieur te beoordelen," *Het Schaap* 5, no. 1 (1981): 23–4; P.J.N. van der Poel and H. Sturkenboom, "Meer aandacht voor produktiviteitsvererving," *Het Schaap* 5, no. 2 (1981): 11–13; Anon., "Mag ik me even voorstellen?" *Het Schaap* 4, no. 6 (1980): 6–8.

64 Anon., "Eendracht maakt macht," *Het Schaap* 3, no. 5 (1979): 3.

65 Anon., "Eendracht maakt macht," *Het Schaap* 3, no. 5 (1979): 3; H.M.P. v.d. Brandt, "Kostprijsverlaging noodzakelijk voor behoud concurrentiepositie," *Het Schaap* 3, no. 6 (1979): 16–18; Van Bodegraven, *Geschiedenis*, 74–7.

66 J. Doeksen, "Rentabiliteit schapenhouderij liep terug," *Het Schaap* 3, no. 3 (1979): 10–13; J. Doeksen, "Rentabiliteit schapenhouderij vorig jaar verder teruggelopen," *Het Schaap* 4, no. 4 (1980): 16–17; Van Bodegraven, *Geschiedenis*, 14–17.

67 The Swifter Flock Book Society, as it was called, kept systematic records of its activities, a rarity among sheep breeders' societies. The society's archives are in personal possession of former board member Anton Bosgoed; they will henceforth be referred to as SFA. For the July 1981 meeting, see: Samenvatting van een bespreking tussen de fokkers van V/T schapen a/d Boerderij "De Kraal" te Bleiswijk op 3 juli '81, SFA.

68 Letter from L.W. Jonker (Heiloo) to Bekedam, 27 April 1982, SFA; Statuten Fokkersvereniging van het Swifter Schaap (1982), SFA; Samenvatting

van een bespreking tussen de fokkers van V/T schapen a/d Boerderij "De Kraal" te Bleiswijk op 3 juli '81, SFA.

69 Verslag van de Algemene Vergadering van de Swifter Fokkersvereniging op 24-11-'82 in Motel Bunnik te Utrecht, SFA; Het Swifter Schaap. Een nieuw ras met een hoog financieel rendement (1983), SFA.

70 Letter from J. Tiggelen, 21 June 1982, SFA.

71 Het Swifter schaap. Een nieuw ras met een hoog financieel rendement (1983), SFA.

72 Verslag van de Algemene Ledenvergadering op 10-05-1983, SFA; Jaarverslag 1984, SFA; Jaarverslag 1986, SFA.

73 Verslag van de Algemene Ledenvergadering op 24-11-1982, SFA.

74 Ibid.

75 Letter from M. van Oorspronk to the Swifter society board, 31 May 1984, SFA.

76 Uitslag van de gehouden enquête 1985, SFA.

77 Letter from Jos Leenders, 17 September 1983, SFA.

78 Verslag van de Bestuursvergadering op 30-10-1985, SFA.

79 Verslag van de Algemene Ledenvergadering op 23-11-1985, SFA.

80 Ibid.

81 Jaarverslag 1990; Jaarverslag 1991, SFA.

82 Uitslag van de gehouden enquête 1985, SFA.

83 Letter to the Swifter breeders, 6 June 1987, SFA; Verslag van de Bestuursvergadering op 20-1-1988, SFA. In 1984, even the number of Flemish sheep (145) outnumbered the newborn $F_2$ sheep (120); Jaarverslag 1984, SFA.

84 Verslag van de Algemene Ledenvergadering op 25-5-1989, SFA.

85 Verslag van de Bestuursvergadering op 18-9-1986, SFA; Verslag van de Algemene Ledenvergadering op 22-1-1986, SFA; Verslag van de Algemene Ledenvergadering op 24-11-1986, SFA.

86 Het Swifter Schaap. Een nieuw ras met een hoog financieel rendement (1983), SFA; Verslag van de Algemene Ledenvergadering op 10-5-1983, SFA; Jaarverslag 1984, SFA; Jaarverslag 1985, SFA; Verslag van de Algemene Ledenvergadering op 22-5-1987, SFA; Jaarverslag 1987, SFA.

87 Verslag van de Algemene Ledenvergadering op 7-6-1986, SFA; Bekedam, "A Crossbreeding Experiment"; Bekedam. "Zuivere teelt en kruising bij schapen"; Visscher, "Mogelijkheden voor de verhoging."

88 Jaarverslag 1987, SFA.

89 Verslag van de Bestuursvergadering op 12-9-1983, SFA.

90 Verslag van de Bestuursvergadering op 12-6-1986; Verslag van de Bestuursvergadering op, 12-12-1987, SFA.

91 Verslag van de Bestuursvergadering op 12-6-1986, SFA.

92 Memo by Bekedam: Aan kopers en gebruikers van de Ir. A.P. Minderhoudhoeve gefokte rammen en ooien, July 1988, SFA; Verslag van de Bestuursvergadering op 26-07-1988, SFA.
93 Verslag van de Bestuursvergadering op 25-3-1986, SFA.
94 Uitgangspunten om de Minderhoudhoeve mee te laten doen aan de Swifter registratie, 7 September 1988, SFA; Verslag van de Bestuursvergadering op 17-10-1988, SFA.
95 Verslag van de Bestuursvergadering op 10-01-90, SFA.
96 Verslag van de Bestuursvergadering op 01-06-1987, SFA.
97 See http://eur-lex.europa.eu/LexUriServ/LexUriServ.do?uri=CONSLEG:1981R1208:19910429:EN:PDF; accessed 17 January 2018.
98 Verslag van de vergadering van de Foktechnische Commissie Swifterschapenstamboek op 08-02-1990, SFA.
99 Letter from the committee on breeding, 23-05-1991, SFA.
100 Verslag van de Bestuursvergadering op 29-01-1992, SFA.
101 Verslag van de Bestuursvergadering op 18-03-1992, SFA; Letter to the Swifter breeders, 08-06-1992, SFA.
102 Letter from the Swifter board to those breeders who sent in rams to the demonstration days in the north and the south, 04-08-1992, SFA.
103 Verslag van de Algemene Ledenvergadering op 09-01-1993, SFA.
104 J.H. Lantinga, "Het oprichtingsjaar van de verschillende schapenstamboeken in ons land," *Het Schaap* 16, no. 2 (1972): 10; W. Pijper, "Grootse manifestatie van schapenfokkend Nederland," *Het Schaap* 15, no. 4 (1971): 1–2; L.W. Biesheuvel, "Officiële mededelingen van het C.B.S.," *Het Schaap* 16, no. 2 (1972): 1–2; Van Bodegraven, *Geschiedenis*, 60–5.
105 L.W. Biesheuvel. "Officiële mededelingen van het C.B.S.," *Het Schaap* 14, no. 2 (1970): 2–3.
106 *Jaarverslag Nederlands Texels Schapenstamboek over 1979* (Leeuwarden: NTS, 1980); Van Bodegraven, *Geschiedenis*, 32–3, 63–5.
107 Interview with Jan Geluk, first president of the NTS, 18 December 2015. Anon., Eén landelijk schapenstamboek nog niet van de grond," *Het Schaap* 3, no. 5 (1979): 9; W. Wisman, "Voorlopig moeten we het maar houden zoals het is," *Het Schaap* no. 7 (1987): 6–7.
108 M. Bekedam, J.A. Beukeboom, and A.H. Visscher, Inrichting van stamboeken voor schapen (1974), Groninger Archieven, Afd. Groningen van het Nederlands Texels Schapenstamboek, 2970, box 14. For the earlier experiments, see J.A. Beukeboom, "Groei en slachtkwaliteit bij lammeren," *Het Schaap* 17, no. 4 (1973): 12–14; Beukeboom, *Groei- en slachtkwaliteit*.
109 W., "Naar één stamboek," *Het Schaap* 3, no. 1 (1979): 1; Anon., "CBS gaat herstructureren," *Het Schaap* 3, no. 1 (1979): 15.

110 Anon., "Beminnelijkheid maakt plaats voor zakelijkheid," *Het Schaap* 4, no. 2 (1980): 7; Anon., "Mag ik me even voorstellen?" *Het Schaap* 4, no. 6 (1980): 6–8.
111 A.H. Visscher, Productiecontrole en selectie in de Texelse stamboekfokkerij. Nota tot stand gekomen op verzoek van het Dagelijks Bestuur van het Nederlands Texels Schapenstamboek (s.l.: IVO, 1982). See also Van Bodegraven, *Geschiedenis*, 117–18.
112 A.H. Visscher, "Proberen om foktechnisch geen achterstand op te lopen," *Het Schaap* 6, no. 1 (1982): 10–15; J. Doeksen, "Met doelmatige fokkerij antwoord geven op buitenlandse ontwikkelingen," *Het Schaap* 6, no. 1 (1982): 16–19; Anon., "Produktiecontrole en selectie. De selectiekenmerken voor een doelmatig fokprogramma," *Het Schaap* 6, no. 5 (1982): 12–13; Anon., "Produktiecontrole en selectie. Erfelijke verbeteringen," *Het Schaap* 6, no. 5 (1982): 14–15.
113 A.H. Visscher, "Proberen om foktechnisch geen achterstand op te lopen," *Het Schaap* 6, no. 1 (1982): 10; A.H. Visscher, Productiecontrole en selectie in de Texelse stamboekfokkerij (see note 111). See also Anon., "Fokdoel is een paal aan de horizon," *Het Schaap* 6, no. 4 (1982): 10; W. Pijper, "Fokken, maar waaraan moet je dan denken?" *Het Schaap* 6, no. 3 (1982): 10–13.
114 De Graaf and Visscher, *De ontwikkeling*.
115 Ibid.
116 Artificial insemination in sheep will be discussed in the next section.
117 Donker and Visscher, *Verificatie*, 45.
118 W. Kistemaker, "Opmeer: adelijke indruk blijft aanwezig," *Het Schaap* 6, no. 6 (1982): 21.
119 K. Geertsema and R. Jongejan "Kanttekeningen bij een aantal commentaren," *Het Schaap* no. 1 (1983): 6–7.
120 C.A. van Oostveen, "Kanttekeningen bij kanttekeningen," *Het Schaap* no. 2 (1983): 4; Anon., "NTS-voorzitter J.C. Geluk. Meisjes van dertien, er net tussenin ..." *Het Schaap* no. 1 (1983): 10–12.
121 *Jaarverslag Nederlands Texels Schapenstamboek over 1986* (Leeuwarden: NTS, 1987).
122 See *Jaarverslag Nederlands Texels Schapenstamboek* over the years 1985–96 (Leeuwarden: NTS, 1986–97).
123 J. Vullings "Ram is pas een fokram als hij zich heeft bewezen," *Het Schaap* no. 7 (1990): 18–19; J. Mariët, "Nieuwe groei-index geeft rammen betrouwbaar cijfer," *Het Schaap* no. 9 (1991): 24–5; H. te Mebel, "Trots op kritische afdeling," *Het Schaap* No. 3 (1992): 40–1; Anon., "Stamboeknieuws," *Het Schaap* no. 1 (1993): 40–1; A.H. Visscher, "Stamboekfokprogramma ten dienste van een economische lamsvleesproduktie," *Het Schaap* no. 8 (1985): 18–19.

124 M. Baeten, "Ook in de topfokkerij gaat het om geld," *Het Schaap* no. 1 (1988): 16–17.

125 J. Vullings, "Cees Kikkert uit het Texelse Den Burg: 'Met 80 fokooien is het druk zat,'"*Het Schaap* no. 4 (1985): 24–7; "G. Everts, "Den Bosch: Kikkert-fokkerij geeft toon aan," *Het Schaap* no. 7 (1985): 29; W. Kistemaker "Texelse invloed op de Nederlandse schapenfokkerij is groot," *Het Schaap* no. 7 (1987): 15.

126 Anon., "Matige belangstelling voor weegprogramma in Noord-Holland," *Het Schaap* no. 5 (1989): 5.

127 G. Everts, "Nieuwe fokrichting duidelijk zichtbaar," *Het Schaap* no. 8 (1989): 22–3; H. Mulder, "Bredere top en minder ondereind," *Het Schaap* no. 8 (1989): 24–5; H. te Mebel, "Winst voor ontwikkeling," *Het Schaap* no. 8 (1989): 26–7; H. te Mebel, "Keuringen Texelaars 1991. Tendens naar groter schaap zet door," *Het Schaap* no. 8 (1991): 25; H. te Mebel, "Tendens naar ruimere Texelaar zet echt door," *Het Schaap* no. 8 (1992): 26–7; H. Mulder, "Beste jeugd met ruimte en ras," *Het Schaap* no. 8 (1991): 32–3.

128 M. Nijssen, "Keuringen 1989. Een opmerkelijk seizoen," *Het Schaap* no. 8 (1989): 15; see also M. Nijssen, "Weerspiegeling van de veranderende fokkerij," *Het Schaap* no. 8 (1990): 14–17; M. Nijssen, "Texelaarkeuringen 1993. Winst voor functioneel exterieur en macht," *Het Schaap* no. 10–11 (1993): 35; M. Nijssen, "Succes voor fokkers en organisatie," *Het Schaap* no. 10–11 (1993): 36–8.

129 Bakker, *De Texelaar*, 216–19; http://www.texelaar.info; accessed 24 February 2018.

130 D. Reijne, "Aparte uitstraling," *Het Schaap* no. 10–11 (1994): 44–5; J. Engelen, "De keuze van twee keurmeesters," *Het Schaap* no. 12 (1994): 17.

131 J. Engelen, "PVV steekt half miljoen in schapensector," *Het Schaap* no. 2 (1990): 16–17.

132 Van Bodegraven, *Geschiedenis*, 8–13.

133 For short overviews of AI in Dutch sheep, see Strikwerda, *Revolution*, 154–9; Van Bodegraven, *Geschiedenis*, 156–7.

134 M. Bekedam, "Voortplanting en vruchtbaarheid bij schaap," *Het Schaap* 3, no. 4 (1959): 1–2; A.J.B. Hammink, "Een onderzoek naar de mogelijkheden voor het vergroten van de worpgrootte bij het schaap," *Het Schaap* 11, no. 2 (1967): 1–2; Willemse, Brand and Muurling, "Oestrussynchronisatie"; Willemse, Brand and Muurling, "Synchronisatie."

135 Willemse, Brand and Muurling, "Oestrussynchronisatie"; Muurling, Brand, and Willemse, "Oestrusinductie bij schapen in het diepe anoestrusseizoen"; Muurling, Brand, and Willemse, "Oestrusinductie bij schapen in het late anoestrusseizoen"; Muurling, Brand, and Willemse, "Oestrusinductie bij schapen in het vroege anoestrusseizoen."

136 W. van Gemert, Schapen K.I. demonstratie and Verslag schapen K.I., Archives of the Nationaal Veeteelt Museum, Beers; C.H. Herweijer, "Europese Vereniging voor Dierlijke Produktie (E.A.A.P.)," *Het Schaap* 13, no. 4 (1969): 1–2.

137 W. van Gemert, Verslag schapen K.I., Archives of the Nationaal Veeteeltmuseum, Beers; W. van Gemert and H. Hoogekamp, "K.I. bij het schaap in combinatie met oestrussynchronisatie," *Tijdschrift voor Diergeneeskunde* 100 (1975): 489–97.

138 W. van Gemert, Aantekeningen, Archives of the Nationaal Veeteeltmuseum, Beers; Van Gemert and Hoogekamp, "K.I. bij het schaap."

139 P.W.Tol, "Kunnen fokrammen intensiever benut worden?" *Het Schaap* no. 2 (1976): 48.

140 W. van Gemert, "Mogelijkheden en onmogelijkheden van de schapen-K.I.," *Het Schaap* 4, no. 5 (1980): 36–7. A.H. Visscher, Productiecontrole en selectie in de Texelse stamboekfokkerij (see note 111).

141 Van Bodegraven, *Geschiedenis*, 154–5.

142 C.D.W. König, "Zwoegerziektebestrijding in de (nabije) toekomst," *Het Schaap* 5, no. 2 (1981): 28; Anon., "Georganiseerde zwoegerziektebestrijding binnenkort van start?" *Het Schaap* 5, no. 7 (1981): 31; Anon., "Zwoegerziekte: op weg naar een grondige aanpak," *Het Schaap* 5, no. 8 (1981): 25; Anon., "Zwoegerziektebestrijding: goed gestart," *Het Schaap* 6, no. 4 (1982): 20–3; Anon., "Veterinaire eisen bij export van schapen," *Het Schaap* no. 3 (1983): 33.

143 Van Gemert, König and Khoe, *Verslag van een studie-reis*; Wietsma and Khoe, *Kunstmatige inseminatie*.

144 Visscher, "Toepassing."

145 W. van Gemert, "Nederlandse KI-proef evenaart resultaten in buitenland," *Het Schaap* no. 2 (1986): 8–9; Hooikamp, *Praktijkproef*; Houterman, *Drachtigheidsresultaten*.

146 Anon., "Schapen-K.I. start 15 september," *Het Schaap* no. 5 (1986): 20–1; Schapen K.I. catalogus 1986, Archives of the Nationaal Veeteeltmuseum, Beers; De Bruin, *Schapen-KI*.

147 J. Vullings, "Benut kansen KI," *Het Schaap* no. 6 (1986): 3; Anon., "Open dag schapen-KI: van alles wat," *Het Schaap* no. 6 (1986): 4.

148 W. van Gemert, "Kwaliteitscontrole van sperma verhoogt bevruchtingsresultaat," *Het Schaap* no. 3 (1986): 16–17.

149 Anon., "Open dag schapen-KI: van alles wat," *Het Schaap* no. 6 (1986): 4.

150 W. Wisman, "De resultaten zullen zeker beter worden," *Het Schaap* no. 7 (1987): 37; De Bruin, *Schapen-KI*.

151 W. van Gemert, "Schapen-KI in 1988: Minder deelname, maar betere resultaten," *Het Schaap* no. 1 (1989): 13–15.

152 Registration forms on which the breeders indicated their preferences are preserved in the Archives of the Nationaal Veeteeltmuseum, Beers.

153 A.H. Visscher, "Stamboeken starten met KI in fokprogramma," *Het Schaap* no. 6 (1989): 14–15; M. Nijssen, "KI-testprogramma komt op gang," *Het Schaap* 2 (1990): 22–3; J. Geluk, "Stamboeknieuws," *Het Schaap* 4 (1990): 44.
154 J. Engelen, "Een hele klus om KI van de grond te krijgen," *Het Schaap* 5 (1991): 8–9; J. Engelen, "Gestopt wegens gebrek aan belangstelling: KI," *Het Schaap* 3 (1993): 16–17; Letter from F.W. van Schie to de Vries of 10-2-1993; Schapen KI 1992, Archives of the Nationaal Veeteeltmuseum, Beers.
155 Between 1987 and 1990 the percentages were 62.6, 51.5, 54.5, and 58.8 respectively (Interne discussienota: Ontwikkeling KI bij schapen, 1992, Stichting Schapen-K.I., 4 maart 1992, Archives of the Nationaal Veeteeltmuseum, Beers).
156 W. van Gemert, Verslag over de schapen K.I. proef 1985, uitgezocht en beschreven door Frank Houterman, 19 November 1986, Archives of the Nationaal Veeteelt Museum, Beers; Houterman, *Drachtigheidsresultaten*; F. Houterman, "De geboortegolf na kunstmatige inseminatie," *Het Schaap* no. 5 (1986): 20–1; W. van Gemert, "Schapen-K.I. in 1988. Minder deelname, maar betere resultaten," *Het Schaap* no. 1 (1989): 13–15.
157 W. van Gemert, "Schapen-KI in 1988. Minder deelname, maar betere resultaten," *Het Schaap* no. 1 (1989): 13–15.
158 Verslag van de Bestuursvergadering op 30-10-1985, SFA; Verslag van de Bestuursvergadering op 25-10-1986; Verslag van de Algemene Ledenvergadering op 22-11-1986, SFA; Verslag van de Bestuursvergadering op 26 April 1987, SFA; Verslag van de Bestuursvergadering op 19-6-1988, SFA.
159 J.J. Pekelder "Zwoegerziektebestrijding. De tijd is rijp voor een nieuwe fase, *Het Schaap* no. 4 (1988): 37; Anon., "Nederlands Texels Schapenstamboek," *Het Schaap* no. 10 (1989): 32–3; "D.J. Houwers, "Zwoegerziekte. Vaak onzichtbaar aanwezig," *Het Schaap* no. 3 (1990): 22.
160 See for instance http://www.texelse-fokschapen.nl/; http://www.texelse-schapen.nl/; accessed 1 April 2018.

## 5. From Farm Horse to Riding Horse: The Dutch Warmbloods

An earlier version of this chapter was published as Theunissen, "The Transformation."

1 Between 1940 and 1951, for instance, the number of tractors in Dutch agriculture grew from 4,000 to 20,000. See Gehrels, *Paard en trekker*; B.J.B. Groeneveld, "Een analyse van de werkpaardenstapel," *In de Strengen* [*IdS*] 20, no. 23 (1958): 6–10; Priester, "Paarden en trekkers."
2 In the north and the south of the Netherlands, the Dutch Coldblood competed with the Warmblood as a draft horse. The tractor would replace the

Coldblood completely. For a history of Coldblood breeding, see Roumen, *De Nederlandse trekpaardenfokkerij*.

3 In recent years the society ranked in the top two (dressage) and the top four (jumping) in the studbook rankings of the World Breeding Federation for Sports Horses. Belgian and German studbooks are its main competitors. See http://www.wbfsh.org/GB.aspx; accessed 7 December 2018.

4 For the history of Dutch horse racing, see Minkema, Jager, and Frerichs, *Dravend door de tijd*; Minkema, *Draf- en renbanen*. For the history of the rural riding associations, see Heuff, *De landelijke ruitersport*; Melissen, Van Tienen, and Brandsen, *Kroon op het werk*. There are two main reasons for the marginality of racing in the Netherlands. Traditionally, racing was "the sport of kings," that is of the nobility. In Dutch history, the nobility played a far less significant and visible role than in other European countries, and racing never gained wide popularity. Secondly, between the early twentieth century and the early 1940s the confessionalist political parties that dominated Dutch politics prohibited racing on Sundays, as well as betting and bookmaking, which resulted in a further decline of the sport. A later attempt to revitalize racing will be discussed below.

5 In 1918 the government transferred the authority to inspect stallions for stud-worthiness to the breeders societies; see Verzijl, *Wet*.

6 For histories of the Dutch Warmblood, see Van Leeuwen, *Geschiedenis der paardenfokkerij*; Slob, *Het Nederlandse paard*. For the rural riders associations, see note 4.

7 Slob, *Het Nederlandse paard*, 66–73, 92–3, 98–9.

8 Ibid., 78–87. For examples of the perpetual debate over the importance of conformation versus performance, see Slob, *Het Nederlandse paard*, 85–7; Heuff, *De landelijke ruitersport*, 49–50.

9 B.J.B. Groeneveld, "Een analyse van de werkpaardenstapel," *IdS* 20, no. 23 (1958): 6–10. By 1968, the number had dropped to 66,400: A. Heuff, "Aantallen paarden," *IdS* 30, no. 17 (1968): 13.

10 For discussions of the new breeding goal, see for instance G.A.R. Nieuhoff, "Ingezonden," *IdS* 22, no. 9 (1960): 4–5; Anon., "Iets over de Hannoverse fokkerij," *IdS* 23, no. 2 (1961): 6–8; J.A. Crebas, "Overpeinzingen over het paard op onze landbouwbedrijven," *IdS* 23, no. 3 (1961): 4; B. Seldenrijk, "Quo vadis V.N.L.-fokkerij, waarheen gaat gij?" *IdS* 23, no. 19 (1961): 2–3.

11 G.A.R. Nieuhoff, "Ingezonden," *IdS* 22, no. 9 (1960): 4–5.

12 G.M. van Charante-Terlingen and Th. Dijkman, "Ingezonden," *IdS* 23, no. 22 (1961): 4–5; J.T. Bos, "Ingezonden. Bij de voorplaat van het kerstnummer," *IdS* 29, no. 2 (1967): 3–4; A.J. Vermond, "V.L.N. 1967. Ontwikkeling van de fokkerij en aanpassing van de fokleiding," *IdS* 29, no. 12 (1967): 3. The *Tuigpaard* type is unique to the Netherlands.

In the 2000s, it was used by American breeder Gene LaCroix to create the Renai horse, by combining it with the Arabian; see Derry, *Horses in Society*, 242–4.

13 A.J. Vermond, "V.L.N. 1967. Ontwikkeling van de fokkerij en aanpassing van de fokleiding," *IdS* 29, no. 12 (1967): 3.

14 In the early nineteenth century, a royal stud had been established at Borculo for this purpose: hot-blooded sires were made available to the Warmblood breeders to produce military horses. The stud was closed down in 1842, because famers showed only limited interest in producing army horses; Slob, *Het Nederlandse paard*, 52–5.

15 For a history of early Thoroughbred breeding, see Russell, *Like Engend'ring Like*, 60–5, 85–6, 98, 218–22. The German Hanoverian, Holstein and Trakehner are examples of Warmbloods that have been crossed with Thoroughbreds and Arabians since at least the nineteenth century; see Hendricks, *International Encyclopedia*, 213–14, 224–7, 421–3.

16 Anon., "Agenda der Algemene Ledenvergadering, te houden op 30 januari 1962," *IdS* 23, no. 24 (1961): 2–3.

17 For this discussion, see for instance J. Roodenburg, "V.L.N. fokkerij met meer bloed," *IdS* 23, nos. 20–1 (1961): 5; C.P.W., "Afdeling Zuiderzeeland," *IdS* 24, no. 4 (1962): 4–7.

18 W. Slob, "De fokkerij in Frankrijk," *IdS* 43, no. 12 (1976): 1; H. Kingmans, "Amor: bouwmeester die zijn tijd vooruit was," *IdS* 46, no. 23 (1979): 15–21.

19 H. Kingmans, "Directe rol van Volbloed nog zeer sterk in nieuwe jaargang," *IdS* 44, 2 (1977): 4–6. For an overview of the different breeding options, see A.J. Vermond, "V.L.N. 1967. Ontwikkeling van de fokkerij en aanpassing van de fokleiding," *IdS* 29, no. 12 (1967): 3.

20 See for instance W. Slob, "Utrecht 1962," *IdS* 24, no. 18 (1962): 2–8.

21 H. Kingmans, "Van Binsbergen (met bolhoed geboren)," *IdS* 41, no. 10 (1974): 10–11.

22 Anon. "Nederlandse halfbloedfokkerij bereikt de internationale rijpaardenmarkt," *IdS* 30, no. 19 (1968): 1; A. Heuff, "Stal Maathuis introduceert Nederlands rijpaard op internationale markt," *IdS* 31, no. 11 (1969): 4–6; A. Heuff, "Utrechtse hengstenshow een manifestatie van internationale allure," *IdS* 36, no. 4 (1971): 2–7.

23 H. Kingmans, "De baas van Henri, de rappe draver. Pieter Abel Meinardi: veelzijdig fenomeen," *IdS* 42, no. 1 (1975): 17–21.

24 There was an extensive debate over these matters in *In de Strengen* that continued for over a decade. See for instance G.M. van Charante-Terlingen, "Ingezonden," *IdS* 25, no. 1 (1963): 3–4; W.C. van Dam, "Iets over het rijpaard-bloedpaard," *IdS* 29, no. 5 (1967): 8–9; A.J. Vermond, "V.N.L. 1967. Ontwikkeling van de fokkerij en aanpassing van de fokleiding," *IdS* 29, no. 12 (1967): 3; P. van Schaik, "Het verloop

van de paardenstapel. Het gaat om het behoud van genoeg oude fokmerries," *IdS* 29, no. 13 (1967): 4–5; P. van Schaik, "Beschouwing over de hedendaagse fokrichting en over toe te passen fokmethoden," *IdS* 30, no. 7 (1968): 1–2; A.J. Vermond, "V.L.N. fokkerij," *IdS* 30, no. 9 (1968): 1–2; P. van Schaik, "De volbloed in de rijpaardfokkerij," *IdS* 33, no. 7 (1971): 1–2; W.P.N.-discussiegroep, "Hoeveel bloed?," *IdS* 39, no. 15 (1972): 3–4; P. van Schaik, "Over het fokdoel," *IdS* 41, no. 7 (1974): 11–12; P. Verhoeven, Een studie van het verleden is een richtsnoer voor de toekomst," *IdS* 42, no. 19 (1975): 9–10.

25 A.M.H. Sänger, "Ervaringen in de volbloedfokkerij en de relatie met de WPN-fokkerij," *IdS* 49, no. 1 (1982): 17–21.

26 A.J. Vermond, "V.L.N. fokkerij," *IdS* 30, no. 9 (1968): 1–2. See also H. Kingmans, "Van Binsbergen (met bolhoed geboren)," *IdS* 41, no. 10 (1974): 10–11.

27 Anon., "Wetenschap en praktijk op de Uithof," *IdS* 30, no. 19 (1968): 3–5.

28 J.F. Eysink, "Publieke tribune. Het WPN warmblood paard van de toekomst," *IdS* 33, no. 9 (1971): 10–11.

29 In 1978 there was only one Groninger stallion left, and some 100 mares. In 1982 a group of enthusiasts established a separate society to maintain what was left of the original type; H. Bouman, "Nog is het Groninger paard niet verloren," *De Boerderij* 67, no. 27 (1982): 60–3. The Groninger is now a rare breed; see http://szh.nl/paarden/groningen-paard/; accessed 23 December 2017.

30 See for instance G.A.R. Nieuhoff, "Betreurenswaardig," *IdS* 30, no. 20 (1968): 4; A. Heuff, "De Gelderse fokmerriën in Bennekom," *IdS* 41, no. 23 (1974): 1–8; Vermond, "Het basispaard," *IdS* 43, no. 5 (1976): 3–4.

31 H. Kingmans, "Liefhebbers basispaard vragen aandacht voor hun wensen," *IdS* 46, no. 25 (1979): 70.

32 The board's reasoning in rejecting this option showed clear parallels to that of the sheep breeders who, in the early 1980s, diverged from Bekedam's plan to produce first-generation crossbreds from Texel and Finnsheep parents, as discussed in the previous chapter.

33 Anon., "Fokkerij van internationale springpaarden," *IdS* 52, no. 1 (1985): 36–8; F.A. van der Lee, "Paardenvolks-verlakkerij," *IdS* 52, no. 6 (1985): 44.

34 L.W.B., "Veelzijdigheidsmeries sterven uit, gezien de partnerkeuze," *IdS* 44, no. 20 (1977): 51–4. The Gelderlander is now a rare breed; see http://szh.nl/paarden/gelders-paard/. In 2005, the remaining breeders of Gelderlanders, like the Groninger breeders, set themselves the aim of preserving the Gelderlander, claiming that it should be continued as a separate breed; see http://www.gelderlanderhorse.nl/; accessed 23 December 2017. Considering its long history as a performance type rather than a breed, this was a surprising move.

35 For the discussions on this topic, see P. van Schaik, "De fokmerriekeuringen van het rijpaardtype op de Utrechtse paardendagen," *IdS* 30, no. 18 (1968): 4–5; N.M. Strik, "V.L.N.-ers, let op uw saeck!," *IdS* 31, no. 4 (1969): 11; P. van Schaik, "Fokrichting en fokkeuze," *IdS* 32, no. 7 (1970): 1–2; P. van Schaik, "De volbloed en de rijpaardfokkerij," *IdS* 33, no. 7 (1971): 1–2; W.P.N.-discussiegroep, "Hoeveel bloed?," *IdS* 39, no. 15 (1972): 3–4; P. Verhoeven, "Een studie van het verleden is een richtsnoer voor de toekomst," *IdS* 42, no. 19 (1975): 9–10.

36 W. Slob, "Welke waarde heeft het exterieur?," *IdS* 40, no. 25 (1973): 4; H. Kingmans, "Kan een springpaardfokkerij toch bestaan?," *IdS* 41, no. 25 (1974): 1–7.

37 H. Kingmans, "De opvallende prestaties van Doruto's kinderen in de dressuurbaan, No. 2," *IdS* 43, no. 25 (1976): 3–9.

38 Exterior evaluation remained an important part of the new selection procedure that was enacted in 1978; see below.

39 A.M.H. Sänger, "Ervaringen in de volbloedfokkerij en de relatie met de WPN-fokkerij," *IdS* 48, no. 23 (1981): 17–20.

40 Anon., "Op- en uitbouw van de WPN-fokkerij. Fokleiding ziet om en kijkt vooruit," *IdS* 48, no. 25 (1981): 9–15; H. Kingmans, "Woorden ten afscheid van P.B. van Binsbergen," *IdS* 49, no. 21 (1982): 3–9.

41 H. Kingmans, "De tijd van de buffels is voorbij," *IdS* 52, no. 9 (1985): 30–4.

42 H. Kingmans, "De fokkerij onderweg (1)," *IdS* 44, no. 12 (1977): 3–7.

43 Grijpstra, *Paardenhouderij*.

44 Slob, *Het Nederlandse paard*, 112–15.

45 *IdS* 45, no. 14 (1978): 12; H. Kingmans, "Paardenwereld in beroering om brief minister," *IdS* 53, no. 24 (1986): 58–60.

46 Van Geffen, *De winnaar*, 16–17. No exact figures are available for the numbers of mare and stallion owners in these years, nor about the proportion of them that worked commercially.

47 E.F. Geessink and H. Kingmans, "Behoefte aan en levensvatbaarheid van fokkerijcentrum moet uit studie blijken," *IdS* 45, no. 3 (1978): 3–6.

48 For Van der Stee, see http://www.parlement.com/id/vg09llg9q6zs/a_p_j_m_m_fons_van_der_stee; accessed 23 December 2017.

49 M.P.M. Vos, "Paardenhouderij, een volwaardige bedrijfstak? Aandacht van de overheid," *IdS* 45, no. 7 (1978): 16–18; M.P.M. Vos, "Waarom gaat het Ministerie van Landbouw zich plotseling bemoeien met de paardenfokkerij?" *IdS* 46, no. 7 (1979): 30–3; Anon., "Goede sfeer op algemene ledenvergadering," *IdS* 46, no. 9 (1979): 12–13.

50 Anon., "Hengstenhouders bijeen," *IdS* 47, no. 6 (1980): 36.

51 On Melchior, see http://www.horses.nl/sport/springen-sport/springen-algemeen/leon-melchior-overleden/; accessed 23 December

2017. Zangersheide was located in Lanaken, just across the southernmost Dutch-Belgian border.

52 Melchior had a brochure printed in which he explained his breeding method: Anon., "*Zangersheide.*" For his breeding system, see also Anon., "Een gesprek tussen het Ministerie van Landbouw en Visserij, het WPN en "Zangersheide," gehouden op 16 januari 1980. Samenvattend verslag," *IdS* 47, no. 3 (1980): 29–30.

53 *IdS* 51, no. 4 (1984): 5.

54 The plans were first announced in *In de Strengen* in October 1978: Anon., "Ministerie actief: Stichting Paardencentrum opgericht," *IdS* 45, no. 21 (1978): 30. Further details were provided in Anon., "Paardencentrum krijgt vooral demonstratiefunctie," *IdS* 45, no. 22 (1978): 21; H. Kingmans, "Hoofdbestuur voorzichtig in benadering samenwerkingsvorm met Stal "Zangersheide,"" *IdS* 46, no. 21 (1979): 20–1.

55 Anon., "Beleidsnota paardenhouderij op komst. Minister van de Stee: essentie van het initiatief doorzetten," *IdS* 46, no. 6 (1979): 28.

56 H. Kingmans, "Peiling op ledenvergaderingen. Het WPN in gesprek," *IdS* 47, no. 3 (1980): 9–12; Anon., "Een gesprek tussen het Ministerie van Landbouw en Visserij, het WPN en "Zangersheide," gehouden op 16 januari 1980. Samenvattend verslag," *IdS* 47, no. 3 (1980): 29–30; Anon., "Ontwikkelingen baren grote zorgen. Afdelingen reageren op discussiepunten," *IdS* 47, no. 4 (1980): 15–16; "WPN-jaarrede prof. dr. G.J.W. van der Mey: In het verleden ligt het heden, in het nu wat worden zal," *IdS* 47, no. 8 (1980): 19–23.

57 Van der Stee explicated his plans in a policy document: Kamerstuk Tweede Kamer 1979–1980, kamerstuknummer 16027, ondernummer 2, Paarden in Nederland; http://resolver.kb.nl/resolve?urn=sgd%3Ampeg21%3A19791980%3A0006962; accessed 23 December 2017. The plans also included facilities for a number of other sports to be built at the same location. For a history of the hippodrome, see Minkema, *Draf- en renbanen*.

58 Anon., "Jaarrede NHS-voorzitter: Minister moet niet buiten organisaties om gaan werken," *IdS* 46, no. 5 (1979): 11; Anon., "*Paarden in Nederland*," 6.

59 For the ministerial policy document, see note 57. For the discussions in Parliament, see Kamerstuk Tweede Kamer 1979–1980, kamerstuknummer 16027, ondernummer 5, Paarden in Nederland; http://www.statengeneraaldigitaal.nl; accessed 30 December 2017.

60 H. Kingmans, "Ook in Nota Paardenhouderij: minister blijft vaag over Limburgse plannen," *IdS* 47, no. 3 (1980): 17–18; Anon., "Ontwikkelingen baren grote zorgen. Afdelingen reageren op discussiepunten," *IdS* 47, no. 4 (1980): 15–16.

61 Hans van der Kolk, "Oorlog in paardenwereld," *De Telegraaf*, 23 February 1980, 5. Available at www.delpher.nl; accessed 30 December 2017.

62 Anon., "Open brief aan minister Ir. G.J.M. Braks," *IdS* 47, no. 5 (1980): 32; J. Hayen a.o., "Ernstige kritiek op plannen in Limburg," *IdS* 47, no. 5 (1980): 43–4.

63 Anon., "Paardenstamboek vreest Melchior," *Nieuwsblad van het Noorden*, 28 February 1980, 23. Available at www.delpher.nl; accessed 30 December 2017.

64 Anon., "Voorstel van dagelijks bestuur: geen ontheffing voor Raimond en Ramiro," *IdS* 47, no. 4 (1980): 11.

65 H. Kingmans, "Minister wil snel beslissen over paardencentrum en het spel buiten de baan." Appendix to *IdS* 47, no. 13 (1980).

66 "Het Binnenhof en de Nederlandse paardenwereld," Extra edition of *IdS* 47, no. 13A (1980): 6.

67 For Braks, see http://www.parlement.com/id/vg09llhykoyz/g_j_m_gerrit_braks; accessed 30 December 2017.

68 Anon., "Tendens naar concentratie van hengstenhouderijen. Minister kiest voor drietal paardencentra," *IdS* 47, no. 18 (1980): 21–3. For the discussions about these new plans in Parliament, see: Tweede Kamer der Staten Generaal, Zitting 1980–1981, Aanhangsel van de Handelingen, Vragen gesteld door leden van de Kamer, met de daarop door de Regering gegeven antwoorden, nr 771; available at www.statengeneraaldigitaal.nl; accessed 30 December 2017. Braks initially envisaged three centres of this kind, but only the one in Limburg would be realized. The WPN had also entertained plans for a centre for raising, training and selling horses, and for some time there were talks about integrating these plans. However, due to lack of funds the WPN centre did not materialize either.

69 Anon., "Hoofdbestuur niet positief over nieuwe Haagse plannen," *IdS* 48, no. 1 (1981): 29–31; H. Kingmans, "Minister geeft toe: overleg kwam als mosterd na de maaltijd," *IdS* 48, no. 8 (1981): 53–5. Questions were also asked in Parliament about these stallions; see note 68.

70 H. Kingmans, "Limburgse plannen krijgen vorm in Merkelbeek. "De Bovenste Hof": proefbedrijf in dienst van kleinschaligheid," *IdS* 49, no. 9 (1982): 3–9; H. Bouwman, "Paardenplan blijkt geen banenplan," *De Boerderij* 67, no. 46 (1982): 40–3.

71 For the ministerial reasons for this decision, see Tweede Kamer der Staten Generaal, Zitting 1982–1983, Aanhangsel van de Handelingen, Vragen gesteld door leden van de Kamer, met de daarop door de Regering gegeven antwoorden, nr 561; available at www.statengeneraaldigitaal.nl; accessed 23 December 2017.

72 Minkema, *Draf en renbanen*.

73 H. Bouwman, "Paardenplan blijkt geen banenplan," *De Boerderij* 67, no. 46 (1982): 40–3. For Ramiro's successful career as a jumper and a stud horse, click on "Ramiro" at https://www.kwpn.nl/over-kwpn/

lidmaatschap/artikelenarchief/kwpn-goedgekeurde--en-erkende-hengsten; accessed 23 December 2017.

74 Anon., "Discussie rond het centraal onderzoek van rijpaardhengsten II," *IdS* 40, no. 19 (1973): 6; Extra edition *IdS* 45, no. 22 (1978), "Verrichtingsonderzoek rijpaardhengsten Uddel 1978"; G. van der Veen, "Hengstenselectiesysteem opnieuw op een rijtje gezet," *IdS* 51, no. 2 (1984): 20–4.

75 H. Kingmans, "Hoe doen de kinderen van WPN-hengsten het in de ruitersport?" *IdS* 45, no. 9 (1978): 3–7; G. van der Veen, Reaction to Heuff, "De aanleg tot springen in onze rijpaarden," *IdS* 45, no. 13 (1978): 27–9; H. Kingmans, Gerangschikte sportgegevens uiterst waardevol voor de fokkerij; de Duitsers beschikken erover. Wanneer wij?" *IdS* 45, no. 15 (1978): 3–5.

76 H. Kingmans, "Zinvolle confrontatie fokkerijbeleid en -techniek," *IdS* 46, no. 14 (1979): 3–9.

77 Landbouwschap Commissie Paardengebruik, "Samenwerking ruiterbonden en paardenfokkers," *IdS* 40, no. 13 (1973): 24.

78 M.P.M Vos, "Paardenhouderij, een volwaardige bedrijfstak? Aandacht van de overheid," *IdS* 45, no. 7 (1978): 16–18.

79 Anon., "Historisch besluit: WPN op NHS-computer," *IdS* 46, no. 13 (1979): 10.

80 Anon., "Samenwerking fokkerij en gebruik. Mijlpaal: minister stelt computer in gebruik," *IdS* 47, no. 25 (1980): 26–7; H. Kingmans, "NHS-jaarboek: schitterende start van koppeling sport- en fokkerij-gegevens," *IdS* 50, no. 11 (1983): 3–6.

81 H.A. Huizinga, "Hengstenindex: hulpmiddel om de koers uit te zetten. Sportgegevens van nafok objectief op een rijtje," *IdS* 54, no. 7 (1987): 4–8. See also Huizinga, *Genetic Studies*.

82 G.J.W. van der Mey, "Bezinning. Jaarrede WPN voorzitter 22 April 1981," *IdS* 48, no. 8 (1981): 10–15.

83 H. Kingmans, "Export sportpaarden neemt toe," *IdS* 47, no. 7 (1980): 3–6; H. Kingmans, "Een jaar omzien. Conclusie: het WPN-paard leeft als nooit tevoren," *IdS* 49, no. 25 (1982): 62–5.

84 Anon., "Hoofdbestuur kiest formeel voor prestatie," *IdS* 47, no. 12 (1980): 14; H. Kingmans, "Hoofdbestuur stelt tweede selectiesysteem voor hengsten vast," *IdS* 47, no. 13 (1980): 17–21.

85 Anon., "Voorstel van dagelijks bestuur: geen ontheffing voor Raimond en Ramiro," *IdS* 47, no. 4 (1980): 11.

86 Noortje Schmeink, "De gedachten van twee hengstenopfokkers," *IdS* 48, no. 4 (1981): 3–8. A stallion in his waiting period might bring in money by doing well in sports, but this implied that the owner had to employ a good rider.

87 For a history of AI in horses in the Netherlands, see Strikwerda, *Revolutie*, 220–39.

88 For some examples of the ongoing discussions about the pros and cons of AI in Thoroughbred breeding, see http://cs.bloodhorse.com/blogs/scot/archive/2009/05/06/live-cover-vs-artificial-insemination-in-thoroughbred-breeding-why-the-jockey-club-has-it-right.aspx; http://equine-reproduction.com/articles/Thoroughbred-AI.shtml; accessed 30 December 2017.

89 Strikwerda, *Revolutie*, 229–30; *IdS* 46, no. 23 (1979): 68.

90 Anon., "Toepassing K.I. bij paarden zal nog niet storm lopen," *IdS* 49, no. 8 (1982): 3–8.

91 H. Kingmans, "Fenomeen spermawinstations uit de startblokken; die in Lexmond ten doop gehouden," *IdS* 52, no. 6 (1985): 15–18; Strikwerda, *Revolutie*, 228–31.

92 Anon., "Geval van CEM in ons land vastgesteld," *IdS* 54, no. 15 (1987): 26–7. Anon., "Hengsten- én merriehouders moeten eendrachtig CEM onder de duim zien te houden," *IdS* 54, no. 25 (1987): 78–9.

93 Strikwerda, *Revolutie*, 228–33.

94 W.F. Gerhardt, "Exterieur en prestatie, een noodzakelijk weerwoord," *IdS* 44, no. 3 (1977); H. Kingmans, "De fokkerij onderweg (2)," *IdS* 44, no. 13 (1977): 3–8.

95 Over the years, the WPN – since 1988 the KWPN, Koninklijk Warmbloed Paardenstamboek Nederland – has sharpened its focus on sport horses. The breeding goal is now to produce horses that can perform at Grand Prix level in dressage or jumping; Kampman et al., *The KWPN Horse*, 10–11. The society's English name reflects this: Studbook of the Royal Dutch Sporthorse.

96 Kampman et al., *The KWPN Horse*. Science would also become more important in other ways, such as screening for diseases and hereditary defects; see https://www.kwpn.nl/over-kwpn/diensten; accessed 31 December 2017.

97 Anon., "Op-en uitbouw van de WPN-fokkerij. Fokleiding ziet om en kijkt vooruit," *IdS* 48, no. 25 (1981): 9–15; H. Kingmans, "De volbloedhengst kan niet worden gemist," *IdS* 51, no. 6 (1984): 19–22.

98 Thurtle, "Harnessing Heredity." For other examples from horse breeding, see Cassidy, *The Sport of Kings*; Krüger, "A Horse Breeder's Perspective"; Swart, *Riding High*; Tyrell, "Bred for the Race."

99 For a breed history of the Friesian horse, see Savelkouls, *Het Friese paard*. For the Friesian Horse Studbook Society see https://www.kfps.nl/; accessed 18 March 2018.

100 Aartsen, Vos and Karssen, *Afscheid dr.ir. M.P.M. Vos*; Maat, *Science Cultivating Practice*, 7–9.

101 J. Melissen, "Bij het afscheid van dr.ir. M.P.M. Vos," *IdS* 50, no. 10 (1983): 3–5.

**Conclusion**

1 Jonsson, "Methods," 2.
2 McAllister, *Beauty and Revolution*. See also Holloway and Morris, "Viewing Animal Bodies."
3 Edgerton, *The Shock of The Old*.
4 For Ús Mem, see Strikwerda, *Koers*, 104. For the Friesian horse statue, see for instance http://www.lc.nl/friesland/Mega-standbeeld-Fries-paard-financieel-een-stuk-dichterbij-22320709.html; accessed 7 December 2018; the plan has not yet been realized.
5 Woods, "Rethinking the History"; Brassley, "The Decline."
6 There was a small, local group of Dutch farmers who protested against the government's modernization policy and who believed they could survive as small farmers – if only the government left them to their own devices. The group was the foundation of a political party, the *Boerenpartij*, that grew into a general protest party that also attracted city dwellers. The party was represented in Parliament between 1963 and 1981. See Nooij, *De Boerenpartij*; Vossen, "De andere jaren zestig."
7 Fitzgerald, *Every Farm a Factory*.
8 Seddon, *The Silent Revolution*.
9 Schot and Van Lente, "Technology."
10 https://www.biojournaal.nl/artikel/14223/Bio-KI-Meer-bio-stieren-op-de-kaart/; https://www.melkvee.nl/artikel/68839-biologische-boeren-richten-cooperatieve-ki-vereniging-op/; accessed 7 December 2018.
11 http://edepot.wur.nl/14563; http://edepot.wur.nl/249672; accessed 7 December 2018.

# Sources

## Archives

Archives of the Nationaal Veeteelt Museum, Beers
Archives of the Swifter Breeders' Society (in private possession)
Municipal Archives, Texel, in Regional Archives, Alkmaar
Groninger Archives, Groningen
Image archives of the journal *Veeteelt* (CRV Holding BV)
National Archives, The Hague
North Holland Archives, Haarlem

## Periodicals Referenced in the Endnotes

References to articles in farming magazines, breeding journals, breeders' society journals, agricultural and general newspapers, and yearly reports of breeders' societies and AI associations are given in full in the endnotes. The periodicals in question are the following:

*Bedrijfspluimveehouder*
*Boerderij*
*Boerderij-Varkenshouderij*
*Friese Veefokkerij*
*In de Strengen*
*Jaarboek KI*
*Jaarverslag Nederlands Texels Schapenstamboek*
*Keurstamboeker*
*Maandblad voor de Varkensfokkerij*
*Nieuwe Veldbode*
*Nederlandsch Landbouw-Weekblad*

*Schaap*
*Schager Courant*
*Telegraaf*
*Texelsche Courant*
*Varkensfokkerij/Mesterij*
*Veeverbetering*
*Veeteelt*
*Veldbode*

Some of the journals on breeding are a bibliographer's nightmare: titles, volume numbers, volume identification (by number or by year), issue identification (by number or by date), and pagination (per issue or consecutively per volume), may all change, sometimes after a merger with another journal, sometimes for no apparent reason. This does not allow for a consistent system of referencing; I have provided whatever information is needed to retrieve the sources. All other references in the endnotes have been shortened and refer to the full titles in the bibliography below.

# Bibliography

Ackrill, R. *The Common Agricultural Policy*. Sheffield: Sheffield Academic Press, 2000.

Anon. "Hybrids on the Nest." *Wallace's Farmer*, 16 October 1948.

– "Miscellaneous. How the Netherlands Government Helps the Dutch Poultry Industry." *World's Poultry Science Journal* 5 (1949): 90–3.

– *De Nederlandse landbouw in een groeiende economie*. 's-Gravenhage: LEI, 1965.

– "Paardenstamboek vreest Melchior." *Nieuwsblad van het Noorden*, 28 February 1980, 23.

– *"Paarden in Nederland" en de Nederlandse paardenhouderij. Een gezamenlijke reactie van het Landbouwschap, de Stichting Nederlandse Draf- en Rensport, de Stichting Nederlandsche Hippische Sportbond [en] de Stichting Nederlandse Hippische opleidingen op de ministeriële nota "Paarden in Nederland."* 's-Gravenhage: s.n., 1980.

– *Schapen K.I. catalogus 1986*. sl.: s.n., 1986.

– "De varkensfokkerij van vandaag." *Diergeneeskundig Memorandum* 52, no. 1 (2005): 1–72.

Atkins, P.J. *A History of Uncertainty. Bovine Tuberculosis in Britain, 1850 to the Present*. Winchester: The University of Winchester Press, 2016.

Bakker, D.L. *Grondbeginselen der algemeene veeteelt*. Zwolle: Tjeenk Willink, 1919.

Bakker, M.S.C. "Voeding in Nederland." In *Geschiedenis van de Techniek in Nederland in de Negentiende Eeuw*, vol. 1, *Techniek en Modernisering, Landbouw en Voeding*, edited by J.W. Schot et al., 39–51. Zutphen: Walburg Pers, 1992.

Bakker, P.A. *De Texelaar. De geschiedenis van een schaap met toekomst*. Norg: Drukware, 2009.

Bakker, P.A., and J.H. Vosjan. "Bewaaïerig weer en hangkonterige schapen." *Uitgave van de Historische Vereniging Texel* no. 74 (March 2005): 6–33.

Bats, E.J. *Schapenfokkerij en -houderij in Nederland*. Meppel: Tjeenk Willink, 1953.

Bekedam, M. "Selectie en gebruik van k.i.-stieren." *Veeteelt- en Zuivelberichten* 6 (1963): 240–8.

– "A Crossbreeding Experiment with Texel and Flemish Sheep; Preliminary Results." In *Proceedings of the Working Symposium on Breed Evaluation and Crossing Experiments with Farm Animals Held at the Research Institute for Animal Husbandry "Schoonoord," Zeist September 15–21, 1974*, 407–19. Zeist: IVO, [1975].

Bekedam, M., and A. van der Greft. "Vruchtbaarheid en lammerensterfte bij Texelse ooien onder Nederlandse bedrijfsomstandigheden." *Bedrijfsontwikkeling/Veehouderij* 2 (1971): 59–63.

Berlan, J-P., and R.C. Lewontin. "The Political Economy of Hybrid Corn." *Monthly Review* 38 (1986): 35–47.

Betteridge, K.J. "A History of Farm Animal Embryo Transfer and some Associated Techniques." *Animal Reproduction Science* 79 (2003): 203–44.

Beukeboom, J.A. *Groei- en slachtkwaliteit van Texelse lammeren: verslag van een rammenselectieproef op Texel.* Alkmaar: s.n., 1976.

Bieleman, J. "De georganiseerde rundveeverbetering." In *Techniek in Nederland in de twintigste eeuw*, edited by Schot et al., 131–53, vol. 3, *Landbouw en voeding*. Zutphen: Walburg Pers, 1992.

– "De legkippenhouderij." In *Techniek in Nederland in de twintigste eeuw*, edited by Schot et al., 155–80, vol. 3, *Landbouw en voeding*. Zutphen: Walburg Pers, 1992.

– *Boeren in Nederland: geschiedenis van de landbouw 1500–2000.* Amsterdam: Boom, 2008.

Bläsing, J.F.E. *Op het spoor van de Körver. Ontstaan, groei en transformatie van de Brabantse familieonderneming. Hendrix' Fabrieken 1979/1930 bedrijfskundig bekeken.* Leiden: Martinus Nijhoff, 1986.

Bonneuil, C. "Mendelism, Plant Breeding and Experimental Cultures: Agriculture and the Development of Genetics in France." *Journal of the History of Biology* 39 (2006): 281–308.

Brassley, P. "Cutting across Nature? The History of Artificial Insemination in Pigs in the United Kingdom." *Studies in History and Philosophy of Science* Part C: *Studies in History and Philosophy of Biological and Biomedical Sciences* 38 (2007): 442–61.

– "The Decline of Pig and Poultry Production on Family Farms in England." Rural History 2015 Annual Meeting, Panel 2: *The Rise of Agribusiness in the Second Half of the 20th Century*; http://ruralhistory2015.org/doc/papers/Panel_2_Brassley.pdf.

Broekhuizen, H., and J. Thijs. "Selectiemesterijen." In *Varkens varia II*, edited by P. Noë. Utrecht: Stichting Land- en Tuinbouwgidsen, 1969.

Bugos, G.E. "Intellectual Property Protection in the American Chicken-Breeding Industry." *Business History Review* 66 (1992): 127–68.

Cassidy, R. *The Sport of Kings: Kinship, Class and Thoroughbred Breeding in Newmarket.* Cambridge: Cambridge University Press, 2002.

Clark, A.E. "Social Worlds/Arenas Theory as Organizational Theory." In *Social Organization and Social Process: Essays in Honor of Anselm Strauss*, edited by D.R. Maines, 119–58. New York: Aldine de Gruyter, 1991.

Clarke, A.E., and S.L. Star. "The Social Worlds Framework: A Theory/Methods Package." In *The Handbook of Science and Technology Studies*, edited by E.J. Hackett, O. Amsterdamska, and M.E. Lynch, 113–37. Cambridge, MA: MIT Press, 2007.

Cleveringa, C.J. "De ontwikkeling in de veehouderij." In *Veehouderij*, Anon., 103–38. 's-Gravenhage: Ministerie van Landbouw en Visserij, 1965.

Clutton-Brock, J. *A Natural History of Domesticated Mammals.* Cambridge: Cambridge University Press, 1987.

Comstock, R.E., H.F. Robinson, and P.H. Harvey. "A Breeding Procedure Designed to Make Maximum Use of Both General and Specific Combining Ability." *Agricultural Journal* 41 (1949): 360–467.

Cooke, K.J. "From Science to Practice, or Practice to Science? Chickens and Eggs in Raymond Pearl's Agricultural Breeding Research, 1907–1916." *Isis* 88 (1997): 62–86.

Crabb, A.R. *The Hybrid Corn Makers: Prophets of Plenty.* New Brunswick: Rutgers University Press, 1947.

Crawford, R.D., eds., *Poultry Keeping and Genetics.* New York: Elsevier, 1990.

Crow, J.F. "Anecdotal, Historical and Critical Commentaries on Genetics. 90 Years Ago: the Beginning of Hybrid Maize." *Genetics* 148 (1998): 923–8.

Darwin, C.R. *On the Origin of Species by Means of Natural Selection, or the Preservation of Favoured Races in the Struggle for Life.* London: J. Murray, 1859.

– *The Effects of Cross- and Self-Fertilisation in the Vegetable Kingdom.* London: J. Murray, 1876.

De Boer, H., and R. Strikwerda. "Zestig jaar Nederlandse Zoötechnische Vereniging." In *Markante ontwikkelingen. Nederlandse Zoötechnische vereniging 1930–1990*, edited by R.D. Politiek, 11–26. Wageningen: Nederlandse Zoötechnische Vereniging, 1990.

De Bruin, A. *Schapen-KI een haalbare zaak?* Dordrecht: Agrarische Hogeschool, 1987.

De Graaf, F., and A.H. Visscher. *De ontwikkeling van een leeftijdscorrectiemethode voor het gewicht van Texelaar lammeren.* IVO Rapport B234, Zeist: IVO, 1984.

De Jonge, J. "Varkensfokkerij en –houderij." In *Het varken I*, edited by E.J. Dommerhold and J. Grashuis, 150–223. Doetinchem: Misset, 1967.

Derry, M.E. *Ontario's Cattle Kingdom: Purebred Breeders and Their World, 1870–1929.* Toronto: University of Toronto Press, 2001.

– *Bred for Perfection. Shorthorn Cattle, Collies, and Arabian Horses since 1800.* Baltimore & London: Johns Hopkins University Press, 2003.

– *Horses in Society: A Story of Animal Breeding and Marketing Culture, 1800–1920.* Toronto: University of Toronto Press, 2006.

– *Art and Science in Breeding. Creating Better Chickens.* Toronto: University of Toronto Press, 2012.
– *Masterminding Nature. The Breeding of Animals 1750–2010.* Toronto: University of Toronto Press, 2015.
Directie van den Landbouw, *Staatszorg voor den landbouw.* 's-Gravenhage: Van Langenhuysen, 1913.
Dommerhold, E.J. *Het uitwending voorkomen van het varken.* Maastricht: Leiter-Nypels, 1920.
Donald, H.P., J.L. Read, and W.S. Russell. "A Comparative Trial of Crossbred Ewes by Finnish Landrace and other Sires." *Animal Production* 10 (1968): 413–21.
Donker, R.A., and A.H.Visscher. *Verificatie van de gebruikte correctiefactoren bij de fokwaardeschatting voor het 135-dagen gewicht van Texelaar lammeren.* IVO Rapport B-281. Zeist: IVO, 1986.
Edgerton, D. *The Shock of the Old: Technology and Global History since 1900.* London: Profile Books, 2006.
El-Shimy, S.A.F. *The Hereditability of Milk Yield and Fat Percentage in the Friesian Cattle in the Province of Friesland.* 's-Gravenhage: Excelsior, 1956.
Ernst, E. "Vergeleichende Untersuchungen der Leistungen von Deutschen Schwarzbunten, Holstein-Friesians und deren Kreuzungen." *Der Tierzüchter* 20 (1968): 798–800, 828–30.
Fitzgerald, D.K. *The Business of Breeding: Hybrid Corn in Illinois, 1890–1940.* Ithaca, NY: Cornell University Press, 1990.
– *Every Farm a Factory. The Industrial Ideal in American Agriculture.* New Haven: Yale University Press, 2003.
Foote, R.H. "The History of Artificial Insemination: Selected Notes and Notables." http://www.asas.org/symposia/esupp2/Footehist.pdf.
Ford, H.W. *Netherlands: Surplus Producer of Egg and Poultry Products.* Foreign Agriculture Circular FPE 2–55. Washington DC: U.S. Department of Agriculture, 1955.
Frankenhuis, M.T. *Over het ontstaan van de bedrijfspluimveehouderij.* Doorn: Gezondheidsdienst voor Pluimvee, 1989.
Freeman, A.E. "C.R. Henderson. Contributions to the Dairy Industry." *Journal of Dairy Science* 74 (1991): 4045–51.
Frost, J. *Die Holländische Landwirtschaft.* Berlin: J. Springer, 1930.
Gaudillière, J.-P., D. Kevles, and H-J. Rheinberger, eds. *Living Properties: Making Knowledge and Controlling Ownership in the History of Biology.* Berlin: Max Planck Institute for the History of Science, 2009. https://www.researchgate.net/publication/38140066_Living_properties_making_knowledge_and_controlling_ownership_in_the_history_of_biology.
Gehrels, J.C. *Paard en trekker in het gemechaniseerde landbouwbedrijf.* Groningen: s.n., 1951.

Govers, E.D. *50 jaar wol.* 's-Gravenhage: CBS, [1966].

Gowen, J.W., ed. *Heterosis: a Record of Researches toward Explaining and Utilizing the Vigor of Hybrids.* Ames, IA: Iowa State College Press, 1952.

Grasseni, C. "Skilled Vision. An Apprenticeship in Breeding Aesthetics." *Social Anthropology* 12 (2004): 41–55.

– "Designer Cows: The Practice of Cattle Breeding between Skill and Standardisation." *Society and Animals* 13 (2005): 33–50.

Grijpstra, J. *Paardenhouderij: paardenfokkerij en paardensport. Discussienota Ministerie van Landbouw, Directie Veehouderij en Zuivel.* 's-Gravenhage: s.n., 1977.

Groenen, M.A.M., et al. "A Consensus Linkage Map of the Chicken Genome." *Genome Research* 10 (2000): 137–47.

Hagedoorn, A.L. *Handboek voor fokkerij en plantenteelt voor Nederland en koloniën.* Maastricht: Leiter-Nypels, 1927.

– "An Improved Method of Testing the Quality of a Breeder's Entire Flock." *Proceedings of the Third World's Poultry Congress*, 95–8. Ottawa: Auburn, 1927.

– *Animal Breeding.* London: Lockwood, 1939.

Hagedoorn, A.L., and G. Sykes. *Poultry Breeding. Theory and Practice.* London: Lockwood, 1953.

Hajer, M. "Discourse Coalitions and the Institutionalisation of Practice: The Case of Acid Rain in Great Britain. In *The Argumentative Turn in Policy Analysis and Planning*, edited by F. Fischer and J. Forester, 43–67. Durham/London: Duke University Press, 1993.

Haley, C.S., and S.A. Knott. "A Simple Regression Method for Mapping Quantitative Trait Loci in Line Crosses Using Flanking Markers." *Heredity* 69 (1992): 315–24.

Hartmann, W. "From Mendel to Multi-National in Poultry Breeding. Gordon Memorial Lecture." *World's Poultry Science Journal* 45 (1989): 5–26.

Harwood, J. "The Reception of Genetic Theory among Academic Plant-Breeders in Germany, 1900–1930." *Sveriges Utsädesförenings Tidskrift* 107 (1997): 187–95.

– "Did Mendelism Transform Plant Breeding? Genetic Theory and Breeding Practice, 1900–1945." In *New Perspectives on the History of Life Sciences and Agriculture*, edited by D. Phillips and S. Kingsland, 345–70. Cham: Springer, 2015.

Havenstein, G.B. "H&N – A Brief History," revised 24 June 2007. http://www.hn-int.com/eng-wAssets/docs/a_brief_history.pdf.

Hazel, L.N. "The Genetic Basis for Constructing Selection Indexes." *Genetics* 28 (1943): 476–90.

Hendricks, B.N. *International Encyclopedia of Horse Breeds.* Norman and London: University of Oklahoma Press, 1995.

Heuff, A. *De landelijke ruitersport.* Doetinchem: Misset, 1968.

Hirschfeld, W.K. "Voor- en nadelen van bedrijfskruisingen." *Verslagen van het eerste pluimveecongres, 18 en 19 november 1948 te Barneveld.* Barneveld: s.n., 1949.

Hoekstra, P. "Kentering in de waardering der exterieurkeuring van runderen." *Tijdschrift voor Diergeneeskunde* 88 (1963): 1590–1600.

Hoekstra, P., and G.J.W. van der Mey. "De betekenis van de exterieurkeuring voor de rundveehouderij." In *Veehouderij*, Anon., 47–64. 's-Gravenhage: Ministerie van Landbouw en Visserij, 1965 .

Holloway, L., and C. Morris. "Viewing Animal Bodies: Truths, Practical Aesthetics and Ethical Considerability in UK Livestock Breeding." *Social and Cultural Geography* 15 (2014): 1–22.

Homburg, E. *Groeien door kunstmest. DSM Agro 1929–2004*. Hilversum: Verloren, 2004.

Hoogland, W.C. *De veeteelt in de Verenigde Staten: Rapport studiegroep veeteelt.* 's-Gravenhage: Contactgroep Opvoering Productiviteit, 1951.

Hooikamp, A.H. *Praktijkproef K.I. bij schapen.* s.l.: Gezondheidsdienst voor Dieren in Gelderland, 1984.

Horowitz, R. "Making the Chicken of Tomorrow. Reworking Poultry as Commodities and as Creatures, 1945–1990." In *Industrializing Organisms*, edited by Schrepfer and Scranton, 215–35.

Houterman, T.F.M. *Drachtigheidsresultaten bij kunstmatig geïnsemineerde schapen.* s.l.: s.n., 1986.

Houwink, R. *De hoenderrassen.* Assen: Stoomdrukkerij Floralia, 1909–16.

Huizinga, H.A. *Genetic Studies on Performance of the Dutch Warmblood Riding Horse.* Utrecht: s.n., 1990.

Hy-Line Nederland. *Hy-Line hybridekippen. Het resultaat van praktisch en wetenschappelijk onderzoek.* Milheeze [1960?].

Janssen, W., C.J. Broos, and P.J. Renders. *Handboek voor den bedrijfspluim-veehouder. Een werkje voor pluimveeteelt- en landbouwhuishoudcursussen, lagere landbouwscholen, landbouwwinterscholen en bedrijfspluimveehouders.* Helmond: Geeris-Roxs, [1930].

Jasiorowski, H.A., M. Stolzman, and Z. Reklewski. "International FAO Black and White Cattle Strain Comparison (1974–84)." *World Animal Review* 62 (1987): 2–15.

Jonsson, P. "Methods of Pig Improvement Through Breeding in the European Countries: A Review." *Livestock Production Science* 2 (1975): 1–28.

Kallweit, E., and U.E. Pfleiderer. "Steigerung der Fruchtbarkeit bei Schafen durch Kreuzung." *Der Tierzüchter* 24 (1972): 181–3.

Kampman, I., et al. *The KWPN Horse: Selection for Performance.* Zeist: KWPN, 2012.

Karel, E.H. *De maakbare boer. Streekverbetering als instrument van het Nederlandse landbouwbeleid 1953–1970.* Groningen: Nederlands Agronomisch Historisch Instituut, 2005.

– *Boeren tussen markt en maatschappij. Essays over de effecten van de modernisering van het boerenbestaan in Nederland (1945–2012).* Groningen/Wageningen: Nederlands Agronomisch Historisch Instituut, 2013.

Kenyon, P.J. "The Effect of CAP on the Pig Industry." In *The Effect of the EEC Common Agricultural Policy on Animal Production and Veterinary Medicine*, edited by D.B. Ross and K.C. Sellers, 45–8. London: Royal College of Veterinary Surgeons, 1986.
Ketelaars, E.H. *Historie van de Nederlandse pluimveehouderij*. Barneveld: BDU, 1992.
Kevles, D. "Patents, Protections, and Privileges: The Establishment of Intellectual Property in Animals and Plants." *Isis* 98 (2007): 323–31.
– "New Blood, New Fruits: Protections for Breeders and Originators, 1789–1930." In *Making and Unmaking Intellectual Property: Creative Production in Legal and Cultural Perspective*, edited by M. Biagioli, P. Jaszi, and M. Woodmansee, 253–68. Chicago: University of Chicago Press, 2011.
Kingsbury, N. *Hybrid. The History and Science of Plant Breeding*. Chicago: The University of Chicago Press, 2009.
Kloppenburg Jr, J.R. *First the Seed: The Political Economy of Plant Biotechnology*. New York: Cambridge University Press, 1988.
Knibbe, M.T. *Agriculture in the Netherlands 1851–1950. Production and Institutional Change*. Amsterdam: NEHA, 1993.
– "De opkomst van de intensieve pluimveeteelt in Nederland 1890–1930." *Tijdschrift voor Sociaalwetenschappelijk Onderzoek van de Landbouw* 10 (1995): 55–75.
Knol, E.F., B. Nielsen, and P.W. Knap. "Genomic Selection in Commercial Pig Breeding." *Animal Frontiers* 6 (2016): 15–22.
Kroon, H.M. *De tegenwoordige richtingen in de fokkerij der landbouw-huisdieren in Nederland*. Maastricht: Leiter-Nypels, 1913.
– *Die Schweinezucht in Holland und ihre Entwicklung in den letzten 100 Jahren*. Bern: s.n., 1915.
Krüger, A. "A Horse Breeder's Perspective: Scientific Racism in Germany, 1870–1933." In *Identity and Intolerance. Nationalism, Racism, and Xenophobia in Germany and the United* States, edited by N. Finzsch and D. Schirmer, 371–96. Cambridge: Cambridge University Press, 1998.
Le Mair, W. "Typering van een tijdvak." In *Boer en markt. Ontwikkeling van de Nederlandse land- en tuinbouw en de Cebeko-Handelsraad-organisatie in de periode 1949–1974*, edited by IJ. de Boer, 29–94. Nijmegen: Thieme, 1976.
Lefever, G. *Wel en wee... bij het Hybro en Hyline agentschap bij Euribrid en in de Belgische Pluimveehouderij*. Maldegem: s.n., 2004.
Leignes Bakhoven, H., and W. de Jong. *De varkensfokkerij en -mesterij in Denemarken*. 's-Gravenhage: Algemeene Landsdrukkerij, 1929.
Löhnis, F.B. *Varkenshouderij in Nederland*. Verslagen en Mededeelingen van de Directie van den Landbouw 1906, no. 1. 's-Gravenhage: Van Langenhuysen, 1906: 1–63.
– *Schapenhouderij*. Verslagen en Mededeelingen van de Directie van den Landbouw 1908, no. 3. 's-Gravenhage: Van Langenhuysen, 1908: 1–70.

Loman, D.C. "Het Texels schaap." *Magazijn voor Landbouw en Kruidkunde* 2 (1862): 66–70.

– "Gemeente Texel." In Anon., *Uitkomsten van het onderzoek naar de toestand van de landbouw in Nederland*, vol. 2, 13–21. 's-Gravenhage: van Cleef, 1890.

Lush, J.L. *Animal Breeding Plans.* Ames, IA: Iowa State College Press, 1943.

– "Family Merit and Individual Merit as Bases for Selection." *The American Naturalist* 81 (1947): 241–61.

– "Genetics and Animal Breeding." In *Genetics in the 20th Century*, edited by L.C. Dunn, 493–525. New York: Macmillan, 1951.

Maat, H. *Science Cultivating Practice: A History of Agricultural Science in The Netherlands and Its Colonies, 1863–1986.* Dordrecht: Kluwer Academic Publishers, 2001.

Maitland, R.T. *Hoenderboek. Hand- en standaardboek voor den hoenderliefhebber.* Amsterdam: s.n., 1882.

Mangelsdorf, P.C. *Donald Forsha Jones 1890–1963. A Biographical Memoir.* National Academy of Science: Washington DC, 1975. http://www.nasonline.org/publications/biographical-memoirs/memoir-pdfs/jones-donald-f.pdf.

Mansfield, R.H. *Progress of the Breed: the History of U.S. Holsteins.* Sandy Creek, NY: Holstein-Friesian World, 1985.

Maris, A. *Het kleine-boeren vraagstuk op de zandgronden. Een economisch-sociografisch onderzoek van het Landbouw-Economisch Instituut.* Assen: Van Gorcum, 1951.

Maso, B. *Rood en zwart: Bedrijfsstrategieën en kennismodellen in de Nederlandse melkveehouderij.* Wageningen: Landbouwuniversiteit, 1986.

Matz, B. "Crossing, Grading, and Keeping Pure: Animal Breeding and Exchange around 1860." *Endeavour* 35, no. 1 (2001): 7–15.

McAllister, J.W. *Beauty and Revolution in Science.* Ithaca, NY: Cornell University Press, 1996.

Melissen, J. *Kroon op het werk: 75 jaar KNF 1926–2001.* Houten: Premium Press, 2001.

Mingay, G. *British Friesians: an Epic of Progress.* Rickmansworth: British Friesian Cattle Society of Great Britain and Ireland, 1982.

Minkema, D. "Bespiegelingen over afstammelingenonderzoek van K.I.-stieren." *Veeteelt- en Zuivelberichten* 4 (1961): 237–44.

– "Het effect van selectie in een rundveefokkerij met kunstmatige inseminatie." *Landbouwkundig Tijdschrift* 75 (1963): 459–73.

– *Draf- en renbanen in Nederland.* Zeist: Minkema, 2004.

Molegraaff, J.H. *Boeren in Brussel: Nederland en het gemeenschappelijk Europees landbouwbeleid 1958–1971.* Utrecht: s.n., 1999.

Molema, M., and B. de Haan. *De boer, hij investeerde voort. Persoonlijke verhalen over agrarisch ondernemerschap tussen 1955 en 1980.* Leeuwarden: Friese Pers Boekerij, 2015.

Mulder, F. "Met pijn in het boerenhart. De meest efficiënte kip ter wereld." *De Groene Amsterdammer*, 8 January 2015, 30–3.

Müller-Wille, S., and H.-J. Rheinberger. *A Cultural History of Heredity*. Chicago: University of Chicago Press, 2014.

Muurling, F., A. Brand, and A.H. Willemse. "Oestrusinductie bij schapen in het diepe anoestrusseizoen." *Tijdschrift voor Diergeneeskunde* 93 (1968): 1008–18.

– "Oestrusinductie bij schapen in het late anoestrusseizoen." *Tijdschrift voor Diergeneeskunde* 94 (1969): 246–54.

– "Oestrusinductie bij schapen in het vroege anoestrusseizoen." *Tijdschrift voor Diergeneeskunde* 94 (1969): 751–7.

Nitter, G., and D. Fewson. "Experimental Designs for Building a Synthetic Dam Line for Meat Production in Sheep." *Livestock Production Science* 1 (1974): 77–85.

Noë, P., ed. *Varkens varia 1971*. Utrecht: s.n., 1970.

Nooij, A.T.J. *De Boerenpartij: desoriëntatie en radikalisme onder de boeren*. Meppel: Boom, 1969.

Numan, A. *Handleiding tot de inlandsche schaaps-teelt inzonderheid met opzigt tot verbetering der wol*. Haarlem: Loosjes, 1835–6.

Ogink, G. "Vooruitgang in de stamboekfokkerij." *Bedrijfsontwikkeling* 8 (1977): 61–3.

Oldenburger, J., and B. Theunissen. "Alexander Numan (1780–1852) en de veredeling van de Nederlandse schapenrassen." *Studium* 8 (2015): 65–83.

Orland, B. "Turbo Cows. Producing a Competitive Animal in the Nineteenth and Early Twentieth Century." In *Industrializing Organisms*, edited by Schrepfer and Scranton, 167–89.

Palladino, P. "Between Craft and Science: Plant Breeding, Mendelian Genetics, and British Universities, 1900–1920." *Technology and Culture* 34 (1993): 300–23.

– "Wizards and Devotees: On the Mendelian Theory of Inheritance and the Professionalization of Agricultural Science in Great Britain and the United States, 1880–1930." *History of Science* 32 (1994): 409–44.

Paridaans, A. *75 Jaar varkensfokkerij in stamboekverband. Invloed van de stamboekorganisatie op de kwaliteitsverbetering van het varken in zuid Nederland*. Veldhoven: s.n., 1987.

Parmalee Prentice, E., *Breeding Profitable Dairy Cattle*. Boston, NY: Houghton Mifflin Company, 1935.

Paul, D., and B. Kimmelman. "Mendel in America: Theory and Practice, 1900–1919." In *The American Development of Biology*, edited by R. Rainger, K.R. Benson, and J. Maienschein, 281–310. Philadelphia: University of Pennsylvania Press, 1988.

Pawley, E. "The Point of Perfection: Cattle Portraiture, Bloodlines, and the Meaning of Breeding, 1760–1860." *Journal of the Early Republic* 36 (2016): 37–72.

Politiek, R.D. *The Influence of Heredity and Environment on the Composition of the Milk of Friesian Cows in the Province of Friesland and the Practical Possibilities of Selection on the Protein Content*. Wageningen: s.n., 1957.
– "De productievererervingsbepaling bij stieren." *Landbouwkundig Tijdschrift* 73 (1961): 481–95.
– *Doel en streven in de rundveefokkerij*. Wageningen: Veenman, 1962.
– "De praktische betekenis van de populatiegenetica voor de rundveeteelt." *Veeteelt- en Zuivelberichten* 6 (1963): 444–52.
– ed. *Problematiek en perspectief van de melkveehouderij. Verslag van de studiegroep melkveehouderij*. Wageningen: Proefstation voor de Akker- en Weidebouw, 1965.
– "Evolutie van theorie en praktijk in de veeteelt." *Veeteelt- en Zuivelberichten* 11 (1968): 271–8.
– "Verleden, heden en toekomst van de Nederlandse rundveehouderij." in *Verleden, heden en toekomst in de Nederlandse veeteelt: 50 jaar Nederlandse Zoötechnische Vereniging 1930–1980*, edited by T.W. Brascamp-Van der Lee. s.l.: Nederlandse Zoötechnische Vereniging, 1981.
Politiek, R.D., and J.J. Bakker, eds. *Livestock Production in Europe: Perspectives and Prospects*. Amsterdam: Elsevier, 1982.
– "Veranderingen in de erfelijke aanleg voor de melkproductie en het vetgehalte bij de koeien in Friesland en Noord-Holland." *Landbouwkundig Tijdschrift* 77 (1965): 36–49.
– "Publikatie en interpretatie van de productievererving van stieren." *Landbouwkundig Tijdschrift* 75 (1963): 1091–1105.
Priester, P.R. "Paarden en trekkers." In *Techniek in Nederland in de twintigste eeuw*, vol. 3, *Landbouw en voeding*, edited by Schot et al., 73–81.
Reens, A. *De vleeschexport van Nederland*. 's-Gravenhage: Nijhoff, 1922.
Reimers, J.H.W.Th. *Die Bedeutung des Mendelismus für die landwirtschaftlichte Tierzucht*. 's-Gravenhage: Martinus Nijhoff, 1916.
Ritvo, H. *The Animal Estate. The English and Other Creatures in the Victorian Age*. Cambridge, MA: Harvard University Press, 1987.
– "Possessing Mother Nature: Genetic Capital in Eighteenth-Century Britain." In *Early Modern Conceptions of Property*, edited by J. Brewer and S. Staves, 413–26. London/New York: Routledge, 1995.
– *The Platypus and the Mermaid and Other Figments of the Classifying Imagination*. Cambridge, MA: Harvard University Press, 1997.
– *Noble Cows and Hybrid Zebras: Essays on Animals and History*. Charlottesville, VA: The University of Virginia Press, 2010.
Robroek, A. *Verslag over den landbouw in Nederland over 1933*. Verslagen en Mededeelingen van de Directie van den Landbouw in 1934. 's-Gravenhage: s.n., 1934.
Rosenthal, G.G. *The Men Behind the Decisions: Cases in European Policy-Making*. Lexington, MA: Heath, 1975.

Roumen, M.P.H.M. *De Nederlandse trekpaardenfokkerij*. Heythuysen, s.n.: 1989.
Russell, N. *Like Engend'ring Like. Heredity and Animal Breeding in Early Modern England*. Cambridge: Cambridge University Press, 1986.
Ryder, M.L. *Sheep and Man*. London: Duckworth, 1983.
Saraiva, T. *Fascist Pigs: Technoscientific Organisms and the History of Fascism*. Cambridge: MIT Press, 2016.
Savelkouls, J. *Het Friese paard*. Gorredijk: Bornmeer, 2016.
Sayer, K. "Battery Birds, "Stimulighting" and "Twilighting": The Ecology of Standardized Poultry Technology." *History of Technology* 28 (2008): 149–68.
– "His Footmarks on her Shoulders": The Place of Women within Poultry Keeping in the British Countryside, c.1880 to c.1980." *Agricultural History Review* 61 (2013): 301–29.
Schapsmeier, E.L., and F.H. Schapsmeier. *Henry A. Wallace of Iowa: The Agrarian Years, 1910–1940*. Ames, IA: The Iowa State University Press, 1968.
Schippers, H.L., P.C.M. Simons, and P. Borst. *Kippen. Geschiedenis, kunst, rassen / Chickens. History, Art, Breeds*. Zutphen: Roodbont Publishers, 2014.
Schot, J.W., et al., eds. *Techniek in Nederland in de twintigste eeuw*, vol. 3, *Landbouw en voeding*. Zutphen: Walburg Pers, 2000.
Schot, J.W., H. Lintsen, and A. Rip, eds. *Technology and the Making of the Netherlands. The Age of Contested Modernization, 1890–1970*. Zutphen: Walburg Press and Cambridge, MA: The MIT Press, 2010.
Schot, J.W., and D. van Lente. "Technology, Industrialization and the Contested Modernization of the Netherlands." In *Technology and the Making of the Netherlands*, edited by Schot, Lintsen, and Rip, 485–541.
Schrepfer S., and P. Scranton, eds. *Industrializing Organisms: Introducing Evolutionary History*. London & New York: Routledge, 2003.
Sebright, J.S. *The Art of Improving the Breeds of Domestic Animals. In a Letter Addressed to the Right Hon. Sir Joseph Banks, K.B.* London: J. Harding, 1809.
Seddon, Q. *The Silent Revolution: Farming and the Countryside into the 21st Century*. London: BBC Books, 1989.
Shull, G.H. "Duplicate Genes for Capsule-Form in *Bursa bursa-pastoris*." *Zeitschrift für induktive Abstammungs- und Vererbungslehre* 12 (1914): 97–149.
– "What is Heterosis." *Genetics* 33 (1948): 439–40.
Siebenga, J. *Kunstmatige inseminatie bij runderen*. Meppel: Agrarische Pers, 1938.
Sijbrandij, S.R. "De verhoging van de melkproductie in de naoorlogse jaren." *Landbouwkundig Tijdschrift* 73 (1961): 471–80.
Skaller, F. "The Hagedoorn "Nucleus-system" of Breeding. A Critical Evaluation Based on an Experiment with Poultry." *Proceedings of the Australian Society of Animal Production* 1 (1956): 165–76.
Slaghuis, H., and R. van der Berg. *Van everzwijn tot vleesvarken: de geschiedenis van de varkensfokkerij in Nederland*. Beers: Nationaal Veeteelt Museum, 2010.

Slob, W. *Het Nederlandse paard. De geschiedenis van de Nederlandse warmbloedfokkerij tot 1950.* Doetinchem: Misset, 1995.

Smith, H.F. "A Discriminant Function for Plant Selection." *Annals of Eugenics* 7 (1936): 240–50.

Smith, K. "The History of Hypeco-CPI-Bovans," 2009. https://hatchability.com/Hypeco.pdf.

– "The History of Euribrid," 2011. http://www.hendrix-genetics.com/~/media/Files/ISA/History/History%20of%20Euribrid%20PDF%201%20january%202011.pdf.

Spahr van der Hoek, J.J. *Geschiedenis van de Friese landbouw.* Drachten: Laverman, 1952.

Speight, D. "The Effect of the EEC on Poultry Production." In *The Effect of the EEC Common Agricultural Policy on Animal Production and Veterinary Medicine,* edited by D.B. Ross and K.C. Sellers, 49–57. London: Royal College of Veterinary Surgeons, 1986.

Sprague, G.F., and L.A. Tatum. "General vs. Specific Combining Ability in Single Crosses of Corn." *Journal of the American Society of Agronomy* 34 (1942): 923–33.

Stanford, J.K. *British Friesians: a History of the Breed.* London: Max Parrish, [1956].

Stapel, K.P. *Rundveefokkerij.* Zutphen: Terra, 1988.

Stegenga, Th. "De Noordamerikaanse zwartbonte." *Landbouwkundig Tijdschrift* 82 (1970): 75–8.

Stichting Instituut voor Veeteeltkundig Onderzoek Schoonoord, *Het Instituut voor Veeteeltkundig Onderzoek "Schoonoord" in 1976.* Zeist: s.n., 1977.

– *Het Instituut voor Veeteeltkundig Onderzoek "Schoonoord" in 1983.* Zeist: s.n., 1984.

Stichting voor het Fokkerijwezen bij de Pluimveehouderij, *50 Jaar pluimveetoetsen.* Zoetermeer: s.n., 2006.

Strauss, A.L. "A Social World Perspective." *Studies in Symbolic Interaction* 1 (1978): 119–28.

Strikwerda, R. [Reimer]. *Een eeuw Fries stamboekvee.* Leeuwarden: Friesch Rundvee-Stamboek, 1979.

– *Melkweg 2000.* Arnhem: CR Delta, 1998.

– *Revolutie in het dierenrijk. De geschiedenis van de kunstmatige inseminatie in Nederland.* Beers/Doetinchem: Reed Business, 2007.

– *Koers van koeien.* [Arnhem]: CRV, 2010.

Strikwerda, R. [Rein]. "Persoonlijke ervaringen rond en met het invriezen van sperma, 1949–1984." *Argos* 22 (2000): 67–74.

Swart, S., *Riding High: Horses, Humans and History in South Africa.* Johannesburg: Wits University Press, 2010.

Tegetmeier, W.B. *The Poultry Book.* London: George Routledge and Sons, 1867.

Theunissen, B. "Closing the Door on Hugo de Vries" Mendelism." *Annals of Science* 51 (1994): 225–48.

– "Knowledge Is Power: Hugo de Vries on Science, Heredity and Social Progress." *The British Journal for the History of Science* 27 (1994): 291–311.

– "Breeding without Mendelism: Theory and Practice of Dairy Cattle Breeding in the Netherlands 1900–1950." *Journal of the History of Biology* 41 (2008): 637–76.

– "Een mooie koe is een goede koe. Wetenschappers en practici over de Nederlandse rundveefokkerij, 1900–1950." *Studium* 1 (2008): 47–61.

– "Breeding for Nobility or for Production? Cultures of Dairy Cattle Breeding in The Netherlands 1945–1995." *Isis* 103 (2012): 278–309.

– "Darwin and His Pigeons. The Analogy Between Artificial and Natural Selection Revisited." *Journal of the History of Biology* 45 (2012): 1–34.

– "De Fries-Hollandse zwartbonte in de twintigste eeuw. Van melkspecialiste naar dubbeldoelkoe en weer terug." *Tijdschrift voor Geschiedenis* 125 (2012): 536–51.

– "Practical Animal Breeding as the Key to an Integrated View of Genetics, Eugenics and Evolutionary Theory: Arend L. Hagedoorn (1885–1953)." *Studies in History and Philosophy of Science* Part C*: Studies in History and Philosophy of Biological and Biomedical Sciences* 46 (2014): 55–64.

– "The Transformation of the Dutch Farm Horse into a Riding Horse: Livestock Breeding, Science, and "Modernization" 1960s–1980s." *Agricultural History* 92 (2018): 24–53.

Thirsk, J., ed. *The Agrarian History of England and Wales*, vol. 5.1, *1640–1750, Regional Farming Systems*. Cambridge: Cambridge University Press, 1984.

Thurlings, T.L.M., and M.T.G. Meulenberg. "De betekenis van de pluimveehouderij voor de Nederlandse economie." *Landbouwkundig Tijdschrift* 73 (1961): 946–54.

Thurtle, P. "Harnessing Heredity in Gilded Age America: Middle Class Mores and Industrial Breeding in a Cultural Context." *Journal of the History of Biology* 35 (2002): 43–78.

Timmermans, J. *Schapenfokkerij en -houderij*. Roermond: N.V. tot Exploitatie van Veeteeltkundige Instituten en Rasfokkerijen, [1940].

Trow-Smith, R. *A History of British Livestock Husbandry to 1700*. London: Routledge and Kegan Paul, 1957.

– *A History of British Livestock Husbandry, 1700–1900*. London: Routledge and Kegan Paul, 1959.

Tyrell, B. "Bred for the Race: Thoroughbred Breeding and Racial Science in the United States." *Historical Studies in the Natural Sciences* 45 (2015): 549–76.

Van Aartsen, J.J., M.P.M. Vos, and C.M. Karssen. *Afscheid van dr.ir. M.P.M. Vos, voorzitter College van Bestuur Landbouwuniversiteit, 29 januari 1977*. Wageningen: Landbouwuniversiteit, 1997.

Van Adrichem Boogaert, D.H. *De ontwikkeling van de Nederlandse rundveehouderij in deze eeuw. Een historisch overzicht over de periode tot 1970.* 's-Gravenhage: Ministerie van Landbouw en Visserij, 1970.

Van Albada, M. *Evolutie in de Nederlandse pluimveefokkerij.* Bericht Instituut voor de Pluimveeteelt "Het Spelderholt," no. 9. s.l., s.n. [1958?].

Van Bodegraven, D. *Geschiedenis van de schapenhouderij in Nederland in de 20e eeuw.* Doetinchem: Tirion Natuur, 1998.

Van den Bosch, I.G.J. *De fokkerij van het zwartbonte Friesch-Hollandsche rundveeras in de V.S. van Amerika in verband met de werkzaamheid van The Holstein-Frisian Association of America.* 's-Gravenhage: Algemeene Landsdrukkerij, 1932.

Van den Hoek, A. "De ontwikkeling van de landbouw." In *Boer en markt. Ontwikkeling van de Nederlandse land- en tuinbouw en de Cebeko-Handelsraad-organisatie in de periode 1949–1974*, edited by IJ. de Boer, 95–199. Nijmegen: Thieme, 1976.

Van der Haar, J., J.A. Faber, and M.E. de Ruiter. *De geschiedenis van de Landbouwuniversiteit.* Wageningen: Landbouwuniversiteit Wageningen, 1993.

Van der Kolk, H. "Oorlog in paardenwereld." *De Telegraaf*, 23 February 1980, 5.

Van der Molen, H., and L. Douw. "Een bedrijfstak in ontwikkeling. De Nederlandsch landbouw in de jaren 1950–1975." In *Omstreden landbouw: bijdragen over technische en ecologische aspecten van de Nederlandse landbouw in de naoorlogse tijd*, edited by H. van der Molen et al., 9–35. Utrecht: Het Spectrum, 1978.

Van der Plank, G.M. "Fokwaardebepaling van melkvee in de U.S.A. en in ons land." *Tijdschrift voor Diergeneeskunde* 73 (1948): 185–92.

– "Theoretische grondslagen voor, en practische toepassing in, de pluimveeteelt," *Tijdschrift voor Diergeneeskunde* 77 (1952): 553–65.

Van der Ploeg, J.D. *De virtuele boer.* Assen: Van Gorcum, 2000.

Van der Vlis, J.A.*'t Lant van Texsel. Een geschiedschrijving.* Den Burg: s.n., 1975.

Van der Waaij, L., and B. Theunissen. "De meest efficiënte kip ter wereld." De Nederlandse legkippenfokkerij in de twintigste eeuw." *Studium* 10 (2017): 61–85.

Van der Wiel, K. *Veehouderij*, Westfriese Historische Reeks, vol. 2. Zwolle: Waanders, 2011.

Van der Wiel, K., and J. Zijlstra. *Paradijs der runderen. Geschiedenis van de rundveeverbetering in Noord-Holland.* Wormerveer: RON, 2001.

Van Geffen, J. *De winnaar heeft altijd gelijk. Het effect van ingrijpen in de paardenhouderij.* Lelystad: IKCL, 1995.

Van Gemert, W., and H. Hoogekamp. "K.I. bij het schaap in combinatie met oestrussynchronisatie." *Tijdschrift voor Diergeneeskunde* 100 (1975): 489–97.

Van Gemert, W., C.D.W. König, and L.H. Khoe. *Verslag van een studie-reis naar Frankrijk.* s.l.: Gezondheidsdienst voor Dieren in Gelderland, 1983.

Van Leeuwen, A. *Geschiedenis der paardenfokkerij in Nederland.* Maastricht: Leiter-Nypels, 1922.

Van Merriënboer, J.C.F.J. *Mansholt. Een biografie.* Amsterdam: Boom, 2006.

Verdonk, D.J. *Het dierloze gerecht. Een vegetarische geschiedenis van Nederland.* Amsterdam: Boom, 2009.

Verzijl, J.H.W. *Wet van den 18den Juni 1918, S. 419, houdende bepalingen betreffende de Staatszorg voor de paardenfokkerij (Paardenwet 1918, S.419).* Zwolle: Tjeenk Willink, 1918.

Visscher, A.H. "Mogelijkheden voor de verhoging van de lammerenproduktie." *Bedrijfsontwikkeling* 9 (1978): 1070–6.

– "Toepassing van kunstmatige inseminaties in de schapenfokkerij." *Bedrijfsontwikkeling* 14 (1983): 780–4.

Vogel, F., and F. Werkman. "Progeny-testing op twee bekende stieren in Nederland." *Tijdschrift voor Diergeneeskunde* 77 (1952): 386–91.

Vos, M.P.M. *Het meten en wegen van runderen voor de selectie op vleesproductie.* Wageningen: Pudoc, 1969.

Vosjan, H.J. "De eerste toepassing van de genetica in de Texelse schapenfokkerij." *Argos* no. 43 (2010): 88–95.

Vosjan, H.J., and P.A. Bakker. "Eén van de eerste beschrijvingen van het type: Texelsch Schaap." *Uitgave van de Historische Vereniging Texel Nr. 86* (March 2008): 5–14.

Vossen, K. "De andere jaren zestig. De opkomst van de Boerenpartij (1963–1967)." In *Jaarboek 2004 Documentatiecentrum Nederlandse Politieke Partijen.* https://dnpp.nl/dnpp/publicaties/jaarboeken/2004.

V.P.N. *Nuthoenderstandaard der Vereeniging tot Bevordering der Pluimveeteelt en Tamme Konijnenteelt in Nederland, goedgekeurd bij Koninklijk Besluit,* 3 Febr. 1912, no. 36. 's-Gravenhage: VPN, [ca. 1920].

Werkgroep Technisch-Genetische Aspecten van de Varkenshouderij, *Mogelijkheden van de varkensfokkerij in stamboekverband.* s.l.: s.n., 1968.

Westerink, G.J. *De pluimveeteelt in Nederland* .'s-Gravenhage: s.n., 1921.

Wieland, T. "Scientific Theory and Agricultural Practice: Plant Breeding in Germany from the Late 19th to the Early 20th Century." *Journal of the History of Biology* 39 (2006): 309–43.

Wietsma, S., and I. Khoe. *Kunstmatige inseminatie bij schapen.* s.l.: Gezondheidsdienst voor Dieren in Gelderland, 1983.

Willemse, A.H., A. Brand, and F. Muurling. "Oestrussynchronisatie bij het Texelse schaap." *Tijdschrift voor Diergeneeskunde* 93 (1968): 66–82.

– "Synchronisatie, inductie en onderdrukking van de oestrus." *Tijdschrift voor Diergeneeskunde* 93 (1968): 283–97.

Wilmot, S. "From 'Public Service' to Artificial Insemination: Animal Breeding Science and Reproductive Research in Early Twentieth-Century Britain."

*Studies in History and Philosophy of Science* Part C: *Studies in History and Philosophy of Biological and Biomedical Sciences* 38 (2007): 411–41.

– ed. "Between the Farm and the Clinic: Agriculture and Reproductive Technology in the Twentieth Century." Special issue of *Studies in History and Philosophy of Science* Part C: *Studies in History and Philosophy of Biological and Biomedical Sciences* 38 (2007): 303–530.

Windig, J.J., D.I. Bohte-Wilhelmus, and R.A.H. Hoving-Bolink. *Huidige staartlengte bij Clun Forest, Hampshire Down en Suffolk: startpunt voor fokken van kortere staarten*, ASG Rapport 270. Wageningen: WUR, 2009.

Wiseman, J. *The Pig: A British History*. London: Duckworth, 2000.

Wood, R.J., and V. Orel. *Genetic Prehistory in Selective Breeding: A Prelude to Mendel*. Oxford: Oxford University Press, 2001.

– "Scientific Breeding in Central Europe during the Early Nineteenth Century: Background to Mendel's Later Work." *Journal of the History of Biology* 38 (2005): 239–72.

Woods, A. "Rethinking the History of Modern Agriculture: British Pig Production, c.1910–65." *Twentieth Century British History* 23 (2012): 165–91.

Woods, R.J.H. *The Herds Shot Round the World. Native Breeds and the British Empire 1800–1900*. Chapel Hill: University of North Carolina Press, 2016.

Wykes, David L. "Robert Bakewell (1725–1795) of Dishley: Farmer and Livestock Improver." *Agricultural History Review* 52 (2004): 38–55.

Zirkle, C. "Early Ideas on Inbreeding and Crossbreeding." In *Heterosis: A Record of Researches toward Explaining and Utilizing the Vigor of Hybrids*, edited by J.W. Gowen, 1–13. Ames, IA: Iowa State College Press, 1952.

# Index

Page numbers in *italics* refer to illustrations.

www.ingramcontent.com/pod-product-compliance
Lightning Source LLC
LaVergne TN
LVHW040151080826
844660LV00014B/918/J